# IDEOLOGY IN THE SUPREME COURT

# Ideology in the Supreme Court

Lawrence Baum

**PRINCETON UNIVERSITY PRESS**

PRINCETON AND OXFORD

Published by Princeton University Press,
41 William Street, Princeton, New Jersey 08540

In the United Kingdom: Princeton University Press,
6 Oxford Street, Woodstock, Oxfordshire OX20 1TR

press.princeton.edu

Jacket design by Amanda Weiss

Library of Congress Cataloging-in-Publication Data

Names: Baum, Lawrence, author.
Title: Ideology in the Supreme Court / Lawrence Baum.
Description: New Jersey : Princeton University Press, 2017. | Includes bibliographical
    references and index.
Identifiers: LCCN 2016055318 | ISBN 9780691175522 (hardback)
Subjects: LCSH: United States. Supreme Court. | Courts of last resort—United States. | BISAC:
    POLITICAL SCIENCE / Government / Judicial Branch. | POLITICAL SCIENCE / Political
    Ideologies / General. | POLITICAL SCIENCE / History & Theory. | LAW / Courts.
Classification: LCC KF8748 .B29 2017 | DDC 347.73/26—dc23
    LC record available at https://lccn.loc.gov/2016055318

British Library Cataloging-in-Publication Data is available

This book has been composed in Adobe Text Pro and Gotham

Printed on acid-free paper. ∞

Printed in the United States of America

10 9 8 7 6 5 4 3 2 1

*To Carol*

# CONTENTS

# FIGURES AND TABLES

## Figures

**Tables**

Observers of politics talk about policies and policy makers in ideological terms. Certainly this is true of the courts, and especially the Supreme Court. To take two examples, news reports and scholarly articles on the Court regularly describe justices and decisions as conservative or liberal.

This book is an effort to probe the meaning of ideology in the Supreme Court and in the world of political elites in which the Court resides. Our sense of ideology is based on the labeling of certain positions on policy issues as liberal or conservative. How and why do those labels get attached to particular positions, linking ideology to issues such as criminal justice and freedom of expression in particular ways?

These "how" and "why" questions have received attention from scholars, but not as much as they merit. That is especially true of the courts. Those of us who study judicial decision making tend to take for granted the identification of some issue positions as conservative and others as liberal. To the extent that scholars think about the linkages between issues and ideology, we tend to assume that judges reason deductively from broad ideological values to positions on the issues they address.

Yet there is considerable evidence that is not entirely consistent with this assumption. In the Supreme Court, for instance, the positions that liberal and conservative justices take on some issues have no clear relationship with broad ideological values. Indeed, some of those positions seem arbitrary and even inconsistent with each other. Occasionally, ideological positions that seemed firmly rooted in fundamental values get uprooted. And the lineup of justices in some cases on an issue is sometimes reversed in other cases on the same issue.

Confronting those kinds of evidence got me started on the inquiry that resulted in this book. In the process of undertaking this inquiry I gave more attention to scholarship on the workings of ideology in American politics, and I thereby gained a better sense of the relationship between ideology and issue positions. I build on what I learned in chapter 1, which lays out a theoretical perspective on issues and ideology. I then probed one puzzling aspect of ideology in the Supreme Court, change over time in the linkage between ideology and a particular issue. My analyses of such changes in three issue areas are presented in chapters 2-4. Less extensive inquiries into other issues, presented in chapter 5, provide additional evidence about the linkages between issues and ideology.

What I found differs considerably from my prior understanding of the workings of ideology in the Court—and, I think, the understanding of most people who study the Court. My best answer to the "how" question is similar to the answers that some other students of American politics have offered: the identification of certain positions on issues as conservative or liberal develops through the creation of what I call shared understandings among political elites. Those understandings rest in part on logical deduction from broad premises, but to a considerable degree they are contingent on circumstances that give them an arbitrary element and make them potentially unstable. Supreme Court justices gain their sense of the connections between issues and ideology largely from these shared understandings, understandings that they help to create.

On the "why" question, I conclude that values play an important part in driving issue positions, but so do people's likes and dislikes for groups in society that are potential beneficiaries of government policies and for groups in politics that advocate certain policies. Affect toward groups stands alongside values, sometimes intertwined with them, as a source of liberal and conservative positions on issues. Further, what I call group affect often modifies issue positions as policy makers address specific policy questions, including the questions that arise in individual Supreme Court cases.

The inquiry in this book provides one vantage point on the workings of ideology in the Supreme Court, and it is neither complete nor definitive. Even so, I think that the results of this inquiry have important implications for our understanding of the Court and for the ways that we study the Court, implications that I discuss in chapter 6. There is no reason to de-emphasize the concern with ideology that pervades research on the Supreme Court, but the ideological element in decision making should be treated as complicated and fluid rather than simple and straightforward. And I think that scholars need to give greater attention to affect toward groups as an element of the thinking and behavior of Supreme Court justices. In these ways, I believe, we can gain a richer sense of decision making in the Court.

# ACKNOWLEDGMENTS

This book represents the culmination of thinking, research, and writing that began almost two decades ago. Not surprisingly, I have accumulated a good many debts to people who helped me move the project forward to its completion.

The project began when Wendy Watson and I wrote a paper on the impact of defendants' social attributes on the justices' votes in criminal cases. As much as the focus of the project has changed since then, the final version still incorporates ideas that we developed together. I am grateful for Wendy's role in getting the project started; I doubt that the book would exist without our work together.

As the project developed, I presented work at seminars at the Moritz College of Law at Ohio State University, at the University of Georgia, and at Georgia Southern University. I also presented papers at meetings of the Western Political Science Association and the Midwest Political Science Association. Participants at those presentations offered a wealth of good suggestions that I have used.

I also had the opportunity to present material from the project in a journal article.[1] The comments from the anonymous reviewers for the journal were very helpful, and I appreciate permission from the University of Chicago Press to use material from the article in chapters 1 and 4.

Several students gave me crucial help as research assistants: Jeffrey Eisenstodt, Paul Filippelli, Marie Rehg, Juliana Wishne, and Alexis Zhang. They assisted me a good deal in collecting data, but

1. Lawrence Baum, "Linking Issues to Ideology in the Supreme Court: The Takings Clause," *Journal of Law and Courts* 1 (March 2013): 89–114.

their more important contribution was working with me to develop and apply rules for case inclusion and for coding of key variables. The book is considerably better because of their efforts.

Several professional colleagues provided useful suggestions, comments, and leads on sources, including Howell Baum, Christine Chabot, Charles Epp, Margaret Hermann, Daniel Lempert, Carol Mock, Richard Pacelle, Paul Parker, Sergio Díaz Sierra, Charles Smith, and Stephan Stohler.

Thomas Nelson and Christopher Devine both helped me develop the theoretical perspective of the book, and their scholarship was also a major resource. James Brudney offered valuable feedback in a series of discussions. David Klein made a fundamental contribution to the book by talking through ideas with me as I was formulating the project. The two anonymous scholars who served as reviewers for Princeton University Press made insightful suggestions for strengthening of the manuscript, suggestions that had substantial impact on the final version.

Andrew Martin and Alicia Uribe took the trouble to provide me with versions of the Martin-Quinn scores from which free expression cases or criminal cases were excluded, thereby improving the analyses of the Supreme Court's polarity in chapters 2 and 3.

The political science department at Ohio State University and its recent and current chairs, Herbert Weisberg and Richard Herrmann, have facilitated my research on this and other projects in several important ways. I appreciate that assistance a great deal.

I have benefited a great deal from the work of people at Princeton University Press. Sara Lerner, Brittany Micka-Foos, and Hannah Zuckerman provided valuable help in the editing and production stages. Eric Crahan, senior editor for political science at the Press, offered a great deal of encouragement and many insightful suggestions, and he played a key part in the development of this book. I am grateful for all that he and his colleagues at the Press have done to assist me.

IDEOLOGY IN THE SUPREME COURT

# 1

# Ideology, Issues, and Group Affect

When people talk about the U.S. Supreme Court, whether they are scholars, commentators, or interested observers, they regularly use the language of ideology. Decisions, justices, and the Court as a whole are described in terms of their liberalism or conservatism.

Yet in all this talk about ideology, there is surprisingly little attention to its meaning.[1] Why are certain positions on affirmative action or government health care programs or regulation of campaign finance labeled as conservative or liberal? Even scholars who study the Court typically apply these labels to issues that the Court addresses without probing their sources. Much of the political science research on the Court does rest implicitly on one conception of the linkages between ideology and the issues in the Court, but the validity of that conception generally goes unexamined.

This book is about the functioning of ideology in the Supreme Court. I argue that the ideological element in decision making by the justices is not as simple as it is generally thought to be. By probing

---

1. I focus on one aspect of the meaning of ideology here. Fischman and Law (2009, 137–42) note a broader inattention to that meaning.

how and why the justices' ideological stances[2] are applied to the issues and specific questions that the Court addresses, I think, we can gain a better understanding of both the Court and ideology.

A good place to start is with the Court's 2000 decision in *Bush v. Gore,* which raised significant questions for people who study the Court. The most fundamental question stemmed from the Court's 5–4 division along ideological lines in the case. Of course, that division was hardly unusual. Rather, it was the apparent basis for the division that concerned some scholars. In a reversal of the justices' usual positions, the conservative justices favored a claim under the equal protection clause of the Fourteenth Amendment and the liberals opposed that claim. The key to that reversal, as some scholars saw it, was simple: every justice voted in favor of the candidate whom that justice presumably favored in the election.

Writing shortly after the decision, Sanford Levinson contrasted the justices' responses to *Bush v. Gore* with the usual form of decision making in the Court: "Though judges are 'political,' the politics are 'high' rather than 'low'; that is, decisions are based on ideology rather than a simple desire to help out one's political friends in the short run."[3] Levinson and his fellow legal scholar Jack Balkin later elaborated on this idea: "We should make a distinction between two kinds of politics—'high politics,' which involves struggles over competing values and ideologies, and 'low politics,' which involves struggles over which group or party will hold power."[4] Political scientist Howard Gillman distinguished between high and low politics in his own analysis of *Bush v. Gore,* contrasting "a form of relatively consistent ideological policymaking" with "mere partisan favoritism."[5]

The dichotomy between high and low politics is both insightful and valuable. Yet the difference between high and low politics is not quite as sharp as it might seem. Balkin and Levinson referred to high

2. I will refer to justices' places on a conservative-liberal scale across all issues as ideological stances; I use the term "stances" to distinguish ideology as a whole from "positions" on specific issues.

3. Levinson (2001).

4. Balkin and Levinson (2001), 1062; see Balkin (2001), 1408–9.

5. Gillman (2001), 7.

politics in terms of values. However, values in their usual meaning are not the only basis for the divisions between liberal and conservative justices that would fit in the category of high politics. Those ideological divisions also reflect favorable and unfavorable attitudes toward social groups whose interests are affected by decisions and toward political groups that advocate positions on issues in general and on individual cases. The justices who participated in *Bush v. Gore* appeared to act on their rooting interests in the success of one political party, but the role of rooting interests in the decision was not an anomaly. Justices' positive feelings about certain social and political groups and their negative feelings about others help to create ideological divisions in a wide range of cases in which partisan considerations do not play a direct part.

An example that Levinson used to differentiate between high and low politics highlights that point.[6] Levinson contrasted the partisan motivations he perceived in *Bush v. Gore* with cases in which Democratic justices vote to uphold legislative districting maps that maximize the number of African American legislators and in which their Republican colleagues vote to strike down those maps, "in spite of reasonably good evidence that" the maps "run contrary to the institutional interest of the Democratic Party." That is a powerful example, one that effectively highlights the distinction between high and low politics that Levinson and others have made. But if the justices do not act on a partisan basis in these districting cases, their affect toward groups in society may still influence their responses to those cases. Indeed, their votes likely are shaped to a degree by their affect toward the African American community and toward political groups that favor or oppose efforts to maximize the community's representation in government.

The conception of ideological decision making as value-based has deep roots in political science scholarship on the role of ideology in the Supreme Court. That scholarship incorporates a second and related conception, the idea that justices work deductively from broad premises to positions on specific issues and then to positions

---

6. Levinson (2013).

on the questions that arise in individual cases. This conception too is accurate only in part. The identification of certain issue positions as conservative or liberal occurs through a social process in which justices and other political elites work out what positions are appropriate for conservatives and liberals to take. In that process of developing shared understandings about the meaning of ideology, general premises are only one basis for those understandings.

In the first two sections of this chapter, I develop a perspective on the linkages between issues and ideology in the Supreme Court and in the world of political elites of which the Court is a part. The first section looks at those linkages in general terms. The second section focuses on affect toward social and political groups (more simply, group affect), with particular attention to its role in the linking of issues to ideology.

The final section of the chapter lays out an analytic approach with which to identify the sources of linkages between ideology and issue positions in the Supreme Court. That approach makes use of changes in the linkages between ideology and issues over time. On certain issues the ideological polarity of the justices has shifted, in that the relationship between justices' stances on a liberal-conservative scale and their positions on an issue came to take a different form. Inquiries into the reasons for those changes provide a way of identifying the reasons why the polarity of an issue takes a particular form at any given time.

Chapters 2 through 4 carry out that analytic approach by applying it to three issues. The first is freedom of expression, an issue on which a relatively recent change in ideological polarity in the Court has received considerable attention. The second is criminal justice, an issue with a polarity that we take for granted because it has lasted for so long, but one that has not always existed in the Court. The final issue is takings, a relatively obscure issue on which the Court's ideological polarity has shifted twice in the past century.

Chapter 5 continues the inquiry by analyzing the ideological polarity of other issues in the Court, giving particular attention to variation in that polarity among cases falling under the same issue. Chapter 6 pulls together the evidence and considers the implications of the study for our understanding of the Court and of the ways that ideology functions in decision making.

## Ideology and Issues: General Considerations

In considering the relationship between ideology and issue positions, the first task is to make clear what I mean by ideology and by issues. As John Gerring demonstrated, the term "ideology" has been used in a bewildering variety of ways.[7] I am concerned with the two facets of ideology that receive the greatest attention from students of American politics.[8]

The first is ideology as a set of policy preferences or policy positions. Hans Noel defined ideology as "a nearly complete set of political issue preferences that is shared by others in the same political system."[9] Noel's definition is another way of describing the well-known concept of constraint among issue positions that Philip Converse emphasized.[10] One set of positions that is widely shared by members of political elites in the United States has been labeled conservative, while another set has been labeled liberal. In the United States, people who are highly educated and politically sophisticated tend to show high levels of constraint, holding predominantly what are considered to be liberal positions or predominantly conservative positions on issues.[11] The existence of constraint facilitates placing people's policy preferences on an ideological scale.

In an analogous process, we can place government officials on an ideological scale on the basis of their votes and decisions on policy

7. Gerring (1997).

8. These facets correspond in part with what have been called the operational and symbolic aspects of ideology. Jost, Federico, and Napier (2009), 312. In focusing on these two facets, I leave aside some complexities about ideology that are important for other analytic purposes, such as the various strains of conservatism and liberalism that scholars of political thought have identified.

9. Noel (2013), 41.

10. Converse (1964).

11. Kritzer (1978); Hagner and Pierce (1982); McClosky and Zaller (1984), 259–62; Jennings (1992); Poole and Rosenthal (1997), 4–5; Lewis-Beck et al. (2008), 280–86; Jost, Federico, and Napier (2009), 314–15.

questions. Both scholars and other observers of government routinely do so for legislators and judges. These policy positions do not necessarily match officials' personal policy preferences; they may stem from other sources as well. The extent to which preferences and positions do match can be expected to vary with the attributes of policy-making bodies.

One important complication is that policy preferences and positions do not fall perfectly along a single dimension. Indeed, some scholars have concluded that a multidimensional characterization of policy preferences and positions is superior to a unidimensional characterization. There is considerable evidence for this conclusion about attitudes of the mass public.[12]

A single dimension fits the preferences of political elites better than it does for the mass public.[13] Still, it is uncertain whether the policy positions of people in government are better described in unidimensional or multidimensional terms. As the analyses of congressional voting by Keith Poole and Howard Rosenthal suggest, the answer may change over time.[14] Major early studies of Supreme Court voting by Glendon Schubert[15] and David Rohde and Harold Spaeth[16] identified multiple dimensions. More recently, quantitative studies of the Court tend to assume a single dimension, in part because of the popularity of unidimensional measures of justices' policy preferences[17] and their voting behavior.[18] Among scholars who have probed this question, some favor a unidimensional interpretation of the Court,[19] others a multidimensional interpretation.[20]

12. Swedlow and Wyckoff (2009); Feldman and Johnston (2014); Gries (2014), ch. 2; Jacoby (2014).

13. Lupton, Myers, and Thornton (2015); Jewitt and Goren (2016).

14. Poole and Rosenthal (1997).

15. Schubert (1965).

16. Rohde and Spaeth (1976).

17. Segal and Cover (1989).

18. Martin and Quinn (2002).

19. Martin and Quinn (2002); Grofman and Brazill (2002).

20. Lauderdale and Clark (2012, 2014); Robinson and Swedlow (2015); see Fischman (2015). Multidimensional interpretations have two versions. In one, the justices' positions in a specific domain are unidimensional, but those single dimensions look different in different domains. That is the classical version, reflected in Schubert

The second key facet of ideology is individuals' self-identifications.[21] A majority of adults in the United States are willing to identify themselves as conservatives or liberals even when they are given the appealing alternative of "moderate."[22] The same is true of political activists and elites, such as national convention delegates.[23] Identification with an ideological group can be an important part of a person's social identity. That is especially likely in a time like the current era, when partisan and ideological identifications tend to reinforce each other.

But just as issue positions can vary among people whom we would identify as liberals or as conservatives, the strength of identifications with an ideological group can also vary. Any degree of identification as a liberal makes that affiliation an element of a person's social identity, but liberals differ in the importance of that element. Thus, when I refer to people's assimilation of shared understandings about what position someone with their ideological identification should take on an issue, it should be kept in mind that as people's identifications with an ideological group strengthen, so does the influence of those shared understandings.

Inevitably, the two facets of ideology are related empirically. Even in the general population, there is a substantial correlation between ideological self-identification and attitudes on political issues, one that increases with political sophistication.[24] If national convention delegates are typical, as they probably are, the correlation for political elites is very strong.[25]

Students of mass political behavior give considerable attention to ideological self-identifications. This is less true of scholarship on

(1965) and Rohde and Spaeth (1976). In the other version, the justices' positions in specific domains fall along multiple dimensions. In this version, the second dimension is not necessarily ideological; rather, it may be based on considerations other than the justices' policy preferences as these preferences are usually defined. Fischman and Jacobi (2016).

21. Devine (2015).
22. Associated Press (2016a, 2016b).
23. Devine (2011), 113.
24. Lewis-Beck et al. (2008), 223–25; Lupton, Myers, and Thornton (2015), 376.
25. Lupton, Myers, and Thornton (2015), 375–76.

public officeholders, primarily because of the difficulty of obtaining accurate self-identifications. In research on the Supreme Court, for instance, justices are nearly always characterized in terms of where their votes and opinions place them on an ideological scale rather than their self-identifications. But it is likely that identification as a conservative or liberal is a significant element in the social identities of many and perhaps most justices. That possibility needs to be taken into account in analyzing the workings of ideology in the Court.

Issues can be defined at varying degrees of generality.[26] In the Supreme Court, the right to counsel could be considered an issue. Alternatively, cases involving that right could be considered part of a broader issue, the procedural rights of criminal defendants. In turn, that issue can be treated as a subset of criminal justice, which also includes the interpretation of statutes that define crimes and establish rules for sentencing. I use the term "issue" to refer to all those levels. The issues that are considered in the next three chapters range from very broad (criminal justice) to moderately broad (freedom of expression) to moderately narrow (takings).

Even relatively narrow issues in this sense of the term can be distinguished from the specific legal and policy issues that appellate courts address in cases, which I call "questions" rather than "issues." For my purposes, the right to counsel is an issue; the choice of rules to determine whether a defendant was deprived of that right by a lawyer's poor performance and the application of those rules to a particular defendant are questions.

The linkages between issues and ideology could be studied in any policy-making body. The Supreme Court is an especially good subject of such a study because justices are relatively free to act on their policy preferences. The justices' life terms and their general lack of interest in other jobs enhance their insulation from

---

26. Beyond degrees of generality, issues can be defined in multiple ways. As a result, the grouping of cases into issues inevitably has an arbitrary element, an element that is heightened if cases are assigned to only a single issue. That arbitrariness is highlighted by criticisms of the assignment of issues to cases in the Supreme Court Database. C. Shapiro (2009, 2010); Harvey and Woodruff (2013).

external influences. With their nearly complete power to set their own agendas, justices select primarily cases in which strong legal arguments can be made on both sides, so the legal merits of cases constrain them less than the legal merits constrain judges on most other courts.

Students of the Court do disagree strongly about the extent to which external influences and the state of the law influence justices' choices.[27] But it seems clear that policy preferences play a more powerful role in shaping those choices than they do in most other policy-making bodies. Moreover, even if other considerations have substantial effects on the justices' choices, differences in policy preferences almost surely are the dominant reason for disagreements among the justices in decisions. This attribute facilitates inquiry into linkages between issues and ideology.

It is important to keep in mind that policy preferences are not synonymous with ideology. Even if justices' ideological stances are characterized as falling along multiple dimensions, individual justices have some policy preferences that do not fit any of these dimensions. But the fact that the preponderance of variation among the justices in votes on case outcomes can be described with a small number of dimensions—to a considerable degree, a single dimension—indicates that patterns of differences among the justices can be understood primarily in ideological terms.

The conceptions of linkages between issues and ideology as deductive and value-based occupy a central place in research on the Supreme Court. In the classic and influential analysis by Glendon Schubert, induction from patterns of justices' votes was used to identify justices' issue positions and values, but the patterns were interpreted in deductive terms.[28] Schubert conceived of political and economic ideology as the primary values guiding the justices. Most issues that the Court addressed fell into those two categories, and

27. The most comprehensive argument for the dominance of policy preferences over those two considerations is presented in Segal and Spaeth (2002). Bailey and Maltzman (2011) present a strong argument for the significance of those considerations.

28. Schubert (1965).

Schubert indicated that in each category liberal and conservative issue positions were derived from the premises of political or economic liberalism and conservatism.[29]

Similarly, in this formulation, issue positions were translated deductively into votes in individual cases. Schubert[30] used psychologist Clyde Coombs's[31] theoretical work to describe a process in which the justices' votes on the questions to be addressed in specific cases rested on the relationship between the justices' issue positions and those specific questions on a linear ideological scale. If a justice's $i$-point was to the left of the $j$-point for a case, the justice would cast a liberal vote.

In the past few decades, students of judicial behavior seldom have described their conception of how ideology functions in the Supreme Court's decision-making process. For this reason it is not clear to what extent they would accept Schubert's formulation of a deductive process that works from values to issue positions to votes in cases. But Court scholars' treatment of ideology is usually consistent with that formulation, and it implicitly incorporates the deductive element of that formulation. In quantitative research, multivariate analyses of justices' voting behavior typically include a measure of their overall ideological stances. Similarly, analyses of the Court's collective decisions use measures of the Court's collective stance. Both usages rest on an assumption that general ideological stances translate into positions on issues and votes in cases.

As I have suggested already, by no means do scholars agree that ideology is the dominant force in Supreme Court decision making. Indeed, studies frequently treat ideology as one force among others, most often the preferences of other political institutions or the general public and the state of the law. But to the extent that scholars see ideology as a component in the justices' decision making—for

29. Rohde and Spaeth (1976, 137–40) were more explicit about values as the basis for issue positions. They identified three overarching values, an economic dimension they labeled "New Dealism" and two civil liberties dimensions called "freedom" and "equality."

30. Schubert (1965), 26–28.

31. Coombs (1964).

most, a quite substantial extent—their treatment of ideology follows the general lines that Schubert laid out.

This is true of both the attitudinal and rational choice conceptions of Supreme Court decision making. In the attitudinal model, justices simply adopt the positions in cases that accord with their policy preferences.[32] Attitudinal justices gain what has been called expressive utility by taking what they see as the right positions.[33] In most strategic models, justices take the positions that best advance their policy goals in the Court's collective decisions and in public policy as a whole.[34] Their utility comes from achieving desirable outcomes.

Different as these two conceptions are in some respects, both rest implicitly on a conception of justices who act deductively on the basis of broad values that are components of their ideological stances. The linkage between ideology and issue positions is not as straightforward in a rational choice conception, because justices may modify the positions that follow from their values on the basis of strategic considerations. But those modifications are likely to be at the margins.

Over the last few decades, judicial scholars have given little explicit attention to the content of justices' values.[35] In contrast, social and political psychologists have been engaged in a continuing inquiry into the values that are elements of liberalism and conservatism. Their research has also done much to identify possible antecedents of these values in more fundamental values, psychological traits, and even genetics.[36]

Most often, two broad values are identified as underlying people's issue positions. Stanley Feldman calls these values economic preferences ("greater equality/compassion vs. market outcomes/ self-interest") and social preferences ("modern vs. traditional

32. Segal and Spaeth (2002).
33. Hillman (2010).
34. L. Epstein and Knight (1998).
35. But see Robinson and Swedlow (2015).
36. Stanley Feldman (2013), 602–16. On possible genetic roots of ideology, see Smith et al. (2011) and Funk et al. (2013). Psychological traits, whether based on genetics or other sources, might shape issue positions independently of ideology.

values or social freedom vs. order").[37] Jost, Federico, and Napier describe the two key values as "rejecting versus accepting inequality" and "advocating versus resisting social change (as opposed to tradition)."[38]

For any formulation of ideological values, perhaps the key question is how these values translate into positions on policy issues. For some values, the translation is straightforward and clear. That is especially true of economic issues such as government benefits for low-income people, which relate directly to attitudes toward equality. But there are also many issues on which the application of general values is at least somewhat ambiguous.[39] Based on the economic and social preferences that Feldman described, what are the liberal and conservative positions on regulation of firearms or support for nuclear power? The application of general values to many foreign policy issues is also far from obvious.[40]

In research on judicial decision making, the absence of clear logical connections between ideology and some issues is suggested by disagreements with the coding of the ideological direction of votes and decisions in the Supreme Court Database, the most widely used source of information for quantitative analyses of Supreme Court decision making.[41] Many of these disagreements would be quite difficult to resolve deductively on the basis of conservative and liberal values. To take one example, it is far from obvious whether liberal values would lead a justice to support protesters at abortion clinics or to support the clinics that seek to limit protest activities.

One consequence of this kind of ambiguity is that the ideological polarity of issues can change over time. As I have noted, substantial changes in polarity that occurred on three issues—both in the

37. Stanley Feldman (2013), 595.

38. Jost, Federico, and Napier (2009), 310.

39. McClosky and Zaller (1984), 259; Tedin (1987), 77; Malka and Lelkes (2010), 158–59.

40. Gries (2014) identified a larger set of values that help to account for foreign policy positions, though the connections between values and positions that he identified were complex and partial.

41. Landes and Posner (2009), 828; C. Shapiro (2009, 2010); Harvey and Woodruff (2013).

Supreme Court and in the larger elite world—are the subjects of the major case studies in this book. To take another example, one involving an issue that the Court barely touches, over the last century there have been several shifts in the polarity of the two sides in debates about military interventions by the United States.

To a degree, change in the polarity of issues could be reconciled with a deductive and value-based explanation of linkages between ideology and issue positions. Changes in the content of the questions that arise on an issue may shift the relationship between an issue and the broad values that relate to it. Such changes in issue content can be substantial, as Richard Pacelle has documented for the Supreme Court.[42] Further, as one analysis of economic issues suggests, polarity can change when justices (or other policy makers) reconsider how their general values apply to an issue.[43] But the existence of fundamental changes in the polarity of issues suggests that something else is going on as well.

What else is there? The mechanism of logical deduction from general premises is only one possibility; the same is true of values as the source of connections between ideology and issues. For mechanisms, the primary alternative to deduction from general premises is the development of shared understandings among political elites about which issue positions are liberal and which are conservative. "Ideas in belief systems go together not because, in some substantive sense, they belong together but, rather, because they have been put together by the course of events."[44] At least in part, these shared understandings arise from direct and indirect interactions among the sets of political thinkers, political activists, and public officials who can be thought of as liberal or conservative camps.[45] The diffusion of what Converse[46] called "packages" of issue positions can create considerable consensus within political elites about the identities of liberal and conservative positions at a

42. Pacelle (1991, 1995).
43. Hagle and Spaeth (1992).
44. Sniderman and Tetlock (1986), 81.
45. See Noel (2013).
46. Converse (1964), 211.

given time, even when it is not obvious which positions logically fall under each heading.[47]

In this way people who think of themselves as conservatives or liberals learn that certain issue positions are appropriate for them to adopt as conservatives or liberals, a process that extends beyond political elites to portions of the mass public.[48] These shared understandings may be stable, but they can also change as members and especially leaders of ideological camps rethink their positions on issues.[49] Some scholars have discussed this process of change. Among them are David Rabban[50] on free speech issues, Ken Kersch[51] on multiple issues relating to civil liberties, and Christopher Schmidt[52] on the broad categories of civil rights and civil liberties.

If the identification of issue positions as liberal and conservative is best understood as a product of shared understandings, this does not mean that deduction from general premises plays no part in that process. After all, some items in the packages of conservative and liberal positions follow in a fairly direct way from the values that underlie conservatism and liberalism. But where the connection between premises and issue positions is unclear, members of political elites such as commentators fill in the gaps.[53] There are also issues on which reasoning by deduction would lead to positions with which members of an ideological camp are uncomfortable for one reason or another, and on those issues the shared understandings that develop may supersede the logic of deduction from general premises.

The concrete questions that government policy makers decide are usually much more specific than issues, and elites outside of government often focus on specific questions as well. For this reason, shared understandings about the ideological content of issues may develop inductively, growing out of responses to various questions

47. Lane (1973), 101–3.
48. Malka and Lelkes (2010); Jewitt and Goren (2016).
49. Noel (2013).
50. Rabban (1997).
51. Kersch (2004).
52. Schmidt (2016).
53. Noel (2013), 46.

on an issue. For that matter, on some issues the shared understandings may be about subsets of issues. In that situation what scholars and other observers perceive as issue positions may really be aggregates of more specific positions.

Supreme Court justices come from the elite world in which shared understandings develop, and they remain part of that world when they serve on the Court. As justices they are not simply passive adopters of those understandings. Because justices confront issues in the form of legal questions and in the context of disputes between specific litigants, they may perceive linkages between issues and ideology somewhat differently from other elites. As a result, they can depart at least marginally from shared understandings about those linkages in their decisions. Moreover, they help to create and solidify these understandings through the ideological polarity of their decisions, which are visible to other segments of the political elite. *The Onion Book of Known Knowledge* touched on this role in jest when it referred to the Roberts Court as a "small but influential Washington, D.C.-based conservative think tank" that "helps shape the national debate."[54]

I think that the case for shared understandings as the mechanism by which linkages are forged is strong. That conception accounts for the development of broad consensus on the identities of conservative and liberal issue positions on a wide range of issues. In any event, the concept of shared understandings provides a very good framework for the analysis of the relationship between ideology and issue positions. The balance between deductive logic and more arbitrary and contingent judgments can be considered within that framework as it is applied to particular issues.

What I call mechanisms relate to the process by which linkages between ideology and issues are forged; what I call sources relates to why those linkages take the form they do. Values are one important source of the linkages. Of other possible sources, the two that stand out are politics and group affect.

54. *The Onion Book of Known Knowledge* (2012), 185.

At least in conceptual terms, politics is fundamentally different from values. Politics involves the adoption of issue positions with the goal of maximizing political support, in either of two senses. The first is success for the policies that people favor. The second, which follows the more conventional definition of politics, is success in winning office for themselves personally or for the political groups they favor.[55] In the scholarship on political parties in the United States, politics in the second sense is the most widely accepted explanation of party positions on issues, since party leaders have strong incentives to win elections.[56] Studies of change in the packages of policies supported by the parties emphasize this explanation: because party leaders and officeholders seek primarily to win elections, they change positions with that goal in mind. In particular, according to these studies, leaders and officeholders try to maintain the support of groups in the electorate that are important to the party coalition and to add new groups to that coalition.[57]

Members of political elites who are not directly involved in political parties and the electoral process do not necessarily have these incentives. But they generally care about politics in the first sense, so they may take potential support for their agendas into account when they adopt particular policy positions.[58] Similarly, if Supreme Court

55. Of course, political considerations also affect positions on specific questions. One example is the tendency for members of Congress to vote for or against increases in the debt ceiling based on which party holds the presidency. Asher and Weisberg (1978), 406–9. Another is the growth in Republican opposition to the idea of an individual mandate to purchase health insurance and to the "Common Core" education standards after President Obama supported them. Klein (2012); Somin (2012); J. Martin (2014). Undoubtedly, affect toward the president and the president's party reinforces politics in those situations.

56. Carmines and Stimson (1989); Karol (2009).

57. Karol (2009). Studies of change in the parties' issue positions include Carmines and Stimson (1989), Berkman (1993), Adams (1997), Burns (1997), Gerring (1998), Wolbrecht (2000), Shoch (2001), Sanbonmatsu (2002), Fordham (2007), and Karol (2009). In contrast, Noel (2013) has made a strong case that changes in the issue positions associated with conservatism and liberalism eventually change the positions that parties take. In an era in which the parties have become more ideologically homogeneous at the elite level, the influence of ideological groups on party positions can be expected to strengthen and to occur more quickly.

58. Noel (2013), 30–31.

justices act strategically in relation to the political world outside the Court, as posited by rational choice models, one motivation is to maximize the impact of the policies they favor. That motivation may be reflected in the content of specific decisions, such as the Court's 1955 decision in *Brown v. Board of Education* on how school desegregation was to be implemented. But it seems less likely to shape the broader positions that liberal and conservative justices develop on issues that the Court addresses.

Some scholars argue that a different political consideration, the desire to maintain support for the Court as an institution, has more extensive effects on the justices' positions.[59] That argument is the primary impetus for studies of the impact of the public's overall ideological stance on the ideological content of Supreme Court decisions.[60] Even if that impact is substantial, however, it is unlikely to shape the basic ideological polarity of issues within the Court.[61]

Political considerations aside, most conservative and liberal justices have rooting interests in the success of the major political party whose ideological stance and issue positions better match their own. Those rooting interests may have a strategic element, because the outcomes of presidential and Senate elections affect the Court's composition. On the whole, however, they are best understood as an element of affect toward social and political groups.

Politics can have an indirect impact on the polarity of issues in the Supreme Court by shaping the shared understandings of conservative and liberal positions that develop in the larger world of political elites. Because those shared understandings affect the justices' own thinking, justices may act in part on the basis of political considerations that are not directly relevant to them. But those shared understandings do not form solely in the segments of political elites in which partisanship is central. Further, even in those segments,

59. E.g., B. Friedman (2009).

60. McGuire and Stimson (2004); Giles, Blackstone, and Vining (2008); Casillas, Enns, and Wohlfarth (2011).

61. That is especially true if the most liberal and most conservative justices are the least likely to be swayed by external influences such as public opinion. See Enns and Wohlfarth (2013).

political considerations are not necessarily dominant as sources of ideological polarity.

Most important, as I have noted, the justices do not just adopt shared understandings that develop elsewhere. They help to shape those understandings and to develop their own specifications of those understandings. Because politics as I have defined it has relatively limited relevance to the justices, its impact on their conceptions of conservative and liberal positions is more limited than that impact in some other segments of political elites.

For those reasons, the chief rival to values as a source of linkages between issues and ideology in the Supreme Court is not politics. Rather, it is affect toward social and political groups. This affect is a powerful basis for policy-relevant attitudes throughout the worlds of elite and mass politics. At the elite level, it is considerably more powerful than is generally recognized. In the next section, I consider group affect in the elite world and specifically in the Court, with special attention to its role in shaping the ideological polarity of issues.

## Group Affect and Ideology

People have positive and negative feelings about the groups that are part of their world. Especially powerful is their positive affect toward groups with which they identify, those that constitute their social identity. In the classic definition, social identity is "that *part* of an individual's self-concept which derives from his knowledge of his membership of a social group (or groups) together with the value and emotional significance attached to that membership."[62] People's attitudes toward other groups can also be strong, especially if they feel a sense of competition with those groups.

People's affect toward groups inevitably comes into play in politics.[63] One object of people's thinking about policy issues is the groups in society whose well-being is affected by policy choices in some

---

62. Tajfel (1978), 63; emphasis in original.
63. Conover (1988); R. Jackson and Carsey (2002).

way. Thomas Nelson and Donald Kinder refer to "group-centric" opinion about policies, "shaped in powerful ways by the attitudes citizens possess toward the social groups they see as the principal beneficiaries (or victims) of the policy."[64] This conception of group-centric opinion can encompass the material or symbolic self-interest of a person's own social groups.[65] A second object of group-oriented thinking is the political groups that advocate positions on the two sides of an issue, including political parties and liberals and conservatives. Affect toward social groups is connected with affect toward political groups, in that attitudes toward social groups shape people's self-identifications with political groups.[66]

In the scholarship on public opinion, group affect is generally portrayed as an alternative to ideology rather than an element of ideology. For the large portion of the mass public that is relatively unsophisticated about politics, ideology is thought to play a minimal role in shaping political choices.[67] Further, some of this scholarship suggests that the most common alternative to ideology is thinking in terms of groups in society. For instance, the classic study *The American Voter* found that many people evaluated political parties and presidential candidates on the basis of "group benefits," which were contrasted with ideology as a basis for choice.[68]

There is considerable evidence that political opinion in the general public does have a large group-centric component. Americans typically hold strong attitudes toward some social groups. Most people also have strong affect toward political groups, especially the Republican and Democratic parties.[69] Personal identification with particular groups and likes or dislikes for other groups affect other political attitudes in powerful ways.[70]

64. Nelson and Kinder (1996), 1055–56.

65. See Noel (2013), 44–45.

66. Green, Palmquist, and Schickler (2002), 10.

67. Converse (1964); Levitin and Miller (1979); Lewis-Beck et al. (2008), 279; but see Peffley and Hurwitz (1985); Sniderman, Brody, and Tetlock (1991), 140–63.

68. Angus Campbell et al. (1960), 249.

69. Iyengar, Sood, and Lelkes (2012); Iyengar and Westwood (2015).

70. Conover (1988); Wlezien and Miller (1997); Zinni, Rohdebeck, and Mattei (1997).

Group-centric opinion extends to the positions that people take on policy issues.[71] "Citizens tend to support policies perceived to benefit groups they like and oppose policies perceived to benefit groups they dislike."[72] Moreover, one reason that Democrats in the mass public adopt different issue positions from Republicans is because positive and negative affect toward the parties causes people to gravitate toward positions that they associate with one party and away from positions identified with the other party.[73] This process is consistent with what we know more generally about the influence of people's identifications with groups and affect toward other groups on their attitudes.[74]

If group-centric thinking is simply a substitute for ideological thinking, then it is irrelevant to political elites who do think in ideological terms. Yet the two types of thinking are compatible. Indeed, affect toward social and political groups can shape ideological thinking in at least two ways. First, people may choose ideological identifications on the basis of their attitudes toward the groups they associate with liberalism and conservatism, groups that are either beneficiaries of liberal and conservative policies or adherents to the ideological camps.[75] Second, the issue positions that are identified as conservative or liberal, identifications that make them attractive to people who think of themselves as conservative or liberal, may reflect the attitudes toward social and political groups that predominate in each ideological camp.

All this would make no difference for the behavior of political elites if people who are politically sophisticated and who think in ideological terms did not feel affect toward social and political groups. But they do. Positive and negative references to social groups are a common feature of elite political discourse, and of

71. Conover (1984); Conover and Feldman (1984).

72. Grant and Rudolph (2003), 456; see Kerlinger (1984), 44, 132.

73. Cohen (2003); Slothuus and de Vreese (2010); Druckman, Peterson, and Slothuus (2013).

74. Prislin and Wood (2005); Hogg and Smith (2007).

75. Sniderman and Tetlock (1986); Zschirnt (2011); see Sullivan, Piereson, and Marcus (1982), 70–76.

course such references to political groups are a staple of that discourse. These attitudes toward groups inevitably shape positions on public policy issues.[76]

Moreover, these attitudes are intertwined with ideology. There is evidence that polarized affect toward conservatives and liberals increases with education and that more intense affect produces greater consistency between ideological self-identifications and positions on issues.[77] The association between ideological stances and affect toward political groups is quite strong among segments of political elites such as delegates to national party conventions.[78] And one study found a degree of constraint in the evaluations of social and political groups by convention delegates that was even greater than the constraint in their positions on policy issues.[79] Partisan sorting and the growth in affective polarization[80]—hostility between ideological and partisan groups—undoubtedly have made these tendencies even stronger.

Group affect could play a substantial part in the process of developing shared understandings about the ideological content of issues. Like values, attitudes toward social groups can serve as general premises that shape those shared understandings. In the mass public, to take one example, affect toward higher-status and lower-status groups differs substantially between people who identify themselves as conservatives and people who identify as liberals.[81] In light of the evidence of constraint in group affect among people who are sophisticated about politics and policy, it seems likely that such attitudes serve as premises for issue positions. Indeed, the central themes of

76. Some suggestive evidence is provided by one study's finding that attitudes about race have a stronger impact on attitudes toward public welfare policy among people with college educations than among those with less education, a finding that the author attributed to an "improved ability to connect predispositions with policy attitudes." Federico (2004), 387.

77. Sniderman, Brody, and Tetlock (1991), 140–63.

78. Zinni, Mattei, and Rhodebeck (1997); Devine (2011), 99–164.

79. Jennings (1992), 426–27; see McClosky, Hoffmann, and O'Hara (1960), 415–17; McClosky (1964), 372–73.

80. Iyengar, Sood, and Lelkes (2012).

81. Nosek, Banaji, and Jost (2009).

conservatism and liberalism since the New Deal era may be more deeply rooted in efforts to serve different segments of society than in abstract values such as equality.[82] David Karol observed that "it seems more apt to say politicians are consistent in their views of 'who' is good and deserving of help than 'what' is good in terms of policy and principles of governmental action."[83]

Indeed, affect toward groups may serve as a more comprehensive basis for deducing issue positions than do values, because the likely beneficiaries of alternative policies are relatively easy to identify across a broad range of issues. Still, there will be issues, especially new issues, on which elites are uncertain about who those beneficiaries are. On these issues, affect toward political groups that take positions on an issue helps people to sort out their own positions. Early on, support for nuclear power was not labeled as a liberal or conservative position. In developing opinions on the issue, according to one study, knowledgeable people did not rely on cues from reference groups to the degree that other citizens did. But their attitudes toward groups on the two sides of the issue shaped their perceptions of where they should stand on the issue as liberals or conservatives.[84]

As an explanation of linkages between issues and ideology, group affect is not entirely distinct from either values or politics. On the value side, to take one key example, attitudes toward equality may be closely tied to attitudes toward upper-status and lower-status groups in society. For people who participate in electoral politics, positive and negative affect toward political groups on the two sides of the ideological divide may reinforce political incentives. The possible intermixing of sources must be taken into account in any inquiry into issues and ideology.

Group affect is highly relevant to the Supreme Court as a potential source of ideological polarity. This would be true even if justices themselves had no affect toward political and social groups other than self-identification as conservative or liberal. In that situation,

82. See Piper (1997), 391–93.
83. Karol (2009), 47.
84. Kuklinski, Metlay, and Kay (1982), 633–34.

the affect of other political elites could influence them by shaping shared understandings of which issue positions are appropriate for conservatives or liberals to adopt.

In reality, justices certainly do feel affect toward political and social groups. As is true of other people, their socialization and experiences lead them to identify with certain groups and to develop positive or negative feelings about other groups. In the current period some of the justices talk about themselves in public a good deal, so evidence about their social identities and their evaluations of groups in society is fairly abundant. The memoirs by Clarence Thomas and Sonia Sotomayor, to take two examples, underline the importance of certain groups to their social identities.[85] The frequent interactions of some justices with political and ideological groups such as the Federalist Society indicate their positive feelings toward those groups.[86] Harry Blackmun's movement to the left during his career on the Court appeared to stem in part from his growing identification with liberal political groups.[87]

At least two justices in the current era have communicated their negative feelings about certain political groups. Justice Antonin Scalia's dissents from the Court's decisions relating to sexual orientation expressed disdain for "the elite class from which the Members of this institution are selected"—by which he meant the liberal segment of that class.[88] Justice Thomas has made his antipathy for political liberals clear,[89] and one year after his 1991 appointment to the Court one of his law clerks reported that Thomas had explained why he would retire in 2034: "The liberals made my life miserable for 43 years, and I'm going to make their lives miserable for 43 years."[90]

The examples of Scalia and Thomas are consistent with the possibility that growth in ideological polarization among political elites

85. Thomas (2007); Sotomayor (2013).

86. Baum (2006), 118–26.

87. Greenhouse (2005).

88. *Romer v. Evans* (1996), 636; see *Romer*, 652–53; *Lawrence v. Texas* (2003), 602–4; *Obergefell v. Hodges* (2015), 658.

89. Baum (2006), 132–35.

90. Lewis (1993).

has given justices stronger positive and negative feelings toward liberals and conservatives than had been true in earlier eras. On the other hand, the sets of justices who were selected prior to the 1970s had considerably more experience in political careers than those who have been chosen since then. The substantial service of many of those earlier justices in elective office or the federal executive branch undoubtedly fostered strong affect toward political groups in its own way.

Justices' attitudes toward political and social groups can affect their votes and opinions in specific ways that are not systematically connected with ideology. One example is the Court's decision in *Wisconsin v. Yoder*, holding that application of a mandatory school attendance law to Amish students violated the free exercise clause of the First Amendment.[91] That decision may have been influenced by the admiration of some justices for the Amish, admiration that comes across clearly in Chief Justice Warren Burger's opinion for the Court. And the negative attitudes toward the news media that were held by Burger and by Justice Byron White may have shaped their responses to cases involving the press.[92]

The question to be considered is the extent to which the group affect of justices and other elites has a more systematic impact along ideological lines, so that it helps to establish the Court's ideological polarity on particular issues. Scholars who analyze Supreme Court decision making in ideological terms have said little about the possible role of group affect in linking ideology with issues. One reason may be a tendency to take these linkages as givens rather than investigating their sources. But the primary reason is probably an implicit belief that these linkages come through the application of broad values to issues, a belief that precludes a search for other possible sources of the linkages.

Much of the quantitative scholarship on decision making in the Supreme Court and in other courts in the United States does consider the impact of litigants' attributes on case outcomes, either as its

91. *Wisconsin v. Yoder* (1972).
92. Journalist Tony Mauro (1998, 219) referred to Burger's "disdain" for journalists. Hutchinson (1998, 4–5) discussed White's attitudes. Mauro did note that Burger's positions in cases involving freedom of the press were generally favorable to the news media.

central concern or as a control in analyses that are focused on other concerns. There is a substantial body of research on the solicitor general as a representative of the federal executive branch in Supreme Court cases and on the success of different types of parties (such as individuals, businesses, and governments) in appellate courts. But this research is concerned chiefly with the capability of parties to make effective cases in court and seldom encompasses judges' affect toward groups.[93]

In the quantitative scholarship, the work that comes closest to focusing on group affect is probably the research by Harold Spaeth and his collaborators that utilized psychologist Milton Rokeach's distinction between attitudes toward objects and attitudes toward situations.[94] As operationalized by Rohde and Spaeth in their classic study of Supreme Court decision making, objects include the social groups to which litigants belong as well as their roles in cases (the most common type of object) and aspects of cases unrelated to the litigants.[95] The inclusion of social groups in this attitude category calls attention to the possibility that the attributes of litigants and other beneficiaries of particular policies shape the justices' responses to cases, and there is some evidence of that shaping in the studies by Spaeth and his collaborators of the impact of attitudes toward objects and toward situations.[96]

Group affect is implicated more directly by scholarship on the impact of criminal defendants' personal attributes, especially race, on sentencing by trial judges.[97] Findings that such attributes affect

93. The research that focuses on party capability derives in part from Marc Galanter's (1974) essay on the success of "haves" and "have-nots" in court. Examples include Wanner (1975); Wheeler et al. (1987); Sheehan, Mishler, and Songer (1992); Kritzer (2003); Songer, Sheehan, and Haire (2003); and Szmer, Songer, and Bowie (2016). Research that focuses on the success of the federal government as a party in the Supreme Court includes McGuire (1998); Pacelle (2003); Bailey, Kamoie, and Maltzman (2005); and Black and Owens (2012).

94. Rokeach (1968), 118, 134–38.

95. Rohde and Spaeth (1976), 161–67.

96. Spaeth and Parker (1969); Spaeth et al. (1972). These studies did find that situations had a more powerful impact on justices' positions than did objects.

97. Clarke and Koch (1976); Spohn and Holleran (2000); Kansal (2005); Steffensmeier and Demuth (2006); Light (2014).

sentencing decisions can be understood as showing primarily the impact of judges' affect toward social groups. Some studies go an important step further, analyzing the relationship between judges' own social attributes, such as race, and the attributes of defendants as a factor in sentencing decisions.[98] Research on the impact of judges' gender and race on their responses to issues that directly relate to women and members of racial minority groups also implicates judges' group affect, though judges' group membership may affect their relevant values as well.[99]

Another vantage point on group affect, specifically in the Supreme Court, was presented in two brief but important discussions by Martin Shapiro.[100] Shapiro argued that in the decades after the Court gained a pro-New Deal majority, its policies reflected a clientele relationship with New Deal constituencies such as union members and African Americans. The famous footnote 4 of *United States v. Carolene Products* articulated a rationale for the Court's use of judicial review on behalf of a new set of beneficiaries, transferring the Court's "patronage from a Republican to a Democratic clientele."[101]

Based on Shapiro's interpretation, the Court's positions on issues such as free expression, labor relations, and racial discrimination in that period could be understood as a product of some justices' positive affect toward social groups with a stake in those issues. Shapiro argued that these justices could have limited the Court's role as a policy maker by adhering to the judicial restraint that liberals had advocated before and during the early New Deal years. But some Franklin Roosevelt appointees chose to use judicial review to serve social groups they favored, perhaps consciously.

The collective sympathy of the justices for the African American community in the mid-twentieth century affected their decisions on an array of issues. For instance, in criminal prosecutions stemming from civil rights protests, the Court collectively did all it could

---

98. Welch, Combs, and Gruhl (1988); Steffensmeier and Britt (2001); Morin (2014).

99. Peresie (2005); Boyd, Epstein, and Martin (2010); Scheurer (2012); Kastellec (2013).

100. M. Shapiro (1978), 188–94; M. Shapiro (1979), 114–17.

101. *United States v. Carolene Products Co.* (1938); M. Shapiro (1978), 190–91.

to overturn protesters' convictions, resting its decisions on narrow grounds in order to avoid establishing broader doctrines that justices were loath to apply to other circumstances.[102] To take another example, the Court dramatically expanded the scope of state action under the Fourteenth Amendment in *Shelley v. Kraemer*, a case involving racial restrictive covenants.[103] That step, which the Court implicitly stepped back from later on, was almost inconceivable except in the context of racial discrimination.

There was a substantial ideological element to these clientele relationships. The Court's support for the African American community extended across the whole ideological spectrum, but it was strongest among the Court's liberals. Support for the interests of some other constituencies such as labor unions was even more concentrated among the Court's liberals. Today, the business community might be viewed as a clientele of the Roberts Court, in that its success in the Court extends to a broad range of issues.[104] That support for the business community is strongest among the Court's conservative members.

Scholars with an historical institutionalist perspective have linked group affect to the ideological polarity of issues in the Court more directly. Ken Kersch analyzed how liberals on the Court and elsewhere addressed conflicts between the interests of two New Deal constituencies, labor unions and African Americans.[105] Kersch and David Rabban have pointed to the impact of changes in the perceived beneficiaries of certain issues on the Court's ideological polarity on those issues. Kersch sketched a shifting polarity in the Court's decisions about the rights of criminal defendants in response to changing perceptions of who benefited from those rights.[106] Rabban discussed how the growth of free expression claims from the political right affected the views of people on the left about the First Amendment.[107]

---

102. Grossman (1969); Tushnet (2006), 121–22.
103. *Shelley v. Kraemer* (1948).
104. L. Epstein, Landes, and Posner (2013b).
105. Kersch (2004), 188–234; Kersch (2006).
106. Kersch (2004), ch. 2.
107. Rabban (1997), 381–92.

In conjunction with the other bodies of scholarship that I have discussed, what we have learned about the Supreme Court suggests that affect toward social and political groups can come into play at three levels. At the broadest level, the justices' ideological self-identifications may reflect their affect toward the groups that they associate with conservatism and liberalism. Second, affect toward advocates and prospective beneficiaries of alternative policies may help define the positions of justices on the issues they address. This process can occur both directly, based on the justices' own group affect, and indirectly, through the role of group affect in the development of shared understandings in the world of political elites. At the third and most specific level, the justices' responses to individual cases may be shaped by their attitudes toward the specific litigants in those cases, the advocates for those litigants, and the perceived broader beneficiaries of prospective decisions.

I will leave aside the potential impact of group affect on the justices' ideological self-identifications, powerful as that impact may be. My primary concern is at the level of issue positions. But the case level is important as well. For one thing, the justices' experiences with specific cases may shape their issue positions, especially if they had not developed a position on a particular issue prior to their service on the Court. As they learn about the litigants and advocates on that issue, their affect toward those groups may lead them to adopt or modify an overall position on the issue. Further, the justices' affect toward the participants in specific cases may serve as a powerful filter between their general issue positions and their responses to those cases. In turn, the issue positions that we perceive and measure may actually be a product of quite different responses to cases with different kinds of litigants.

There are also occasional cases for which the justices' issue positions are essentially irrelevant. The justices had little reason to develop positions that would apply to the question of of how vote recounts should be conducted before they encountered *Bush v. Gore*. And before they faced *Department of Commerce v. U.S. House of Representatives* a year earlier, they had no reason to develop issue positions that encompassed the question of whether sampling techniques can be used in the federal census.[108] In that void, it is not surprising that the justices' affect toward the contending political groups structured their responses to the cases: the justices divided along the same ideological lines in the census decision as they did a year later in *Bush v. Gore*.[109]

I have referred to the justices' affect toward advocates alongside their affect toward prospective beneficiaries of the Court's policies, and I should say more about the roles of advocates in linking ideology to issue positions and specific decisions. Most directly, justices' positive or negative attitudes toward groups such as the American Civil Liberties Union (ACLU), the National Association for the Advancement of Colored People (NAACP), or the U.S. Chamber of Commerce may shape their reactions to issues and cases in which those groups participate. It is not obvious which groups in society benefit from the competing positions on government regulation of firearms, and indeed perceptions of those beneficiaries have changed over time.[110] In that situation, attitudes toward gun policy in the Court and in the larger world of political elites are shaped by the lineups of political groups on the two sides of the issue at a given time. And just as sponsors of litigation seek out litigants who might attract justices' sympathies, they may also seek amicus support from groups that justices view favorably. One widely noticed example is the briefs from businesses and retired military officers in the University of Michigan affirmative action cases, briefs designed to appeal to the Court's moderate conservatives.[111]

The identities of the advocates for the two sides in a case can also help inform the justices about the prospective beneficiaries of their decisions. If any justice was initially unaware of the stakes in the 1999 census case for the litigants and other groups, the signers of the

---

108. *Department of Commerce v. U.S. House of Representatives* (1999).

109. Cases involving election law often fall into this "no-issue" category, and some lower-court studies have found patterns of partisan voting in those cases as well as election cases that do implicate judges' issue positions to a degree. Lloyd (1995); McKenzie (2012); Kopko (2015); Kang and Shepherd (2016); but see Kopko (2008).

110. *McDonald v. City of Chicago* (2010), 770–80, 843–50; Winkler (2011), 230–53.

111. *Gratz v. Bollinger* (2003); *Grutter v. Bollinger* (2003).

amicus briefs on the two sides would have made those stakes clear. In *Coker v. Georgia*, the question was whether the death penalty was allowable as a penalty for sexual assault of an adult.[112] A justice who was sympathetic to feminist groups might have assumed that upholding the death penalty would support those groups' advocacy of stronger enforcement of laws against sexual assault. But an amicus brief from the ACLU and several women's groups opposed imposition of the death penalty for sexual assault—partly on the ground that a possible death sentence for that offense made it more difficult to secure convictions. That brief probably helps to explain the votes for Coker by four justices who had voted to uphold the death penalty for murder a year earlier, but whose positions in other cases indicated their support for gender equality.[113]

Both as sources of information about beneficiaries and as objects of affect in themselves, then, advocates for competing positions may be important in shaping the justices' perceptions of individual cases and of the issues under which those cases fall. Thus an inquiry into the sources of linkages between ideology and issues needs to take advocates into account.

## An Analytic Approach

The conception of shared understandings that I presented in this chapter is a background assumption for the book's empirical inquiries, though I give attention to the question of how much those understandings are shaped by general premises. The more important question is the relative importance of values and affect as sources of the linkages between ideology and issue positions in the Supreme Court.

In the inquiries presented in the next three chapters, the approach I take is to analyze changes over time in the linkages between issues and ideology. The polarity of the justices' voting on an issue can be understood as taking any of three states. In antitrust law, for

112. *Coker v. Georgia* (1977).
113. *Gregg v. Georgia* (1976). Those justices were Byron White, Potter Stewart, Harry Blackmun, and John Paul Stevens.

instance, most cases involve plaintiffs who seek enforcement of the laws against businesses. One possibility is that the justices who vote for plaintiffs in non-unanimous decisions are regularly more liberal (as defined by their overall voting records across issues) than the pro-defendant justices in the great majority of cases. Alternatively, pro-plaintiff justices might regularly be more conservative than justices on the other side, or there might be no clear tendency in either direction. Changes in the linkage between ideology and a particular issue involve movement from one state to another.

Of course, this trichotomy oversimplifies reality. For one thing, no matter how strong the ideological polarity of an issue, there are almost always some cases in which the justices divide along non-ideological lines.[114] There are also occasional cases in which the lineup of justices is more or less the opposite of the usual polarity on an issue. Still, the trichotomy provides a good framework for identification of the changes in polarity that occur on some issues.

I focus on changes in ideological polarity because changes provide a very good window on the bases for linkages between issues and ideology. When the polarity of an issue shifts, the conditions that are associated with that shift can be traced. Identification of those conditions provides an understanding of the sources of linkages more generally. Some care is needed in generalizing from issues on which polarity has changed, since those issues are not necessarily representative of all issues that the Court addresses. In part for this reason, I analyze several other issues in less detail in chapter 5.

The expectations that follow from the two alternative sources of ideological polarity on which I focus can be illustrated with antitrust law. Antitrust fits reasonably well into the economic value that Stanley Feldman and others have described, in that support for strong enforcement of antitrust laws is widely perceived as a means to advance equality, while more lenient enforcement gives weight to outcomes that result from an unregulated market. Indeed, when justices divide in antitrust cases, there is a strong tendency for

---

114. Edelman, Klein, and Lindquist (2008, 2012).

justices who favor the plaintiff to be more liberal than justices who favor the defendant.[115]

Suppose, however, that at some time in the future this polarity disappears, so that conservative and liberal justices favor antitrust plaintiffs at about the same rate. If that development reflects values, then we should see evidence of a change in thinking about the relationship between antitrust policy and conservative and liberal values. For instance, work by economists demonstrating that strong enforcement of antitrust laws actually undermines economic equality might circulate among political elites and change liberals' understanding of the issue.

In contrast, if such a change in the polarity of antitrust reflects group affect, we should see evidence of change in the identities of the advocates for competing positions, the perceived beneficiaries of those positions, or both. In contrast with the historical pattern, for instance, a pattern might arise in which a high proportion of antitrust suits were filed by large corporations against smaller enterprises. To take another possibility, the Republican Party and interest groups associated with the party might become as favorable to antitrust enforcement as the Democratic coalition.

In reality, both the relevant evidence on a change in polarity and its best interpretation are likely to be ambiguous. Changes in the perceived relationship between an issue and a broad ideological value often can be expected to occur alongside changes in the identities of advocates for competing positions and the perceived beneficiaries of alternative policies. In that situation, the causal ordering of values and group affect and their relative importance will not necessarily be clear. On issues relating to equality, there is an additional complication: it can be difficult to distinguish between attitudes toward equality as an abstract value and affect toward high-status and low-status segments of society.

Still, even in such ambiguous situations the evidence can be probed for its implications. One important source of hints is the extent and form of variation in polarity among cases on an issue during

---

115. That tendency is documented in chapter 5.

a particular period. For instance, do justices seem to differentiate among cases based on the identities of the litigants, the interests they represent, or the advocates for the two sides? To the extent they do so, that differentiation provides evidence of the impact of justices' affect toward groups. Other kinds of evidence such as the temporal orderings of relevant developments may be relevant as well. Still, it may be that on some issues a close probe into the evidence does not dispel uncertainty about the relative importance of values and affect, and for those issues it will be necessary to accept a non-definitive result. Of course, such a result itself is informative on the sources of linkages between ideology and issues.

In choosing issues to analyze, I started by setting aside structural issues, those that involve the distribution of power between the federal and state governments and among the three branches of the federal government. Those issues are sometimes characterized in ideological terms,[116] but public policy makers respond to structural issues largely—if not primarily—in terms of their attitudes toward other, substantive issues.[117]

Certainly this is true of Supreme Court justices. Although liberal justices favor the federal government on federalism questions more than conservatives, for instance, the positions of both conservatives and liberals are largely determined by their attitudes toward the substantive issues that underlie particular disputes between the federal and state governments.[118] To take one example, conservative justices tend to support the federal government more than liberals in decisions about whether federal law preempts state policies that benefit workers or consumers.[119] Because of this complication, structural issues are not very useful for my inquiry.

116. The Supreme Court Database treats support for the federal government and for the executive branch as liberal positions (http://scdb.wustl.edu/documentation.php?var=decisionDirection).

117. Piper (1997).

118. Baybeck and Lowry (2000); Parker (2011).

119. Examples from recent years include *Cuomo v. The Clearing House Association* (2009); *Wyeth v. Levine* (2009); *AT&T Mobility LLC v. Concepcion* (2011); and *Pliva v. Mensing* (2011). Greve and Klick (2006) discuss justices' responses to preemption cases as a whole.

Possible substantive issues to analyze were selected on the basis of evidence that the ideological polarity of the justices' positions on an issue might have changed over time. Freedom of expression was an easy choice, because observers of the Court have pointed to a shift in the polarity of the Court's decisions on that issue over the past few decades.[120] I did find a very substantial shift: what had been a strong tendency for liberal justices to give disproportionate support to free expression claims has given way to a mixed relationship between the justices' ideological stances and their support for freedom of expression.

Criminal law and procedure is a less obvious issue to analyze, because there is a widespread perception that the current liberal-conservative divide on the Court and in other arenas is firmly grounded in the premises of conservative and liberal ideology. But historical evidence suggested that this divide did not always exist.[121] Indeed, there was a shift in the Court's ideological polarity in criminal justice during the first half of the twentieth century, from a mixed pattern to the clear ideological division that has become prevalent. The fact that ideological lines we take for granted have not always existed makes this an interesting issue to examine.

Interpretation of the takings clause of the Fifth Amendment is a somewhat narrower issue than the other two. It is also relatively obscure. I explored this issue because I was intrigued by the liberal-conservative division on the Court in *Kelo v. City of New London*, the most visible and controversial takings case in several decades.[122] That division was not an especially good reason to suspect that the ideological polarity of the issue changed over time. However, I learned that there have been two periods of change in the ideological polarity of the issue, and the changes (running in opposite directions) are noteworthy. Because the Court decides a relatively small number of takings cases, this issue requires a closer examination of individual

---

120. E.g., Balkin (1993); Volokh (2001); L. Epstein and Segal (2006); L. Epstein, Parker, and Segal (2013).
121. Kersch (2004), ch. 2.
122. *Kelo v. City of New London* (2005).

decisions than do free expression and criminal justice, and that difference in approach has some analytic value in itself.

Undoubtedly, there are other issues on which there has been substantial change over time in the ideological polarity of the justices' positions. But these three issues provide a good basis for consideration of the sources of such changes. I summarize the methodology for the studies of these issues here. The appendix provides more detail on the identification of cases to analyze for each issue, coding of justices' votes, measurement of ideological polarity, and gathering of information on amicus curiae participation and certiorari petitions.[123]

Each case study covered the 1910 through 2012 Terms of the Court. That time period was long enough to encompass the changes in polarity that occurred on the three issues. It also coincided with the availability of suitable measures of the justices' ideological positions relative to each other. For freedom of expression, the change in polarity came quite late in that century-long period, so the case study of that issue gives only limited attention to the period prior to 1946. Analyses of the other two issues take full account of the whole study period.

The first task in each case study was to ascertain the change or changes in ideological polarity that occurred on the issue. My approach was to compare the lineups of justices in non-unanimous decisions on an issue with the general ideological stances of the justices relative to each other across all issues. For the 1937–2012 Terms, justices' ideological stances were measured by the Martin-Quinn ideological scores, and the ideological stances of the sets of justices on the two sides in a case were computed as the median of the Martin-Quinn scores of each set of justices.[124] For the 1910–36 Terms, other ideological scores were used in an analogous way.[125] Each decision on an issue could then be classified according to whether the justices

123. The last section of the appendix discusses why tests of statistical significance are not presented in the book's case studies, a choice that is somewhat unusual.

124. On the scores, see Martin and Quinn (2002). The appendix discusses how the attributes of those scores relate to their use in this study.

125. Snyder (1958), 235; Leavitt (1970), 146, 186.

who took a particular side—such as voting in favor of a criminal defendant—were more liberal or more conservative than the justices on the other side. The magnitude of the ideological differences between the two sides could be determined and classified as well.[126] The Court's overall polarity on an issue for a particular time period was characterized on the basis of all the non-unanimous decisions during that period. In turn, changes in polarity over time could be identified and their timing ascertained.

This approach serves the purposes of my inquiry, whether the justices' voting behavior is conceived as falling along a single ideological dimension or along multiple dimensions. Even if the justices' ideological stances across all cases were simply averages of quite different lineups on different issues, those stances would still provide a meaningful reference point. The reality is that there is considerable ideological constraint among the justices' positions on different issues. For instance, even in an era in which some Roosevelt and Truman appointees had distinctly more liberal positions on economic issues than on civil liberties issues, there was a correlation of .75 between justices' scale scores on those two dimensions in Schubert's analysis[127] and correlations ranging from .75 to .83 between scale scores on Rohde and Spaeth's three issue dimensions.[128] To the extent that the justices' relative positions on more specific issues or subsets of issues deviate from the overall ideological spectrum on the Court, that deviation can provide insights into the forging of linkages between issues and ideology.

Although the use of votes as indicators of the justices' positions on an issue is standard procedure, it merits consideration. The doctrinal positions presented in opinions are generally more important for public policy than the outcomes on which justices vote. Analysis of votes rather than doctrinal positions in research on judicial behavior results in large part from the difficulty of measuring

126. For reasons that are discussed in the appendix, I analyzed the justices' votes on the outcomes of cases for the litigants in freedom of expression and criminal justice but used their votes specifically on the takings claim in takings cases.

127. Schubert (1965), 125, 145.

128. Rohde and Spaeth (1976), 143.

doctrinal positions in opinions.[129] However, there are reasons other than convenience in data gathering to focus on votes, and one reason is especially relevant to the inquiries in this book. Justices do care about case outcomes, often a great deal, and they may have rooting interests in those outcomes that are based on their affect toward the litigants and other participants in specific cases. Thus analysis of justices' votes facilitates inquiry into the sources of linkages between issues and ideology.

After identifying the form and timing of a change in polarity on an issue, I probe how and why it came about in several stages. The first stage focuses on the world of political elites as a whole, examining developments that occurred in that world. The initial question is whether there was a change in the ideological polarity of the issue among elites that preceded or paralleled the change that occurred in the Court. If such a change occurred, the task is to trace how and why it occurred. These questions are addressed with information from an array of primary and secondary sources, such as reports in the news media and writings by advocates on the issue.

The second stage concerns the cases that the Court decided on an issue: the kinds of questions that it addressed, the identities of the litigants and (where relevant) attorneys on the two sides, and the identities of the groups that participated as amici. The kinds of questions that the Court addressed provide information relevant to the impact of both values and group affect on the justices, and the identities of participants in cases provide information relevant to group affect. These analyses of cases draw primarily on briefs and opinions in the Court. I am also interested in the kinds of cases that were brought to the Court, and analysis of these cases is based on summaries of petitions for certiorari.

The third and most extensive stage of the analyses concerns the justices' responses to the cases they heard on an issue. To what extent were changes in case attributes associated with a change in the ideological polarity of the issue? To the extent that polarity in one

---

129. See Clark and Lauderdale (2010).

period varied among cases, what do the attributes associated with that variation suggest about the sources of the divisions between liberal and conservative justices? I also analyze the justices' responses to cases in a more conventional way, examining patterns in the voting behavior of individual justices in different periods and across different kinds of cases.

In each chapter I assess the evidence for what it indicates about the sources of the change or changes in polarity that occurred on an issue. In chapter 5, I present evidence about other issues more briefly to build a broader picture of how and why linkages between issues and ideology are forged.

It is important to keep in mind that ideological polarity is only one facet of decision making in the Court. By definition, a study of polarity focuses on decisions in which justices disagree with each other. As a result, it leaves aside the cases in which the justices agree on the appropriate outcome for the litigants—a substantial minority of decisions in the period since the 1940s, a distinct majority prior to that time. The book's analyses do make use of information on the Court's full sets of decisions on an issue, especially when they consider the content of the Court's agenda and the voting behavior of individual justices.

Still, the focus is on the positions of justices relative to each other rather than their positions in themselves. Thus it should be kept in mind that, to take one example, justices who are distinctly more favorable to free expression claims than their colleagues in general or in a particular class of cases are not necessarily taking a strongly pro-expression position in absolute terms. More broadly, a focus on disagreements among the justices—and the ideological element in those disagreements—provides only a partial picture of decision making in the Court.

An inquiry into polarity does get to the heart of the ideological dimension in decision making that is a fundamental part of Supreme Court decision making. What we can learn about the relationships between justices' ideological stances and their positions on issues and responses to individual cases can add much to our understanding of the justices' choices as decision makers.

And because the functioning of ideology in the Supreme Court is intertwined with its functioning in the world of elite politics as a whole, the lessons of an inquiry into polarity in the Court can inform our understanding of other institutions as well. Those are the aims of the book.

# 2

# Freedom of Expression

The concept of change in the relationship between justices' ideological stances and their positions on issues that the Supreme Court addresses might seem technical and abstruse. But on the issue of free expression, an apparent change in the ideological polarity of the issue in the Court has received considerable attention.[1] Freedom of expression was long perceived as a field in which the justices' positions followed neat ideological lines. In areas ranging from obscenity to national security, justices whose overall voting records labeled them as liberals were distinctly more favorable to broad interpretations of First Amendment rights than were their conservative colleagues. For that reason, students of the Court regularly characterized votes and decisions supporting free expression claims as liberal.[2]

In the last quarter century, however, observers of the Court have noted a shift in the way that the justices divide. Some non-unanimous decisions follow the accustomed pattern in which liberal justices give disproportionate support to free expression claims. But there are other decisions in which the Court's conservatives are

1. See, for instance, Balkin (1993); Sunstein (1993); Volokh (2001); L. Epstein and Segal (2006); and L. Epstein, Parker, and Segal (2013).
2. Schubert (1965), 101; Rohde and Spaeth (1976), 138.

more favorable to free expression claims than its liberals, and such decisions seem to be growing in frequency. Thus it appears that the Court has moved from a clear ideological polarity in First Amendment cases to a muddled and inconsistent polarity.

That impression of change in the Court's polarity is basically accurate. The question, then, is why it has occurred. To what extent have justices responded to a shift in the relationship between broad values connected with liberal and conservative ideology and the questions that arise in free expression cases, and to what extent have they responded to a shift in the prospective beneficiaries of First Amendment claims and the advocates who support and oppose those claims?

That question is the focus of this chapter. After a brief discussion of free expression as an issue, I document the change that occurred in the ideological polarity of this issue in the Court. The remaining sections of the chapter probe the ways that values and affect toward groups have figured into the shift in polarity by examining evidence on this issue outside the Court, the content of cases that the Court decided, and the justices' responses to those cases.

## Freedom of Expression in the Supreme Court

I use the terms "freedom of expression" and "free expression" to refer to the rights protected by the First Amendment, other than those related to religion. Students of the Supreme Court are familiar with the general contours of the Court's work in the field of freedom of expression, but it is useful to note some attributes of that work. To start with, the Court was essentially inactive on this issue until the second decade of the twentieth century. It appears that there were only about a half dozen decisions interpreting the expression clauses of the First Amendment prior to the Court's 1910 Term.[3]

3. Potential cases for the pre-1910 period were identified through Lexis searches with "first w/1 amendment" and the terms of the relevant clauses in the First Amendment. The decisions in which the Court addressed expression issues under the First Amendment (other than the applicability of the First Amendment to the states) were *Ex parte Jackson* (1878); *Ex parte Curtis* (1882); *In re Rapier* (1892); *Horner v. United*

At about that time, the Court began to hear and decide free expression cases at a somewhat higher rate—an average of about one a year over the next quarter century, under the criteria for classification of cases that I used in this study.[4] Beginning with the 1936 Term, the volume of expression cases increased substantially. Over the years since then, the number of free expression cases and their share of the Court's agenda have fluctuated, but this field has been a regular fixture of the Court's work.

The Court's support for parties with free expression claims has also fluctuated. In the 1910–20 Terms, claimants won less than 5 percent of the time, but they were successful in more than half the Court's decisions in the 1921–45 Terms. The rate of success for claimants dipped to 21 percent in the Vinson Court, then jumped to 74 percent in the Warren Court. In the Burger, Rehnquist, and early Roberts Courts, claimants were successful about half the time.[5]

In light of the wide variety of questions that arise in free expression and the difficulties presented by many of those questions, it is not surprising that the Court's legal rules on the issue are complex. What stands out is the overlap among multiple sets of tests and doctrines. Among them are general tests such as preferred position and balancing, special rules to protect expression such as the void for vagueness doctrine and limits on prior restraint, and specific rules for particular types of expression such as the three-part test for obscenity and the actual malice requirement in libel.

Surveying these varying approaches, First Amendment scholar Thomas Emerson wrote at the end of the Warren Court that the Court "has totally failed to settle on any coherent approach or to

---

*States* (1892); *United States ex rel. Turner v. Williams* (1904); and *Patterson v. Colorado* (1907). In cases such as *Davis v. Massachusetts* (1897), the Court avoided directly addressing First Amendment issues. See Rabban (1997), 173–75.

4. Those criteria are described in the appendix.

5. The success rate was 48 percent in the Burger Court, 54 percent in the Rehnquist Court, and 44 percent in the Roberts Court through the 2012 Term. If the Rehnquist Court is divided into two parts after the 1993 Term, as it is in analyses that follow, the success rate was 56 percent in the first part and 52 percent in the second part.

bring together its various doctrines into a consistent whole."[6] Since then, the Court's application of an analytic scheme with three tiers of review has enhanced the coherence of its approach, but there is still a good deal of what Emerson characterized as chaos.[7] Two commentators said in 2014 that "nobody would nominate 'simplicity' as a defining virtue of the First Amendment."[8]

## The Ideological Polarity of Decisions

As with the other two issues on which the book focuses, I analyzed the justices' votes in freedom of expression cases in the Supreme Court's 1910–2012 Terms. Cases were included if First Amendment claims were made or if there were strong free expression implications, even if a case was ultimately decided on the basis of other legal provisions.

As summarized in chapter 1 and detailed in the appendix, I determined the ideological polarity of each non-unanimous decision by comparing ideological scores for the justices on the two sides of the case based on their voting across all issues. In dichotomous terms, were the justices who favored the party with a free expression claimant in a case more liberal or more conservative than the anti-claimant justices? The magnitude of the ideological difference between the two sides in a case could also be determined.

Because the change in the Court's polarity did not come until the 1990s, I focus primarily on the 1946–2012 Terms. Martin-Quinn scores were available from 1937 on, so a single ideological measure could be employed throughout the period of greatest interest.

Table 2.1 dichotomizes the polarity of the Court's decisions over time. The 1910–36 Terms were combined into a single period because of the relatively small number of non-unanimous decisions

6. Emerson (1970), 16.

7. Bartels (2009); Richards (2013).

8. Tribe and Matz (2014), 152. In contrast, legal scholar Geoffrey Stone argued that "on the whole, free-speech doctrine . . . leads to generally predictable and sound decisions." Bollinger and Stone (2002), 14.

TABLE 2.1. Ideological patterns of votes in non-unanimous freedom of expression decisions, 1910–2012 Terms

| Period | Side with more liberal ideology score | | Percent with pro-claimant side more liberal |
| | Pro-claimant | Anti-claimant | |
| --- | --- | --- | --- |
| 1910–36 Terms | 13 | 3 | 81.3 |
| 1937–45 Terms | 22 | 5 | 81.5 |
| 1946–52 Terms (Vinson Court) | 27 | 1 | 96.4 |
| 1953–68 Terms (Warren Court) | 88 | 9 | 90.7 |
| 1969–85 Terms (Burger Court) | 137 | 10 | 93.2 |
| 1986–93 Terms (early Rehnquist Court) | 49 | 5 | 90.7 |
| 1994–2004 Terms (late Rehnquist Court) | 28 | 21 | 57.1 |
| 2005–12 Terms (Roberts Court) | 12 | 10 | 54.5 |

during those years. The 1946–2012 period was divided by chief justice, with the Rehnquist Court subdivided because of the change in polarity that occurred during that period.[9]

The results are striking. In the period from the White Court of the 1910–20 Terms through the Stone Court of the 1941–45 Terms, the justices who voted for free expression claimants usually were more liberal than their colleagues in opposition. That tendency became even stronger in the Vinson Court, and the proportion of cases in which the pro-claimant justices were more liberal than the justices on the other side remained above 90 percent through the early Rehnquist Court. But in the long natural court that began in the 1994 Term, the proportion was considerably lower.[10] It remained

9. About 16 percent of the cases were decided on bases other than the free expression claims; the temporal patterns are quite similar if those cases are excluded.

10. There was no clear breakpoint between the period of a strong ideological polarity to the Court's divisions in free expression cases and the period of mixed polarity. In every term between 1946 and 1992, the pro-claimant justices in non-unanimous cases were more liberal than the anti-claimant justices at least 70 percent of the time. In the 1990–92 Terms, the pro-claimant justices were more liberal in sixteen of eighteen cases (89 percent). In the 1993–95 Terms, the balance shifted somewhat: the

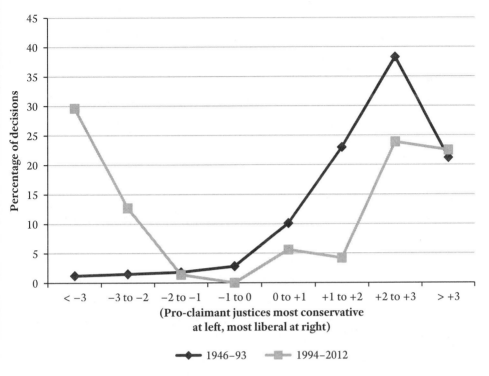

FIGURE 2.1. Magnitude of ideological differences between pro-claimant and anti-claimant justices, non-unanimous decisions, 1946–2012 Terms.

*Notes*: Dates shown are Court terms. Intervals shown on the horizontal axis are for the difference between the median Martin-Quinn scores of justices who voted for the free expression claimant in a case and the median scores of justices who voted against the claimant. Positive differences indicate that the pro-claimant justices were more liberal than the anti-claimant justices.

at that lower level in the early Roberts Court of the 2005–12 Terms. Thus the Court moved from a pattern in which the justices who voted for a free speech claimant in a non-unanimous decision were more liberal than their colleagues the great majority of the time to one in which the pro-claimant justices were more conservative than those voting against a claimant nearly half the time.

If the scores for ideological differences between the two sides are put into a larger set of categories, as they are in figure 2.1, a fuller

pro-claimant justices were more liberal in ten of fifteen cases (67 percent). Another shift occurred in the 1996–99 Terms, when the pro-claimant justices were more liberal in seven of fourteen cases (50 percent). I adopt a dividing line between the 1993 and 1994 Terms because of the long natural court that began in 1994.

picture emerges. Across the full 1946–2012 period the justices divided sharply along ideological lines in the preponderance of cases. There were relatively few cases in which the median Martin-Quinn scores for justices on the two sides were close to each other; overall, only 12 percent of the difference scores were between −1.0 and +1.0. (In free expression cases, positive difference scores indicate that the pro-claimant justices were more liberal than their colleagues on the other side.)

But the ideological polarity of decisions changed dramatically in the late Rehnquist Court and the Roberts Court. For one thing, the Court became even more polarized in individual cases. In the 1946–93 Terms, 64 percent of the non-unanimous decisions had difference scores above +2.0 or below −2.0, scores that indicated quite substantial ideological differences between the two sides. In the 1994–2012 Terms, that proportion jumped to 89 percent. Even more striking was the change in the direction of the differences. In 1946–93, 60 percent of the scores were above +2.0 and 3 percent were below −2.0. In 1994–2012, the equivalent percentages were 46 percent and 42 percent. Thus the Court moved from a pattern in which there was a single peak to its divisions, with pro-claimant justices distinctly more liberal than anti-claimant justices, to a pattern in which that peak was paired with a second peak at which pro-claimant justices were distinctly more conservative than their colleagues on the other side.

Another way to gauge the change in ideological polarity is by examining the justices' voting support for free expression claims in natural courts, periods of stable Court membership, that lasted for at least three terms. For each natural court, each justice's voting support for free expression was measured as the proportion of cases in which the justice cast a vote for the free expression claimant. Both unanimous and non-unanimous decisions were included. Because the early Roberts Court decided relatively few free expression cases, I combined the 2006–12 Terms and analyzed the seven justices who served throughout that period. The correlations between the justices' support for free expression and the means of their Martin-Quinn scores across the free expression cases decided during a natural court are shown in table 2.2,

TABLE 2.2. Measures of support for free expression claims, periods of stable court membership, 1946–2012 Terms

| Terms | Correlation between Martin-Quinn scores and support for expression claims | Standard deviation of percent support for expression claims |
|---|---|---|
| 1949–52 | .959 | 29.0 |
| 1958–61 | .808 | 26.5 |
| 1962–64 | .672 | 23.0 |
| 1972–74 | .855 | 28.5 |
| 1976–80 | .924 | 19.4 |
| 1981–85 | .926 | 18.2 |
| 1994–2004 | .060 | 9.0 |
| 2006–12 | −.402 | 7.5 |

*Notes:* The Martin-Quinn scores for each justice are the means of their term-level scores across all free expression cases decided during the indicated terms. Positive correlations indicate that more liberal justices were more likely to support expression claims. The standard deviations are for the various justices' overall percentages of votes favorable to free expression claims across the indicated terms.

Each period listed included nine justices, except for 2006–12, in which the seven justices who served throughout the period were analyzed. Justice Byron White joined the Court during the 1961 Term but is not included in the calculations for the 1958–61 Terms.

along with the standard deviations of the various justices' proportions of votes for expression claims in each natural court.

In each of the six periods of stable membership between the late 1940s and the mid-1980s, the correlation between voting on free expression and overall ideological voting was quite high, with more liberal justices more favorable to free expression claims. The standard deviations, of course, capture how much the justices differed in the frequency with which they supported expression claims. Those differences were considerably lower in the last two of those six periods, but there was still substantial variation among justices in support for free expression claims as late as the early 1980s.

The last two periods shown are quite different from the earlier ones. The standard deviations dropped considerably, so that the justices differed much less in their overall support for free expression claimants. In the long natural court of the 1994–2004 Terms, there was essentially no relationship between the justices' positions on a liberal-conservative scale and their voting in freedom of expression cases. The negative correlation for the 2006–12 Terms should be

treated as suggestive, since it was based on only twenty-seven decisions. But at the least, it is clear that freedom of expression was no
longer a liberal cause in the Court.

Thus the justices' voting patterns in free expression cases verify
the widespread perception of change in the ideological polarity of
free expression decisions in the Supreme Court. The extent of the
change and the speed with which it occurred are striking, perhaps
more so than is generally recognized. Thus there is an important
phenomenon to explain.

## Explaining the Change

Scholars who give attention to the ideological transformation of free
expression in the Court have also offered explanations of that transformation.[11] Their explanations refer or allude to two themes. The
first is that liberals came to perceive free expression as frequently
conflicting with other values that are important to them, especially
equality. The second is that free expression claims in the Court
increasingly have been brought on behalf of interests that conservatives favor more than liberals, such as the business community.
Those themes largely correspond with the two potential sources
of change in ideological polarity that I have emphasized, and the
relevant evidence can be used to trace the impact of those sources.

Before proceeding further, it is important to consider what values that differentiate liberals from conservatives might underlie the
polarity of free expression at a given time. To return to the char-
acterizations of values that were discussed in chapter 1, Feldman
referred to a dichotomy between social freedom and order, with
liberals giving more weight to social freedom and conservatives to
order.[12] That characterization, like the more specific characteriza-
tions by early students of Supreme Court behavior,[13] suggests that
liberal and conservative values lead directly to a higher priority for

11. See Dorsen and Gora (1982); Balkin (1990, 1993); Graber (1991); Rabban
(1997), ch. 9; L. Epstein and Segal (2006); and L. Epstein, Parker, and Segal (2013).
12. Stanley Feldman (2013), 595.
13. Schubert (1965), 159; Rohde and Spaeth (1976), 138.

freedom of expression among liberals. That conception seemed quite reasonable so long as the Supreme Court followed its traditional polarity in free expression, but it does not help to explain the change in polarity that has occurred since then.

Potentially more helpful are the differential weights given to equality by liberals and conservatives in the formulations by Feldman, by Jost, Federico, and Napier,[14] and by others.[15] In some formulations, conservatives give higher priority to freedom than liberals, who focus more heavily on equality.[16] If shared understandings of the relationship between freedom of expression and equality changed over time, then values might have driven the breakdown of the traditional polarity of free expression in the Court and the larger elite world. That possibility presents a challenge for identification of the sources of the change in polarity, because it may be difficult to distinguish between the impact of equality as a value and the impact of attitudes toward advantaged and disadvantaged social groups. The high priority to order that Feldman identified with conservatism may help to explain the polarity of certain kinds of free expression questions, such as those relating to national security and obscenity, and changes in the prominence of those questions could help to drive changes in the overall polarity of free expression.

### FREE EXPRESSION OUTSIDE THE COURT

Scholars who have studied the politics of freedom of expression during the early twentieth century differ somewhat in their conclusions about the segments of political elites that supported freedom of expression prior to World War I. But their accounts converge in pointing to repression of political dissent during and after that war as a key development: for the first time, free expression became a significant concern for mainstream Progressives and liberals.[17] From

14. Jost, Federico, and Napier (2009), 310.
15. E.g., Rokeach (1973), 169–70; Kerlinger (1984), 17.
16. Kerlinger (1984), 17; see Gerring (1998), 20.
17. Murphy (1972), chs. 2–6; Murphy (1979); Graber (1991), chs. 1–4; Rabban (1997).

that point on, liberals were distinctly more likely than conservatives to support freedom of expression.

To a considerable degree, these alignments reflected the identification of free speech as a cause for the labor movement. Prior to World War I, the International Workers of the World (IWW) had been a major target of government action to limit freedom of expression.[18] After the war, mainstream labor organizations also were targets, and they fought against legislation that impinged on their activities.[19] For their part, business groups supported such legislation.[20]

The American Civil Liberties Union, founded in 1920, both reflected and fostered the linkage between free expression and the labor movement. From the start, leaders of the ACLU sought to protect freedom of expression and other liberties for groups across the whole ideological spectrum. But the early ACLU closely identified with the labor movement, and much of its activity was on behalf of that movement.[21] As Roger Baldwin, the first head of the ACLU, saw it, "The cause we now serve is labor."[22] The connection between organized labor and advocacy for free speech began to loosen in the 1930s and 1940s, but that loosening occurred slowly.[23]

A second connection was also important: government policies that impinged on freedom of speech and freedom of the press were aimed largely at the political left and very little at the political right. From World War I to the Cold War, governments at all levels adopted a variety of legislation and other practices that were directed at the Communist Party and other movements on the left. In practice, these policies had an impact on the mainstream left as well, and largely for that reason they evoked differential responses from liberals and conservatives.

Even if liberal support for freedom of expression originated primarily in group interests and loyalties, that support became firmly

18. Rabban (1997), ch. 2.
19. Murphy (1972), chs. 4, 9.
20. Murphy (1972), 50–51.
21. Johnson (1963), 198–99; Auerbach (1966), 18–32;
22. Walker (1999), 47.
23. See Kersch (2004), 226–30.

established as a tenet of liberalism. The depth and breadth of this support is suggested by the support that groups committed to racial equality sometimes gave to protection of racist speech.[24] Arguments for limitations on expression and policies that created limits came primarily from conservatives. This was true, to take two examples, of criminal sanctions for obscenity and for actions that arguably threatened national security.[25]

Perhaps the first sign of movement toward a more complicated ideological alignment on free speech came from the New Left of the 1960s, some of whose adherents argued that the legal status of freedom of expression served the political right. Most fundamentally, they charged that traditional protections of freedom of expression bolstered the conservative status quo.[26] The most visible presentation of that argument was Herbert Marcuse's essay, "Repressive Tolerance."[27]

In the decades that followed, mainstream liberals, the radical left, or both identified several forms of expression that they saw as harmful. One form was "hate speech."[28] When the ACLU represented the Nazis who sought to march in Skokie, Illinois, in 1977, the organization was following its traditional expansive interpretation of freedom of expression.[29] But the ACLU received heated criticism from some liberals for its role in the Skokie controversy, and it temporarily suffered a substantial decline in membership.

This criticism was a harbinger of the broader concern about hate speech and related expression that developed in later years. Some individuals and groups on the left supported statutes and university rules to address what they saw as the dangers of speech attacking women, members of racial minority groups, and gays and lesbians.[30] Some feminists on the left argued for regulation of pornography on the ground that it did serious harm to women,[31] and liberals

24. Walker (1994), 15–16, 23–24, 83–85; Woeste (2012), 333.
25. Buckley (1962).
26. Emerson (1970), 724–27.
27. Marcuse (1965).
28. Walker (1994); Gould (2005).
29. Goldberger (1978); Downs (1985); Strum (1999).
30. E.g., Delgado (1982); Matsuda et al. (1993).
31. MacKinnon (1986).

supported legal prohibitions of sexual harassment even where those prohibitions had First Amendment implications.[32]

Another form of expression that concerned liberals was campaign finance. Revelations about fundraising and spending in President Nixon's campaign for reelection in 1972 spurred liberals in Congress to support tighter regulation of contributions and expenditures. Their efforts resulted in enactment of the 1974 amendments to the Federal Election Campaign Act. Later, perceptions that large contributions to campaigns and independent spending on behalf of candidates tended to benefit Republican candidates reinforced liberals' concern about the impact of money on politics and made regulation of campaign finance a continuing concern for them.[33] The Court's *Citizens United* decision in 2010 intensified this concern. That decision also helped to trigger a broader concern about the impact of free expression rights for corporations.[34] The leader of one liberal organization, Public Citizen, argued for a constitutional amendment "to remove corporate speech from the ambit of the First Amendment."[35]

A third form was more specific. Liberals were more sympathetic than conservatives to picketing and related activities so long as these modes of expression were undertaken by labor unions and civil rights groups. But when pro-life groups engaged in similar activities at abortion clinics, liberal supporters of abortion rights supported legislation and other legal action to limit picketing and demonstrations that they viewed as efforts to intimidate women who sought abortions and to disrupt the clinics' work.

---

32. See Volokh (1992); Estlund (1997); MacKinnon and Siegel (2004), chs. 21–26.

33. E.g., Wright (1982).

34. See Wu (2013).

35. Weissman (2011), 979. Liberals' support for regulation of campaign finance could be interpreted as reflecting pro-expression values, in that regulation supports the functioning of a meaningful marketplace of ideas. That conception is especially relevant to public funding of campaigns, most notably an Arizona statute that funded candidates whose opponents spent large amounts of money that they raised themselves. The Supreme Court struck down the statute in *Arizona Free Enterprise Club's Freedom Club PAC v. Bennett* (2011), with the Court's conservatives in the majority and its liberals dissenting.

Some of the considerations that undercut support for certain types of expression on the left bolstered that support on the right.[36] Conservatives were considerably less favorable to regulation of campaign finance and restrictions on picketing of abortion clinics than were liberals. Despite its title, the Bipartisan Campaign Reform Act of 2002 passed the House and Senate with support from about only one-fifth of the Republicans in the two houses.[37] Similarly, Democrats and Republicans divided sharply on the Freedom of Access to Clinic Entrances Act in 1994.[38] Conservatives widely attacked efforts to prohibit some types of expression under the rubric of hate speech as a form of "political correctness." Conservative support for certain forms of free expression included the development of constitutional arguments against restrictions on those forms, especially regulation of campaign finance.[39]

The growth of these new types of free expression issues made support for expression rights more situational: depending on the type, either conservatives or liberals gave disproportionate support to protection of speech from government limitations. This change was reflected in the title of a 1992 book by long-time civil libertarian Nat Hentoff: *Free Speech for Me—but Not for Thee: How the Left and Right Relentlessly Censor Each Other.* To adapt a term used by legal scholar Frederick Schauer, groups on both sides of the ideological divide engaged in "First Amendment opportunism."[40]

Like adherents to the New Left in the 1960s, some mainstream liberals later became more suspicious of free expression claims as a whole. That suspicion arose from their perception that the primary beneficiaries of protection for free expression had shifted from the

36. Balkin (1990), 384.
37. In the House, 94 percent of Democrats and 19 percent of Republicans voted for final passage of the bill; in the Senate, the proportions were 96 percent and 22 percent, respectively.
38. In the House, 82 percent of Democrats and 23 percent of Republicans voted to accept the conference report on the bill; in the Senate, the proportions were 95 percent and 39 percent, respectively.
39. Hollis-Brusky (2015), 61–89.
40. Schauer (2002).

left to the right.[41] One leading legal scholar complained that "the first amendment has replaced the due process clause as the primary guarantor of the privileged" and that it "stands as a general obstruction to all progressive legislative efforts."[42]

For their part, conservatives increasingly indicated their support for free expression in general. That support is reflected in the work of some leading public interest law firms. The Institute for Justice lists free speech as one of its "four pillars." Similarly, the Center for Individual Rights lists free speech as one of its three major areas of litigation activity.[43] As part of this process, conservatives advocate free speech claims in a wide range of contexts. Business groups, for instance, cite the First Amendment in challenges to government regulatory policies on matters such as disclosure of total prices for airline tickets,[44] prohibition of surcharges for use of credit cards,[45] and differential treatment of franchisees under local minimum wage laws.[46] Some conservative commentators champion free speech, pointing to what they see as repression of speech on a political basis by people and institutions on the left.[47]

One scholar of freedom of expression summarized what he saw as the shift that had occurred:[48]

> Yesterday liberals hailed the First Amendment; today it is conservatives. Yesterday the First Amendment was the rallying cry of anti-federalists, Bolsheviks, Communists, and anti-war demonstrators; today it is the banner flown by corporations, big-money political PACs, tobacco companies, and advertising agents along with a motley crew of crackpots.

41. Fiss (1986), 1406–7; Horwitz (1993), 109–10; White (1996), 376–77.
42. Tushnet (1984), 1387.
43. The work of these two groups in free expression is described at their websites, http://www.ij.org/cases/firstamendment (Institute for Justice) and https://www.cir-usa.org/case-types/first-amendment/ (Center for Individual Rights).
44. *Spirit Airlines, Inc. v. U.S. Department of Transportation* (2012).
45. *David's Railroad Supply v. Attorney General* (2015).
46. *International Franchise Association v. City of Seattle* (2015).
47. Ham and Benson (2015); Powers (2015); see Sanneh (2015).
48. Collins (2012), 409.

## FREE EXPRESSION CASES IN THE COURT

In themselves, these developments outside the Court could reshape justices' attitudes toward freedom of expression and their perceptions of the relationship between ideology and free expression questions. The cases that the justices considered and decided created a more direct conduit between changes in the larger world of political elites and the Court. Shifts in the kinds of questions raised by these cases could cause reconsideration of how conservative and liberal values apply to free expression. Changes in the identities of free expression claimants and in the advocates for the two sides might modify the justices' perceptions of the issue by triggering their affect toward the relevant social and political groups.[49]

### Questions

In analyzing the kinds of questions that appeared in free expression cases, the first step was to classify cases in conventional subject-matter terms, using categories such as national security, libel, obscenity, and regulation of groups and their members. Of the categories, the agenda shares of two were at least 5 percentage points higher in the 1994–2012 Terms than they had been in the 1946–93 Terms: "mainstream" political activity (+17.3%) and commercial speech (+7.8%). The mainstream category includes regulation of campaign funding, other campaign activities, and non-campaign activities such as lobbying. The agenda shares of two other categories dropped by at least 5 percentage points: national security (−19.4%) and libel (−8.4%).

I also coded cases according to the value that conflicted with freedom of expression—put differently, the justification for limiting expression. There is considerable overlap between these countervailing values and conventional categories such as national security, but coding by value gets more directly at the relationships between

---

49. I should note that in this analysis of the Court's agenda and similar analyses in the chapters that follow, both unanimous and non-unanimous cases are included unless I indicate otherwise.

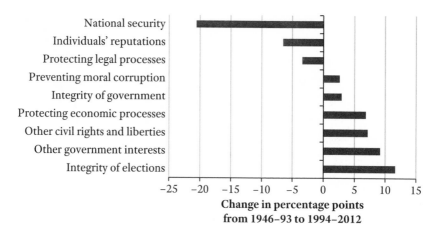

FIGURE 2.2. Change in agenda shares of selected case categories based on countervailing values, 1946–93 Terms to 1994–2012 Terms.
*Notes*: Categories are included if they accounted for at least 5 percent of free expression cases in one or both of the two periods.

cases and values that are associated with liberalism and conservatism. Comparisons of the two periods are shown in figure 2.2.

Cases involving three of the value categories with substantial increases or decreases overlapped considerably with subject-matter categories that also showed large increases or decreases: integrity of elections as value and mainstream political activity as subject, individuals' reputation and libel, and (of course) national security as value and as subject. A plurality of the cases involving protection of economic processes as a value fell in the commercial speech category, but there were also substantial numbers of cases involving picketing and other aspects of labor-management relations as well as others spread across subject-matter categories. The "other government interests" category was quite diverse in subject matter, with the largest numbers of cases involving public speech and speech in prisons.

The other category of values with a substantial increase was other civil rights and liberties—that is, rights other than free expression. This category is of particular interest, because so much attention has been given to situations in which there is a perceived conflict between freedom of expression and rights related to equality. In the 1946–93 Terms, only 4 percent of all cases involved this kind of conflict between rights. Most of these cases arose from efforts by governments to protect against discrimination. In the 1994–2012 Terms, when the proportion in this category increased to 11 percent, a slight majority of the conflicting-rights cases involved conflicts between abortion rights and the free speech rights of pro-life groups. The other cases ranged widely in the questions involved.

The changes that occurred in the kinds of questions raised by free expression cases could well have contributed to the Court's ideological realignment on this issue. Some kinds of questions on which the differences between liberal and conservative attitudes in the elite world as a whole have been especially sharp, such as national security, came to take smaller portions of the Court's agenda. In contrast, there was a growth in cases involving some kinds of questions on which liberals' tendency to favor free expression more than conservatives seems weaker or—in the case of conflicting rights and liberties—that tendency does not exist at all.

### Beneficiaries and Advocates

One way to identify the prospective beneficiaries of free expression claims is through the types of litigants that make those claims. I categorized claimants as government employees, participants in politics, other individuals, news media organizations and owners, non-media businesses and businesspeople, political organizations and leaders, labor unions and members, and other organizations.

There were some substantial increases and decreases in the agenda shares for particular categories. The largest change was an increase from 9.9 percent to 25.5 percent for political organizations and leaders. But some other shifts were even more noteworthy. There were declines for three groups toward which liberals are generally more sympathetic than conservatives: government employees, news media, and labor. Collectively, those three groups were the claimants in 43.1 percent of the cases that the Court decided in the 1946–93 Terms and 24.5 percent in the 1994–2012 Terms. Meanwhile, the proportion of cases with claims by the non-media business community, toward which conservatives are generally more sympathetic, doubled from 8.6 percent to 17.3 percent.

Although claimants' roles capture elements of the justices' sympathies, what can be called their ideological coloration does so even more directly. Ideological colorations were defined in two different ways. In the narrower definition, only political actors whose ideological position could be identified from the case were treated as standing on the left or right. (Thus, I will sometimes refer to this narrower definition as distinguishing between the political left and the political right.) On the left, these included five categories: the Democratic Party and people associated with it, civil rights groups and activists, other liberal interest groups and parties (including organized labor when it acted politically), the Communist Party and associated groups,[50] and other groups and parties on the extreme left. On the right, there were three categories: the Republican Party and people associated with it, pro-life groups and individuals, and other conservative groups and parties.[51]

In the broader definition, all claimants associated with labor unions were also treated as standing on the left, and all claimants in the business world (other than the mass media) were treated as standing on the right. It should be noted that many labor and business claimants had an identifiable ideological position and thus were included in the political left or political right as well as this broader definition of left and right.

The pattern of change for these variables, shown in figure 2.3, is striking. Leaving aside the sizeable proportion of cases that fit into neither ideological category, the Court moved from an era in which it heard predominately cases brought by claimants who can be identified as standing on the left to an era in which it heard predominately cases brought by claimants on the right. In that respect,

50. This category includes people who were charged with association with the Communist Party and associated groups, whether or not those charges were accurate. With that exception, claimants were categorized on the basis of their actual affiliations or expressed beliefs.

51. Extreme right-wing groups were excluded because support for the rights of those groups has been important to liberal conceptions of free expression and is reflected in the work of the American Civil Liberties Union. In each of the seven non-unanimous decisions involving claims by far-right groups, the pro-claimant justices were more liberal than the justices who rejected the free expression claim.

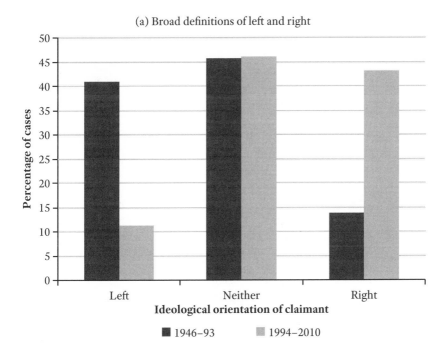

(a) Broad definitions of left and right

Percentage of cases

Ideological orientation of claimant

■ 1946–93    ▨ 1994–2010

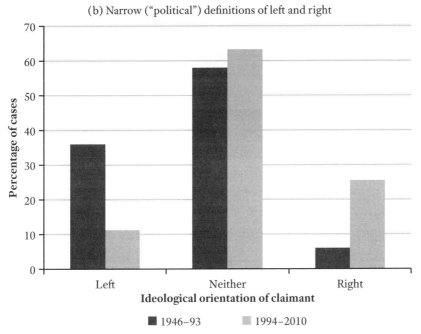

(b) Narrow ("political") definitions of left and right

Percentage of cases

Ideological orientation of claimant

■ 1946–93    ▨ 1994–2010

FIGURE 2.3. Proportions of free expression claimants in three ideological categories. Note: Definitions of left and right are presented in the text.

more than any other, the Court's free expression business changed fundamentally.[52]

The shift in the ideological coloration of claimants began well before the 1994 Term. People and groups on the political left (that is, by the narrow definition of left) constituted 65 percent of all claimants in the Warren Court, 23 percent in the Burger Court, 16 percent in the early Rehnquist Court, and 8 percent in the late Rehnquist Court. Meanwhile, claimants on the political right were scarce in the Vinson and Warren Courts but appeared in 9 percent of the Burger Court cases, 10 percent in the early Rehnquist Court, and 25 percent—vastly outnumbering their counterparts on the left—in the late Rehnquist Court.

In free expression cases, the beneficiaries of a decision are usually clear from the identities of the litigants and the claims they make. However, the identities of the lawyers who represent litigants and of the groups that file and join amicus curiae briefs provide additional information to the justices about the political and ideological interests on either side.

In the Rehnquist and Roberts Courts, traditional civil libertarian lawyers Floyd Abrams and Bruce Ennis each presented arguments for claimants on the right as broadly defined, and so did liberal law professor Laurence Tribe. But even more prominent were two lawyers on the right: James Bopp, Jr., affiliated with several conservative groups, and Jay Sekulow of the American Center for Law and Justice, who each argued for several claimants. Some other claimants on the right were represented by lawyers whom the justices would recognize as conservative, such as former solicitor general Theodore Olson. Among the smaller number of claimants from the political left, several were represented either by ACLU-affiliated lawyers such as Ennis and Burt Neuborne or by lawyers identified as liberal (such as Tribe) or radical (William Kunstler).

---

52. This change is symbolized by the trend for claimants who were on the far left (or who were accused of being on the far left) and civil rights advocates. Together, they appeared in 24 percent of all free expression cases in the 1946–93 Terms, and they constituted 58 percent of all claimants with an identifiable ideological coloration by the narrow definition. In the 1994–2012 Terms, these claimants had essentially disappeared.

As we would expect, a great many claimants on both sides had lawyers who lacked a visible ideological leaning. Even so, the mix of lawyers who presented arguments for claimants on the right may have helped signal the justices that freedom of expression was no longer a cause for which support came overwhelmingly from the political left. Rather, the identities of these lawyers was consistent with the impression that free expression had become a conservative cause when the interests making free expression claims were political conservatives or businesses.

Amicus briefs provide more systematic information to justices about the ideological stakes in cases. In the two decades after World War II, amicus briefs were distinctly more common in free expression cases than they were across all fields of legal policy, and their frequency surged ahead of the average again in the 1986–95 Terms.[53] Briefs favoring free expression claims greatly outnumbered those opposing these claims in the Vinson and Warren Courts; in the Warren Court, the ratio was 3.35 to 1. But after that time, the anti-expression briefs grew more quickly than the pro-expression briefs, so that they became nearly as common; the ratio was 1.09:1 in the 1994–2004 Terms and 1.37:1 in the 2005–12 Terms.[54] This change does not necessarily mean that free expression questions became more controversial, but it indicates that interest groups increasingly found free expression claims antithetical to their interests and sought to defend those interests in the Supreme Court.

The amici that appeared in the Rehnquist and Roberts Court cases are of particular interest. One source of briefs favoring free expression claims was groups that had a direct stake in the Court's decisions, such as media groups in cases involving the mass media. Similarly, governmental groups often appeared in support of government regulations of expression. Both types of amici, along with specialized groups such as those that favored regulation of obscenity, had been prominent in prior periods.

---

53. See Kearney and Merrill (2000), 752–53.
54. These figures are for briefs at the merits stage, so the small numbers of cases decided without oral argument are excluded.

But what stands out in the Rehnquist and Roberts Courts is the frequency with which groups that had a clear ideological identification appeared as amici. Some of these were groups that specialized in the field in question, such as abortion rights groups that supported the government's position in cases involving pro-life demonstrations. Others were groups with broader interests, such as conservative public interest law firms. By their presence, these groups helped to define the ideological sides in cases. Some cases featured large alliances of amici opposing each other; between the 1985 and 2012 Terms, there were ten cases with at least ten briefs on each side. In these cases, groups with a stake in the specific question in the case typically were accompanied by groups with broader ideological agendas, with liberal and conservative groups generally on opposite sides.

One amicus may be especially important as a source of cues to the justices: the ACLU. The ACLU has a general reputation for giving unwavering support to free expression, though some commentators have contested the basis for that reputation.[55] Beyond its role as sponsor of litigation, the ACLU as amicus does support claimants in the overwhelming majority of free expression cases in which it takes a position—93 percent in the 1946–2012 Terms.[56] For this reason, an ACLU amicus brief that opposes a party making free expression claim is likely to send a strong signal to the justices.

In the 1946–2012 Terms, the national ACLU or an affiliate signed or cosigned an amicus brief opposing the party with a free expression claim in fifteen cases, all of them coming after the 1967 Term.[57] In a few of these cases, the free expression claim was peripheral rather than central to the Court's decision. Notably, in thirteen of the fifteen cases, the countervailing value on the anti-claimant side was another right. Thus, for instance, the ACLU favored racial equality,[58]

55. E.g., Bernstein (2003), 145–53.
56. The ACLU occasionally participates as a direct party in free expression cases (e.g., *Ashcroft v. American Civil Liberties Union,* 2002), and attorneys who participate in cases on behalf of the ACLU sometimes represent private parties and amici in free expression cases. In both instances, the participation is almost always on behalf of the free expression claim.
57. In one of those cases, *Wisconsin v. Mitchell* (1993), the ACLU opposed the free expression claim but a state affiliate favored that claim.
58. *Runyon v. McCrary* (1976).

gender equality,[59] and access to abortion[60] over competing free expression claims. By doing so, the ACLU may have helped to alert liberal justices that these cases were more complex ideologically than First Amendment cases traditionally had been.

Like the kinds of questions raised by cases, the identities of beneficiaries and advocates could have contributed to the shift in the Court's polarity. In the cases that the Court heard, free expression claims and their supporters increasingly came from the political right rather than the political left and from the business world rather than organized labor. To the extent that the justices act on their affect toward social and political groups, this change in the composition of cases almost inevitably would lead to a weakening of the traditional polarity of freedom of expression.

In discussing change in the Court's free expression agenda, I have not yet addressed the process of creating that agenda. Of course, the attributes of cases that the Court decides on the merits reflect both the mix of cases brought to the Court and the justices' choices about which of those cases to hear. Listings of paid petitions in *United States Law Week* since the mid-1960s indicate that changes in the Court's agenda of accepted cases have broadly tracked changes in the composition of petitions. In 1966, the petitions were dominated by obscenity cases, with libel second in frequency. The 1976 cases were similar, but by 1986 there were a few petitions in commercial speech and abortion protest cases.

In the 1996, 2001, 2006, and 2011 Terms, the petitions were considerably more heterogeneous, with conservative participants in politics and businesses other than the mass media far better represented than in the earlier years (at least if petitions from non-media businesses in obscenity cases are excluded). Undoubtedly, this change reflected both growth in conservative interest in the First Amendment and perceptions that the Court was becoming receptive to the kinds of cases that conservatives wanted to bring. In any event, by the 1990s

59. *Pittsburgh Press Co. v. Pittsburgh Commission on Human Relations* (1973); *Grove City College v. Bell* (1984); *Hishon v. King & Spalding* (1984); *Roberts v. United States Jaycees* (1984).

60. *Bray v. Alexandria Women's Health Clinic* (1993); *Schenck v. Pro-Choice Network* (1997).

the justices had a wide range of free expression cases to choose from. Collectively, they used that range of choice to create an agenda that differed considerably from the Court's traditional agenda on this issue.

### JUSTICES' RESPONSES TO CASES

Developments outside the Court and attributes of cases on the Court's agenda provide evidence about the bases for the shift in polarity of free expression cases. Patterns in the justices' responses to cases provide more direct evidence on the mechanisms and sources of that shift. I give primary attention to the Court as a whole, probing changes in the Court's polarity by examining the relationship between that polarity and the attributes of cases—first, the kinds of free expression questions, then the ideological coloration of claimants. Finally, I examine patterns of responses to cases by individual justices.

### Questions

The discussion of the subject matter of cases and the countervailing values that arise in those cases indicated a shift in the kinds of questions that the Court heard between the 1946–93 and 1994–2012 periods. If questions that became more prominent on the agenda were those in which the Court's traditional polarity had been relatively weak, or if questions that faded from the agenda were those in which that traditional polarity had been unusually strong, those changes could account for much of the shift in polarity.

Subject-matter and countervailing categories were included in table 2.3 if there were meaningful increases or decreases in their agenda shares. Public speech was also included because of the substantial change in the Court's polarity in that category. Because national security cases were especially strong in their polarity, their virtual disappearance played a role in the overall shift in the Court's polarity, albeit a small one. That was not true of the disappearance of libel cases,[61] because their polarity had been relatively weak.

---

61. One post-1993 case, *Snyder v. Phelps* (2011), might be classified as a libel case; instead, with the libel claim gone from the case by the time it reached the Supreme Court, it was classified as a public speech case.

TABLE 2.3. Agenda shares and ideological polarity for selected categories of cases, 1946–93 and 1994–2012 Terms

| | Percent of free expression agenda | | | Percent of non-unanimous decisions with pro-claimant justices more liberal | | |
|---|---|---|---|---|---|---|
| SUBJECT/VALUE | 1946–93 | 1994–2012 | Change | 1946–93 | 1994–2012 | Change |
| NATIONAL SECURITY (S) | 20.5 | 1.0 | −19.5 | 97.3 | --- | --- |
| LIBEL (S) | 8.4 | 0.0 | −8.4 | 73.9 | --- | --- |
| COMMERCIAL SPEECH (S) | 6.5 | 14.3 | +7.8 | 100.0 | 33.3 | −66.7 |
| MAINSTREAM POLITICS (S) | 10.1 | 27.6 | +17.4 | 80.0 | 26.1 | −53.9 |
|    CAMPAIGN INTEGRITY (V) | 7.8 | 19.4 | +11.6 | 70.0 | 22.2 | −47.8 |
| OTHER RIGHTS (V) | 4.1 | 11.2 | +7.1 | (42.9) | (12.5) | −30.4 |
| PUBLIC SPEECH (S) | 17.7 | 16.3 | −1.3 | 95.0 | 63.6 | −31.4 |
| ALL CASES | | | | 92.6 | 56.3 | −36.3 |

*Notes*: "S" refers to a subject matter category, "V" to a countervailing value category. "---" indicates that there were fewer than five non-unanimous decisions in a period; parentheses indicate that there were between five and nine non-unanimous decisions. All campaign integrity cases are within the mainstream politics category. "Change" is the increase or decrease in the percentages from 1946–93 to 1994–2012; because of rounding errors, the percentage change does not always match the percentages in the preceding two columns.

Because the Court's polarity in mainstream politics cases and in the cases involving elections was relatively weak in the 1946–93 Terms, their growth contributed to the shift in polarity. To a degree (though a lesser one because of their small numbers) the same is true of cases involving conflicts between freedom of expression and other rights.

In each of the categories in the table whose agenda share increased, there was also a substantial change in polarity in the 1994–2012 period. Indeed, the increase in the proportion of cases in which pro-claimant justices were more conservative than their colleagues was more striking than the increase in their frequency. An examination of patterns of polarity within these categories and in public speech can help in understanding what changed.

When the Court began to provide substantial protection for *commercial speech* in the 1970s and 1980s, that departure from its long-standing position garnered disproportionate support from liberal justices. That polarity is striking, because the Court's new position had the effect of limiting government regulation of business activity. One critical commentary suggested that the Court was returning to an earlier era of limits to government regulation, albeit an era in which it supported such limitations against liberal opposition.[62]

The polarity of the commercial speech cases in that period can be explained primarily by the kinds of cases that the Court heard. In most cases the speech in question was especially appealing to liberals.[63] One key case involved advertising of abortion, and another early case involved distribution of contraceptives.[64] Other cases concerned advertising that was perceived to benefit consumers by reducing prices and expanding the availability of products and services—most often, legal services.[65] And most of the early challenges to prohibitions on commercial speech were brought by liberal lawyers or interest groups.

Later, the Court's polarity in commercial speech cases shifted. In the 1994–2012 Terms there were nine non-unanimous commercial speech cases, in six of which the Court's conservatives provided highly disproportionate support for free speech claims. Two of those six cases involved challenges to types of government regulation that liberals were likely to find more benign than conservatives, "must carry" requirements for cable television and limits on tobacco advertising.[66] The other four cases are more difficult to interpret: two involved federally mandated contributions to generic advertising of agricultural products,[67] and two involved pharmaceutical marketing.[68] The drug cases may have reflected a shift in the views of liberals and conservatives about the benefits of product marketing; the generic advertising cases may be more idiosyncratic. But in these six cases as a whole, amicus support for free speech claims came primarily from

62. T. Jackson and Jeffries (1979).

63. See Graetz and Greenhouse (2016), 245–49.

64. *Bigelow v. Virginia* (1975); *Carey v. Population Services* (1977).

65. Examples include *Virginia State Board of Pharmacy v. Virginia Citizens Consumer Council* (1976), the key case expanding constitutional protection for commercial speech, and *Bates v. State Bar of Arizona* (1977), the first of several cases involving advertising by lawyers.

66. *Turner Broadcasting System v. Federal Communications Commission* (1997); *Altadis U.S.A. v. Reilly* (2001).

67. *Glickman v. Wileman Brothers* (1997); *United States v. United Foods* (2001).

68. *Thompson v. Western States Medical Center* (2002); *Sorrell v. IMS Health Inc.* (2011).

businesses and conservative groups, and several liberal groups supported restrictions on speech.[69] This lineup of amici reflected changes in perceptions of commercial speech, so that free expression claims in this field increasingly were identified as serving business interests.[70]

Because there were relatively few divided decisions in the commercial speech category, they contributed only a little to the change in ideological polarity in free expression as a whole. The more numerous *mainstream politics* cases made them a bigger contributor. The ideological polarity of the Court's decisions shifted over time across all types of cases within this category, but the primary source of the change between the two periods was cases involving campaign finance. These cases quadrupled as a proportion of all free expression cases (to 12.2 percent) between the 1946–93 and 1994–2012 Terms. Even in the 1946–93 period, the pro-claimant justices were more conservative than the anti-claimant justices in six of eight decisions. What distinguished these six cases from the other three cases was that they were brought by conservative claimants.[71] In the 1994–2012 Terms, the pro-claimant justices were more conservative than the anti-claimant justices in all eleven non-unanimous decisions involving campaign finance, in ten of which the claimant was on the political right.[72] Indeed, cases involving government regulation of campaign finance came to divide liberal and conservative justices sharply. That division mirrored the division among political elites as a whole.

There was a less dramatic change in the justices' polarity in other types of mainstream politics cases. Relative to their liberal colleagues, conservative justices became increasingly unfriendly to regulation of

69. The three commercial speech cases in the 1994–2012 Terms in which the pro-claimant justices were more liberal than the anti-claimant justices included a lawyer advertising case (*Florida Bar v. Went for It, Inc.*, 1995), a copyright case (*Eldred v. Ashcroft*, 2003), and a case involving mandated contributions to generic advertising that differed from the other cases of this type in that it involved governmental rather than private speech (*Johanns v. Livestock Marketing Association*, 2005).

70. Piety (2012).

71. In *Buckley v. Valeo* (1976), one of the six cases, the challenge to regulation of campaign finance was brought by a coalition of liberals and (in greater numbers) conservatives.

72. The exception was *Davis v. Federal Election Commission* (2008), brought by a Democratic congressional candidate.

political parties and electoral activity. One reason was the increased presence of conservative individuals and groups as challengers to regulation. In non-unanimous decisions on this subject in the 1946–93 Terms, only one of the seven claimants whose ideological coloration was evident came from the political right; in the 1994–2012 Terms, it was five of seven. In the 1994–2012 cases, justices who supported claimants on the left were more liberal than their colleagues in both cases; justices who supported claimants on the right were more liberal than their colleagues in only one of the five cases.

Some of the divisions among the justices in mainstream politics cases have at least tinges of "low politics," in that justices took positions favoring the electoral prospects of groups that shared the justices' partisan or ideological identifications. Restrictions on campaign finance are generally thought to benefit Democratic candidates as a whole. In *Republican Party v. White*, the Court's five conservative justices provided the 5–4 majority to strike down a Minnesota limitation on announcement of policy positions by candidates for judgeships.[73] That division may have reflected the Republican challenge to the Minnesota law and the perception that conservative candidates for judgeships are more likely than liberals to benefit from issue-based campaigns.[74]

In *public speech*, the change in polarity is explained almost entirely by the ideological coloration of claimants. In the 1946–93 Terms, only three of the sixty claimants in non-unanimous public speech decisions were identified with the political right, with the others divided about equally between those on the left and those who could not be placed on either side. Two of the three cases in which the pro-claimant justices were more conservative than their colleagues were also two of the three cases in which the claimant stood on the right.

There were eleven non-unanimous public speech decisions in the 1994–2012 Terms. In the three cases involving pro-life groups, the justices supporting their claims were substantially more conservative than the justices on the other side. In seven of the other eight cases, none of which involved speakers who stood visibly on either

73. *Republican Party v. White* (2002).
74. See Gibson (2012), 133.

the left or the right, the justices supporting the claimants were more liberal than their colleagues. In both periods, then, liberal justices had a strong tendency to favor public speech claims more than the Court's conservatives, except when the claimant was conservative.

The cases involving conflicts between freedom of expression and *other rights* fell under several subject-matter categories, most often public speech (23 percent). When the justices divided in these cases, the pro-claimant justices were more conservative overall than the anti-claimant justices—in four of seven decisions in the 1946–93 Terms and seven of eight decisions in the 1994–2012 Terms. All eleven cases in which the pro-claimant justices were more conservative than the justices on the other side had a strong polarity in that direction. Five involved restrictions on anti-abortion activities, two involved conflicts between freedom of expression and the prohibition of an establishment of religion, three involved conflicts between free expression and equality claims, and in one a First Amendment claim by two newspapers in an antitrust case was countered by free expression considerations on the other side.[75]

Although the conflicting-rights cases account for little of the change in the Court's overall polarity, they are consistent with the idea that the ideological polarity of an issue reflects the relationship between the issue and broad values associated with liberalism and conservatism. For liberals, the rights that weighed against free expression claims may have occupied a more fundamental place in their value systems.[76] The Court's shift of polarity in commercial speech cases can be interpreted in multiple ways. It seems to reflect both values and the justices' attitudes toward the groups whose speech was involved. The ideological identities of the advocates for the competing positions may have provided important cues to the justices about the implications of cases for the justices' values and about the stakes in cases for social groups toward which the justices felt positive or negative affect.

---

75. *Citizen Publishing Co. v. United States* (1969).

76. Another analysis of free expression cases that focused on conflicts between values also can be interpreted as supporting that conclusion (L. Epstein and Segal 2006).

The mainstream politics and public speech cases are different. In those fields, the primary basis for divisions among the justices seemed to be the ideological coloration of the political groups that made free expression claims. Because of the large numbers of cases and the substantial change in the justices' polarity in these two categories, they were responsible for a substantial share of the overall shift in the Court's polarity. In turn, this suggests that group affect played a key role in that shift. The validity of that interpretation can be probed with a comprehensive analysis of the relationship between claimants' ideological coloration and the Court's polarity.

### Claimants

Beginning with the Burger Court, the proportion of free expression claimants from the left declined and the proportion from the right increased, by both broad and narrow definitions of left and right. By the late Rehnquist Court, claimants from the right outnumbered those from the left by a considerable margin. That was also the period when the Court's overall polarity shifted from one in which justices supporting free expression claims were more liberal than their colleagues the great majority of the time to one in which there was no sharp difference between the Court's conservatives and liberals in their overall levels of support for free expression. The relationship between these two trends can be assessed by looking at time periods and the political coloration of claimants together.

Table 2.4 shows this relationship for the dichotomized measure of polarity, and figure 2.4 for the mean differences in the ideological stances of justices on the two sides. The patterns are striking. In the 1946–93 Terms, the strong tendency for pro-claimant justices to be more liberal than their colleagues who opposed free expression claims applied to both cases with claimants on the left and those in which claimants had no political coloration. But this polarity weakened when claimants came from the right. For claimants from the political right (under the narrow definition of left and right), the pro-claimant justices were actually more conservative than their colleagues a majority of the time.

This suggests that the appearance of highly disproportionate support for free expression from the Court's liberals during the 1946–93

TABLE 2.4. Relationship between ideological position of free expression claimants and ideological polarity of non-unanimous decisions, 1946–93 Terms and 1994–2012 Terms (in percentages)

| | Side with more liberal ideology score | | | | | |
| | 1946–93 | | | 1994–2012 | | |
| Claimants | Pro-claimant | Anti-claimant | N | Pro-claimant | Anti-claimant | N |
|---|---|---|---|---|---|---|
| Left and right defined broadly | | | | | | |
| LEFT | 97.9 | 2.1 | 141 | 83.3 | 16.7 | 6 |
| NEITHER | 92.3 | 7.7 | 143 | 81.3 | 18.7 | 32 |
| RIGHT | 73.8 | 26.2 | 42 | 27.3 | 72.7 | 33 |
| Left and right defined narrowly ("political") | | | | | | |
| LEFT | 98.4 | 1.6 | 122 | 83.3 | 16.7 | 6 |
| NEITHER | 93.0 | 7.0 | 187 | 75.0 | 25.0 | 44 |
| RIGHT | 41.2 | 58.8 | 17 | 9.5 | 90.5 | 21 |

era resulted in part from the dearth of cases in which that support was tested by claimants on the mainstream right and in the business world. Once such cases became more common, during the Burger Court, so did decisions in which the justices reversed their traditional ideological polarity in free expression cases.

In the 1994–2012 Terms, there were too few non-unanimous decisions with claimants on the left to identify a temporal trend. Claimants who were on neither the right nor the left continued to receive disproportionate support from more liberal justices, though that tendency weakened somewhat. The really striking change involved claimants from the right. Now the dominant pattern was one in which those claimants received disproportionate support from the more conservative justices. In cases involving the political right, that pattern was overwhelming. Thus there was a sharp difference in the Court's polarity between cases with claimants on the right and the other two categories.[77]

77. L. Epstein, Parker, and Segal (2013) investigated a related phenomenon, the impact of the interaction between justices' overall ideological positions and "the ideological direction of the expression (or expresser)" on justices' votes in First Amendment cases in the 1953–2010 Terms. They also took into account the ideological direction of the law that was challenged. They found that the expresser's ideological grouping had considerable impact, with liberal and conservative justices much closer to each other in the likelihood of supporting a free expression claim when the expresser was identified as conservative. That finding provides additional evidence of the impact of group affect on justices' responses to free expression cases.

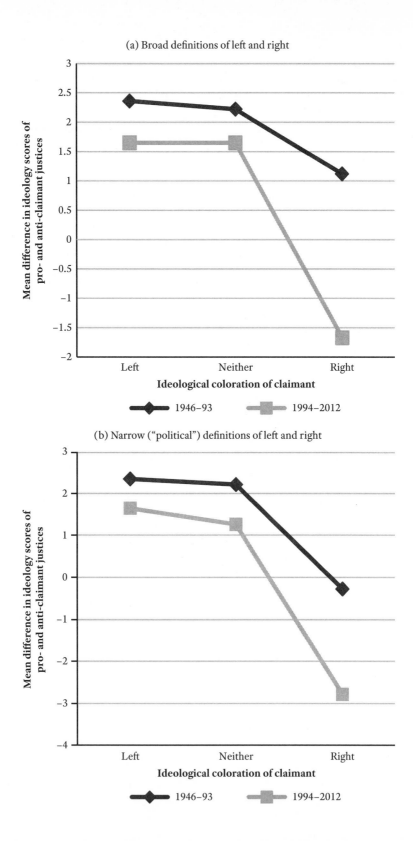

(a) Broad definitions of left and right

(b) Narrow ("political") definitions of left and right

FIGURE 2.4. Mean difference between median Martin-Quinn scores of justices voting for and against free expression claimants, 1946–93 Terms and 1994–2012 Terms.
*Notes*: Because the scales of the two graphs differ, the differences among categories of claimants in the second graph are understated compared with those in the first graph.

The success rates of claimants on the left and right in the Court are also of interest. In the Burger Court, by both definitions of left and right, the two types of claimants were about equally likely to win their cases. In the early Rehnquist Court (through the 1993 Term), by the broad definition of left and right, claimants on the right did substantially better (by a 17 percentage-point margin) than those on the left, a result that reflects the success of businesses as claimants. The reduced numbers of cases after that time made comparisons less meaningful, but the differences in the Roberts Court are striking: claimants on the right were far more successful than those on the left by both definitions (75 percent versus 17 percent by the broad definition, 89 percent versus 17 percent by the narrow definition).

On their face, then, the patterns in the data provide strong evidence that the Court's polarity was powerfully shaped by the ideological identities of the parties with free expression claims. However, we would expect cases with claimants that differed by their ideological coloration to differ in other respects, and it might be that those other differences play a substantial role in shaping the Court's polarity.

Indeed, the distributions of question types and countervailing values differed among the categories of cases defined by the claimants' ideological coloration. For instance, by the broad definition of left and right, across the whole 1946–2012 period the cases with claimants on the left were dominated by the national security (47 percent) and public speech (26 percent) cases. In contrast, the most common categories in cases with claimants on the right were commercial speech (30 percent) and mainstream politics (29 percent).

Because of these differences, I undertook regression analyses that included variables for claimants' ideological coloration and for the substance of cases. In linear regression analyses, the dependent variable was the difference between the median Martin-Quinn scores of the pro-claimant and anti-claimant justices; in logistic regression analyses, the dependent variable was whether the pro-claimant justices were more liberal or more conservative than their colleagues. The independent variables were the broad subject-matter categories or the countervailing value categories and, in alternate analyses, the two variables capturing the ideological orientation of the claimant. Analyses covered the whole 1946–2012 period and the two major subsets of that period.

In all of the analyses, the claimant's ideological coloration had a strong impact on the Court's ideological polarity even with the controls for subject matter or countervailing values. This finding provides additional evidence that the justices responded differentially to free expression claimants on the basis of where those claimants stood ideologically.

In each of the analyses, at least one of the subject types or countervailing values also had a substantial impact on the Court's polarity. Overall, the strongest effects were for mainstream politics cases, especially those involving electoral campaigns, and for cases involving conflicts between free expression and other constitutional rights. In each instance, cases in those categories were substantially less likely to have pro-claimant justices who were more liberal than their colleagues, even with a control for the ideological coloration of the claimant. But even within specific case categories, as discussed earlier, the Court's polarity differed considerably among claimants with different ideological positions. For the 1946–2012 period as a whole, those differences were especially striking in mainstream politics and public speech.

The impact of claimants' identities on the polarity of free expression decisions is symbolized by two sets of cases. The first set concerns campaign finance. In *United States v. Congress of Industrial Organizations* (CIO) (1948)[78] and *United States v. United Auto Workers* (UAW) (1957),[79] the Supreme Court addressed federal statutes that prohibited independent expenditures in federal elections by

78. *United States v. Congress of Industrial Organizations* (1948).
79. *United States v. United Auto Workers* (1957).

corporations and labor unions. In both cases, the Court avoided deciding whether the provision in question violated the First Amendment, and in the *UAW* case, it reinstated a prosecution of the union under that provision. Both decisions elicited minority opinions arguing that the provisions were unconstitutional, a concurring opinion by the four most liberal members of the Court in *CIO* and a dissenting opinion by the three most liberal justices in *UAW*.[80] In *Citizens United v. Federal Election Commission (2010)*, in contrast, the Court addressed another statutory prohibition on certain independent expenditures in federal campaigns by corporations and unions.[81] The Court held that the prohibition violated the First Amendment, with its four most liberal justices dissenting.

A great many things changed between 1957 and 2010, but two connected changes were the keys to the difference in the ideological polarity of the earlier and later decisions. The more specific change was in the challenger to the law: labor unions in the earlier cases, a conservative organization in *Citizens United*. The broader change was in perceptions of the groups that had stakes in the decisions. The provisions challenged in 1948 and 1957 were perceived as a limitation primarily on unions, part of the Taft-Hartley statute that was aimed at union activities; the provision challenged in 2010 was perceived as a limitation primarily on businesses and political groups on the right. The justices responded to those perceptions.

The other set of cases concerns the rights of public employees. When the Court divides in cases involving restrictions by government employers on their employees' speech on the job, the pro-employee justices are nearly always more liberal than the justices who vote against an employee's claim. But when public employees protest mandatory financial contributions to labor unions, it is primarily conservative justices who support their claims.[82] In *Harris v. Quinn*, the Court ruled that collection of union fees from certain

80. See Abrams (2013), 312.
81. *Citizens United v. Federal Election Commission* (2010).
82. Examples of cases in the first category are *Arnett v. Kennedy* (1974) and *Garcetti v. Ceballos* (2006). Examples of cases in the second category are *Lehnert v. Ferris Faculty Association* (1991) and *Knox v. Service Employees International Union* (2012).

government employees violated the First Amendment, with the justices splitting along ideological lines.[83] Justice Kagan pointed out in her dissenting opinion that the Court operates under a doctrine that substantially limits the speech rights of government employees but that it regularly diverges from this doctrine in cases involving employees' objections to union fees. What Kagan did not say, but undoubtedly had in mind, was that the Court's conservative majority had created this difference.

Earlier I discussed anti-claimant amicus briefs from the ACLU as possible cues to the justices about the ideological stakes in cases. The justices' responses to cases are consistent with that possibility. The justices divided in eight of the fifteen cases in which the ACLU took an anti-claimant position, all eight of which involved conflicts between rights. In all but one of those eight cases, the justices on the pro-claimant side were more conservative than those on the anti-claimant side. That pattern contrasted sharply with the cases with non-unanimous decisions in which the ACLU took a pro-claimant position, took a neutral position, or did not file an amicus brief: in 87 percent of those cases (and 85 percent from the 1968 Term on), the pro-claimant justices were more liberal than the justices on the other side. Whether or not the ACLU's briefs served as cues to the justices, its positions reflected the growing ideological complexity of free expression, a complexity that was also reflected in the Court's changed polarity.

### Justices

The voting records of individual justices on free expression claims provide another perspective. Among the seven justices who served both before and after the Court's shift in polarity (with the line drawn between the 1993 and 1994 Terms), overall support for free expression claimants increased among the conservatives and declined among the liberals. However, the changes were substantial

---

In *Friedrichs v. California Teachers Association* (2016), another union fees case, the Court's tie vote was widely assumed to have fallen along ideological lines.

83. *Harris v. Quinn* (2014).

TABLE 2.5. Percentage of justices' votes favoring free expression claimants in cases with claimants on the right minus percentage in cases with claimants on the left, 1946–2012 Terms

| Justice | Definition of left and right | |
|---|---|---|
| | Broad | Narrow |
| Douglas | −38.3 | --- |
| Black | −55.4 | --- |
| Marshall | −27.5 | −36.7 |
| Brennan | −27.6 | −35.5 |
| Ginsburg | −10.0 | −16.7 |
| Stevens | −2.4 | −21.7 |
| Blackmun 2 | −1.1 | −33.9 |
| Souter | −7.5 | −20.2 |
| Breyer | −14.5 | −17.5 |
| Stewart | −20.3 | −15.1 |
| White | +2.0 | −3.3 |
| Blackmun 1 | +25.9 | +24.1 |
| Kennedy | +31.0 | +33.0 |
| Powell | +3.1 | +9.1 |
| O'Connor | +19.4 | +25.3 |
| Roberts | +65.1 | +72.2 |
| Scalia | +38.3 | +51.5 |
| Alito | +57.8 | +65.7 |
| Burger | +6.0 | +21.6 |
| Thomas | +39.0 | +52.4 |
| Rehnquist | +15.0 | +22.2 |

*Notes*: Justices are listed in the order of the percentage of liberal votes they cast in all cases with oral argument during the 1946–2012 Terms, based on coding of votes in the Supreme Court Database. They are included if they participated in at least five decisions in both the "left" and "right" categories. Hugo Black and William O. Douglas met this criterion only for the broad definition of left and right. "Blackmun 1" covers the 1970–81 Terms; "Blackmun 2" covers the 1982–93 Terms. As the table title indicates, a positive percentage indicates that the justice voted for claimants on the right a higher proportion of the time than claimants on the left.

only for William Rehnquist (+15.9 percentage points), John Paul Stevens (−12.8%), and David Souter (−15.3%), and Souter participated in relatively few cases prior to the time break.

More relevant than the justices' overall voting records are their responses to free expression claims from litigants of different ideological coloration. Table 2.5 shows differences in voting support for claimants on the left and right by justices who served during the 1946–2012 Terms and who participated in enough cases involving claimants on both sides to allow for meaningful comparisons. The justices are placed in order of their general liberalism and conservatism, as measured by their votes across all issue areas.

The order of the justices in the table (and the order in similar tables in later chapters) is only an approximate measure of their overall ideological positions, because of changes in the case mix over time. For instance, most observers of the Court would view Samuel Alito as more conservative than Warren Burger. Still, the table shows that liberal justices had a strong tendency to support free expression claims more often when the claimants were on the left than when they were on the right, while conservative justices had the opposite tendency. The relationship between claimant ideology and justices' responses to free expression cases is illustrated in another way by the difference between the first (conservative) and second (liberal) halves of Justice Harry Blackmun's tenure on the Court.

Justices who served early in the period are poorly represented in the table because of the dearth of claimants on the right in that era, but the findings for justices such as Hugo Black and William O. Douglas indicate that justices responded differently to claimants on the left and the right well before the shift in the Court's polarity in the early 1990s. However, there are signs that the tendency has strengthened over time. Among the five justices who served for several terms both before and after the break in 1994, the differences between a justice's support for claimants on the left and those on the right were almost always higher—sometimes considerably higher—after the break.[84]

This leaves only one plausible alternative to a simple explanation that is based on the justices' affect toward the groups represented by litigants: differences in subject matter or countervailing values

84. The five justices were Rehnquist, Stevens, O'Connor, Scalia, and Kennedy. Of the ten comparisons (for broad and narrow definitions of left and right for each justice), only Rehnquist for the narrow definition showed a smaller difference between his support for claimants on the left and for those on the right in the second period than in the first period. The mean of the differences between left and right claimants for the five justices was 14 percentage points higher in the post-1993 period for the broad definition of left and right, 10 percentage points higher for the narrow definition.

between the cases with litigants on the left and those with litigants on the right. As the earlier discussion of this possibility showed, there were meaningful differences in subject matter and conflicting values between those two sets of cases, but those differences do not go far toward explaining the relationship between the ideological identities of litigants and the Court's polarity. Moreover, that relationship is not limited to the past quarter century, when the traditional tendency of liberal justices to lead the Court in support for freedom of expression has weakened considerably.

It is noteworthy that the differences between individual justices' voting support for claimants on the left and their support for claimants on the right are generally higher—in several instances, substantially higher—when claims by business and labor in non-political roles are removed and only the political left and right are included. Although the cases brought by litigants on the political right and left are not identical in their subject matter or in the values that conflict with free expression, the differences in those attributes are hardly sufficient to account for the voting tendencies shown in table 2.5. Rather, justices clearly differentiated between free speech claims brought by their political compatriots and their political opponents. What the data cannot tell us is the extent to which they did so consciously.

### LOOKING BACK TO THE 1910–45 TERMS

The Court's record in its first era of substantial work in freedom of expression provides additional evidence about the ideological dimension in its decisions. As table 2.1 showed, once the Court started to hear significant numbers of free expression cases, the familiar liberal-conservative polarity developed. Of the forty-three non-unanimous decisions in the 1910–45 Terms, the pro-claimant justices were more liberal than their anti-claimant colleagues in thirty-five.

Of those thirty-five cases, twenty-one had claimants on the left, by the broad definition that includes labor unions. Another seven were brought by Jehovah's Witnesses, a group whose outsider status made their claims more attractive to liberals than to conservatives. Only one of the thirty-five cases involved a claimant on the right under the broad definition, a business owner whose challenge to a fraud order by a postmaster attracted a lone dissent by Justice Oliver Wendell Holmes.[85]

Seven of the eight decisions in which the pro-claimant justices were more conservative than their colleagues involved claims by businesses, although four of the claimants did not fall in the "right" category because they were part of the news media. Four of the seven cases involved regulation of labor-management relations, and two involved antitrust law or antitrust-like regulation by the Federal Communication Commission.[86]

As this pattern of polarity indicates, support for free expression in the Supreme Court of the late 1930s and 1940s was linked with economic liberalism, and that linkage came through most clearly in labor-management cases. In contrast, the Court—and especially its most liberal justices—were decidedly less sympathetic to the free speech rights of businesses in the context of labor disputes.[87] Justice Robert Jackson complained about what he saw as the Court's inconsistency in this respect in *Thomas v. Collins*,[88] a complaint that bothered Justices Douglas, Black, and Frank Murphy enough to elicit a rebuttal from them.[89] Jackson's complaint is a culmination of the evidence from this early period that the justices' responses to free expression cases were always shaped by their attitudes toward the claimants in those cases and toward the segments of society they represented.

### Conclusions

Among political elites, support for freedom of expression was associated with liberalism for most of the twentieth century. That is no longer true. Support for free expression has become more situational,

---

85. *Leach v. Carlile* (1922).

86. The one non-business case was *Minersville School District v. Gobitis* (1940), the first school flag salute case, in which freedom of speech was peripheral to the Court's opinion upholding the compulsory flag salute. Justice Harlan Fiske Stone was the lone dissenter.

87. Pritchett (1948), 229–30.

88. *Thomas v. Collins* (1945), 547.

89. *Thomas*, 543–44.

with the strongest support for some kinds of free expression coming from liberals and for other kinds from conservatives.

That pattern of change has been reflected in the Supreme Court. Beginning with the Court's first substantial work in freedom of expression in the second decade of the twentieth century and continuing into the 1990s, the justices who voted for free speech claimants were more liberal than their colleagues in the great majority of non-unanimous decisions. That proportion was especially high in the period from the Vinson Court through the early Rehnquist Court. But in the late Rehnquist Court and early Roberts Court, conservative and liberal justices were about equally likely to provide disproportionate voting support for claimants.

It is tempting to characterize the more recent era, one that has continued since the end of this study, as a time when both liberals and conservatives simply support speech they like and oppose speech they dislike.[90] That characterization oversimplifies a complex reality. It is especially important to keep in mind that we cannot infer absolute levels of support for different kinds of speech claims from the relative levels of support that have been the focus of this chapter. We *can* say that some kinds of speech receive the strongest support from conservatives and other kinds from liberals. To the extent that conservatives and liberals do like different kinds of speech, the question is what determines which kinds they like. In the terms that I have used, how much of the difference in their positions reflects values, and how much reflects affect toward social and political groups?

The difficulty of separating values and group affect empirically makes a precise answer impossible, but the evidence presented in this chapter helps in sorting out the explanations. Perhaps the best place to start is by asking how far a value-based explanation can take us.

How freedom as a value relates to ideology is a matter of disagreement. But if freedom is identified with liberalism, then the traditional polarity of freedom of expression in the Court and elsewhere can be interpreted as a direct reflection of the higher priority of

90. See Stern (2015).

freedom for liberals than for conservatives. One weakness in that interpretation is that liberals and conservatives each give disproportionate support to certain freedoms, so it is not obvious why liberals should be especially supportive of free expression. Further, the change in the polarity of freedom of expression in the current era belies the assumption that support for freedom of expression is deeply embedded in liberal values.

To a degree, connections between broad values and specific types of free expression questions may come into play. National security questions tap the high value of order that has been identified as an element of conservatism, so the sharp decline in national security cases in the Court might have facilitated a shift in the polarity of free expression cases. The growth in commercial speech cases might tap conservative support for economic markets. On the other hand, free expression decisions in the 1946–93 Terms had a strong polarity even if national security cases are excluded, and in the early commercial speech cases it was liberal justices who were more favorable to free expression claims.

Perhaps equality can come to the rescue. For most of the twentieth century, liberal political elites had reason to identify free expression as serving the goal of equality by helping people with low socioeconomic status (such as labor union members) and politically weak outsiders (such as radicals and Jehovah's Witnesses) to advance their goals. By the end of the century, however, they had reason to question whether some forms of free expression actually foster equality rather than hinder it; racist speech and corporate political spending are two prominent examples. Both in the Supreme Court and in the political world as a whole, the growing prominence of free expression claims by "upperdogs" rather than "underdogs" might lead to a broader questioning of the relationship between free expression and equality.

Of course, this evidence can also be interpreted as a reflection of affect toward social groups. Perhaps conservative and liberal positions on freedom of expression are driven primarily by people's feelings about upperdogs and underdogs rather than more abstract views about equality. It is impossible to make a definitive judgment about the relative strength of those two explanations. But I think that the evidence as a whole is more consistent with an explanation based on group affect, one in which both liberals and conservatives respond to individual free expression claims and freedom of expression as a whole largely on the basis of their attitudes toward the prospective beneficiaries of decisions.

The strongest reason for this judgment is that not all the groups whose claims get disproportionate support from either liberal justices or conservative justices are easily connected with equality as a goal. The news media, whose rights receive greater support from liberals, are one example. A broader example is political groups on the left and right that bring free expression cases.

Thus, it seems fair to conclude that the ideological polarity of freedom of expression is based heavily on group affect. That affect shapes both overall positions on free expression and responses to individual cases. Largely because of the identification of free expression with groups for which liberals had greater sympathy than conservatives, support for freedom of expression came to be understood as a liberal position. That understanding extended to cases in which the claimants were not liberal clienteles—even, to a limited degree, claimants with a conservative coloration. In the current era, even with substantial changes in perceptions of who is advantaged by a broad interpretation of the First Amendment, claims by litigants who are associated with neither the right nor the left still get disproportionate support from liberal justices.

At the same time, the ideological polarity of free expression decisions during both past and current eras has differed considerably with the ideological identification of claimants. That difference existed even in the 1946–93 Terms, with claims from the right deviating from other cases in their polarity. That deviation is even sharper today, so that the justices' positions on free expression relative to each other seem less general and more situational than they were in the past.

Change in the Court's free expression agenda facilitated change in its overall polarity. Most free expression cases in the 1946–93 period had claimants who would generally evoke greater sympathy from liberals than from conservatives—people and organizations on the political left, government employees, the news media, and organized labor. For all decisions, the proportion of claimants who fell into those categories was 72 percent; for non-unanimous decisions it was 73 percent. Cases with claimants who would generally evoke greater sympathy from conservatives—people on the mainstream political right and non-media businesses—were much less common, appearing in 14 percent of all decisions and 13 percent of non-unanimous decisions. In the 1994–2012 Terms, in contrast, those two groups accounted for 43 percent of all decisions and 46 percent of non-unanimous decisions. In that period they vastly outnumbered claimants from liberal clienteles.

In considerable part, that agenda change reflected the justices' own choices of cases to hear. But it also reflected change in the mix of cases brought to the Court and, moving backward one more step, new patterns of advocacy for freedom of expression among interest groups. More broadly, the justices' perceptions of free expression and of the ideological stakes in the issue were shaped by the shared understandings that developed and changed in that larger world. The justices themselves participated in the evolution of those understandings. But on this issue as on others, their conceptions of conservative and liberal positions have been largely a product of the prevailing conceptions among political elites as a whole. Thus the justices' responses to free expression cases have had powerful connections to developments in the larger world of political elites.

# 3

# Criminal Justice

In contrast with freedom of expression, the Supreme Court's ideological polarity in criminal justice appears to be a model of stability. From the Warren Court on, the Court has played a highly visible role in this field with its decisions on criminal procedure under the Constitution. And throughout that period, the linkage between the justices' ideological stances and their overall positions in criminal justice has been straightforward: the more liberal a justice is, the more support that justice gives to the legal claims of criminal defendants.

The 2010–12 Terms exemplify this pattern. Chief Justice Roberts and Justices Scalia, Thomas, and Alito voted for the prosecution[1] between 73 percent and 84 percent of the time, Justice Kennedy 59 percent, Justice Breyer 51 percent, and Justices Ginsburg, Sotomayor, and Kagan between 40 percent and 45 percent.[2] In the Warren Court's major expansions of defendants' procedural rights,

1. Although not all criminal justice questions directly involve contention between the defense and the prosecution, for convenience I will refer to those questions in terms of a pro-prosecution and pro-defendant dichotomy.

2. These votes and other statistics on votes and outcomes were in the set of cases defined as involving the criminal justice issue for purposes of the analyses in this chapter. Under this definition, cases are counted as criminal if they were decided on the basis of a question in criminal law or criminal procedure. That definition encompasses many cases that fall outside the criminal procedure issue area in the Supreme Court

the justices who dissented from most of those decisions were generally the Court's conservatives. In the more conservative Courts that narrowed some of those rights, the preponderance of dissents came from the Court's liberals.[3]

The long duration of this polarity makes it seem natural and inevitable. Moreover, conservatives and liberals in the elite world as a whole divide on criminal justice issues along the same lines that Supreme Court justices do. This consistency suggests that the polarity of criminal justice is inherent in the premises of liberalism and conservatism.

Yet the linkage between ideology and criminal justice to which we are accustomed has not always existed in the Supreme Court. In the early twentieth century, the relationship between ideology and positions on criminal justice in the Court was mixed and muddled. To provide another vantage point on the linkages between issues and ideology, this chapter analyzes how and why that muddled polarity turned into the clear polarity of the last several decades.

## Criminal Justice in the Supreme Court

Measured by numbers of decisions, the Supreme Court gives more attention to criminal justice than to any other broad issue.[4] With some oversimplification, the Court's work in the criminal justice field can be divided into two categories. The first category concerns the procedures used in the criminal justice process. Most cases in this category involve interpretations of procedural protections in the Constitution, such as the prohibition of unreasonable searches

---

Database, but it also excludes many criminal prosecutions (as well as some civil cases that are included in the criminal procedure issue area in the Database).

3. The most prominent Warren Court examples were *Mapp v. Ohio* (1961) and *Miranda v. Arizona* (1966). Perhaps the most noteworthy examples in the post-Warren Court period are the decisions in which the Court has applied a good faith exception to the exclusionary rule for illegal searches and seizures—among others, *United States v. Leon* (1984) and *Herring v. United States* (2009).

4. The issue area variable in the Supreme Court Database provides an approximate measure of the proportion of decisions involving criminal law and procedure. The criminal procedure issue ranks first among the twelve issue areas in the Database for the 1946–2012 Terms.

and seizures and the right to the assistance of counsel. These protections became more significant as the Supreme Court applied the great majority of the provisions in the Bill of Rights to the states by incorporating them into the due process clause of the Fourteenth Amendment. For rights related to criminal justice, that incorporation came primarily in the 1960s; prior to that time, most of those rights were incorporated only in part or not at all.

Other procedural questions arise under federal statutes and the Federal Rules of Criminal Procedure. In the current era, the most important of the statutes is the Antiterrorism and Effective Death Penalty Act of 1996 (AEDPA). The Court has decided a long series of cases interpreting AEDPA's limits on the power of federal courts to issue writs of habeas corpus when state prisoners challenge their convictions.

The second category of criminal cases concerns interpretation of federal statutes that define crimes and set rules of sentencing for those crimes, what can be called substantive questions. As the scope of federal criminal law and the number of federal prosecutions grew, so did questions about definitions of crimes. Adoption of the federal sentencing guidelines after enactment of the Sentencing Reform Act of 1984 opened up a new series of questions about sentencing, and the Court has continued to address some of those questions since it made the guidelines voluntary in *United States v. Booker*.[5]

Criminal cases have constituted a substantial part of the Supreme Court's work throughout the past century, but expansion of the reach of federal criminal statutes and nationalization of the Bill of Rights have increased their share of the Court's agenda. From the Vinson Court of the 1946–52 Terms through the Roberts Court of the 2005–12 Terms, the proportion of the Court's decisions on the merits that concerned criminal justice rose from about one in six to about three in ten. There was an increase in the agenda share of criminal justice from each chief justice to the next, with the biggest increase coming in the Roberts Court.

The success of defendants in criminal justice cases has fluctuated over time. During the 1946–2012 Terms, the success rate was

5. *United States v. Booker* (2005).

strikingly high in the Warren Court, at 63 percent. In the other periods defined by chief justice, the success rate ranged from 36 percent in the Rehnquist Court to 45 percent in the Vinson Court. The Warren Court was also a period of dramatic expansions in the procedural rights of criminal defendants, with the Courts before and after that period less favorable to those rights on the whole.

On some issues such as freedom of expression, the Court has developed general tests and doctrines with which to analyze cases. That has not been true of criminal procedure. In interpretation of constitutional protections of procedural rights, separate bodies of legal rules have been created for each right. In interpretation of federal criminal statutes, justices have largely applied the general rules and approaches that they use in statutory interpretation as a whole.[6] As a result, the broad disagreements among justices over means of interpretation such as the value of legislative history have been reflected in the Court's reading of criminal statutes.

## The Ideological Polarity of Decisions on Criminal Justice

Like the analyses of takings and free expression, the analysis of criminal justice decisions covered the 1910–2012 Terms of the Court. For the 1910–45 Terms, only non-unanimous decisions were analyzed. Cases were included if they arose from criminal prosecutions or potential prosecutions and if they were decided on the basis of questions in criminal procedure or substantive criminal law. Thus, both statutory and constitutional decisions were included. Additional information on identification and inclusion of cases, as well as attributes of cases that are analyzed in later sections, is in the appendix. As in the analysis of free expression, the ideological polarity of non-unanimous decisions was determined by comparing the median ideological scores of the justices on the two sides in a decision. Table 3.1 shows the results by time period.

---

6. One important rule specific to criminal cases is the rule of lenity, under which highly ambiguous questions of interpretation of criminal statutes are to be resolved in favor of the defendant. See *Lockhart v. United States* (2016).

TABLE 3.1. Ideological patterns of votes in non-unanimous criminal justice decisions, 1910–2012 Terms

| Period | Side with more liberal ideology score | | Percent with pro-defendant side more liberal |
| --- | --- | --- | --- |
| | Pro-defendant | Pro-prosecution | |
| 1910–20 Terms | 18 | 15 | 54.5 |
| 1921–36 Terms | 11 | 15 | 42.3 |
| 1937–45 Terms | 48 | 19 | 71.6 |
| 1946–52 Terms (Vinson Court) | 87 | 16 | 84.5 |
| 1953–68 Terms (Warren Court) | 252 | 20 | 92.6 |
| 1969–85 Terms (Burger Court) | 409 | 17 | 96.0 |
| 1986–2004 Terms (Rehnquist Court) | 321 | 18 | 94.7 |
| 2005–12 Terms (Roberts Court) | 112 | 10 | 91.8 |

The results are consistent with the image of the Court beginning in the Warren era: in the overwhelming majority of non-unanimous decisions, the pro-defendant justices were more liberal than their colleagues. But the results for earlier periods show that the Court's current polarity took some time to develop. In the period from the 1910 Term through the 1936 Term, pro-defendant justices were about equally likely to lean in a liberal or conservative direction relative to pro-prosecution justices, and after that time the Court moved only gradually to the strong polarity that we now take for granted.

The ideological differences between the two sides as the Court's polarity shifted can be examined in greater detail. Because Martin-Quinn scores are not available for the first two periods, and because different alternative scores were used for the two periods, direct comparisons involving the first two periods are not possible; only an overview of the distribution of the difference scores can be sketched. For the 1910–20 Terms, the differences between the ideological scores of the pro-defendant and pro-prosecution justices in individual cases were distributed in a basically symmetrical pattern around zero. For the 1921–36 Terms, the pattern was

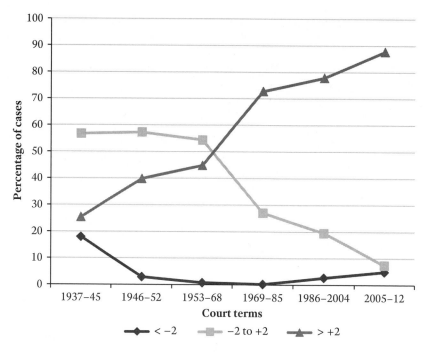

**FIGURE 3.1.** Magnitude of ideological differences between pro-defendant and pro-prosecution justices by category, non-unanimous decisions, 1937–2012 Terms.
*Notes:* Positive differences mean that pro-defendant justices were more liberal than pro-prosecution justices.

somewhat asymmetrical, in that there were four cases in which the pro-defendant coalitions were skewed in a more conservative direction than the liberal skew in any of the cases. In both periods, the mean difference between the ideological scores of the pro-defendant and pro-prosecution justices leaned in the same direction as the dichotomous ideological orientations shown in table 3.1.

For later periods, the ideological differences between the two sides can be analyzed by breaking the differences between median Martin-Quinn scores into categories: higher than +2.0, indicating that the pro-defendant justices were substantially more liberal than the pro-prosecution justices; lower than −2.0, indicating that the pro-defendant justices were substantially more conservative; and the interval between those two extremes. The temporal pattern is shown in figure 3.1.

As late as the New Deal Court of 1937–45, decisions in which pro-defendant justices were considerably more conservative than their colleagues were nearly as common as those in which the justices voting for the defendant were considerably more liberal. After that time, there was a rapid decline in the proportion of decisions with that surprising polarity, followed by a slight increase in the Roberts Court. More gradually, decisions with a relatively weak polarity declined substantially, with a corresponding increase in cases in which the pro-defendant justices were distinctly more liberal than their colleagues.

The temporal trends in the polarity of decisions in criminal justice make it clear that we should not take the Court's current polarity for granted. The development of that polarity requires explanation.

### Explaining the Change

Because the change in the linkage between ideology and freedom of expression was relatively recent, and because it has attracted considerable attention, it was easy to identify credible explanations for that change. That is not true of criminal justice, so the search for explanations needs to be more open-ended. But the central concern is the same: the roles of values and group affect in the change.

How might conservative and liberal values apply to criminal justice? One possibility is a higher priority for "order" in conservatism, as noted by Feldman.[7] That priority potentially translates into a pro-prosecution position. Two legal scholars have suggested that liberals and conservatives begin with different beliefs about the extent to which individuals are responsible and culpable for their actions, beliefs that lead to differing views about desirable criminal justice policy.[8] This perspective is supported by some work in political and social psychology, which indicates that conservatives and liberals diverge in fundamental attitudes about matters such as punishment of rule breakers[9] and the importance of fair procedure.[10] All these

7. Stanley Feldman (2013), 595.
8. Harcourt (1995), 1222–24; Seidman (2004), 25.
9. Smith et al. (2011), 381–85.
10. Feygina and Tyler (2009).

possibilities are consistent with the polarity of criminal justice in the Supreme Court over the last several decades, but not with the more muddled polarity that preceded it.

Because attitudes toward equality are so central to liberalism and conservatism, they might play an important role in shaping positions on criminal justice. But there is not an obvious path from the weight of equality as a value to positions on criminal justice. For that matter, the same is true of affect toward social groups. In both instances, the connection between those premises and criminal justice seems likely to depend on the contexts in which shared understandings develop.

### CRIMINAL JUSTICE OUTSIDE THE COURT

In thinking about the polarity of criminal justice in the elite world as a whole, a good place to start is with the distinction between substantive and procedural questions. The most fundamental substantive questions concern what behavior will be treated as criminal, a matter determined primarily by legislatures.[11] As noted earlier, the Supreme Court addresses a range of other substantive questions alongside Congress.

In broad terms, the positions that people hold on questions of criminal procedure reflect how they balance the efficiency and effectiveness of the criminal justice system in attacking crime against protection of suspects and defendants from wrongful conviction and unfair treatment. Herbert Packer summarized the competing positions on this balance in terms of "crime control" and "due process" models.[12]

Logic does not require any correlation between people's positions on substantive and procedural issues. But in practice, those who favor strong criminal sanctions tend to favor narrow procedural rights as well. Indeed, attitudes toward particular offenses affect people's positions on procedural rights relating to those offenses.

11. See L. Friedman and Percival (1981), 10–11.
12. Packer (1968), ch. 8.

As legal scholar William Stuntz concluded, "to a surprising degree, the history of criminal procedure is not really about procedure at all but about substantive issues, about what conduct the government should and should not be able to punish."[13] This reality moves elite attitudes on criminal justice toward a single dimension.

In the early twentieth century, the period when there was no clear ideological polarity to Supreme Court voting on criminal justice, it is difficult to characterize the positions of conservatives and liberals on criminal justice. In part this is because the federal government played only a limited role in this field, so that political parties and public officials at the national level had little reason to take positions on it.

The positions of the Progressive movement, essentially liberal in today's terms,[14] suggest a complicated relationship between ideology and criminal justice policy during that era. On the one hand, Progressives emphasized the fundamental role of social conditions in producing criminal behavior, and this emphasis led to an interest in "treatment" of criminal defendants rather than punishment. Creation of the juvenile court was the most visible manifestation of this view.[15] On the other hand, Progressives also favored extensions of the criminal law to address what they identified as social problems. The treatment-oriented courts they proposed did not always produce results that were favorable to criminal defendants, and these courts certainly were not bastions of procedural rights for defendants.[16]

At the federal level, probably the most prominent criminal justice concern in that era was corporate crime. Growth in the scope of criminal law in the late nineteenth century and the early twentieth century was driven largely by successful efforts to create criminal penalties for a range of business practices that were deemed undesirable.[17] "Legislators would attach a criminal tail to every important

13. Stuntz (1995b), 394.
14. Milkis (1999), 6–9; Dawley (2003), 4–5.
15. Polsky (1989); Tanenhaus (2004).
16. Willrich (2003), pt. 2; Baum (2011), 205–14. Progressive views on criminal justice are discussed in Rothman (1978) and Willrich (2003).
17. Pound (1930), 15–20; L. Hall (1937).

regulatory law."[18] This movement included the federal government. Regulatory laws enacted by Congress in that era, such as the Sherman Antitrust Act of 1890 and the Federal Food and Drugs Act of 1906, typically provided for criminal penalties. That practice continued in the New Deal era.

At least in the early part of that period, support for such laws with their criminal penalties spanned partisan and ideological lines. There was only one vote against the Sherman Act in either house of Congress. But economic liberals were the strongest supporters of such laws, and there was a degree of moral zeal behind their efforts to attack what they saw as corporate wrongdoing. This perspective was symbolized by a book by a Progressive-minded academic that analyzed unsavory business practices as a form of "sin," a book that featured an endorsement by sitting President Theodore Roosevelt.[19] Democratic Party platforms in the early twentieth century gave strong support to laws that criminalized certain business practices. In contrast, once Progressive influence on the Republican Party had waned, the party's 1916 platform paired its support for punishment of people who violate business regulatory laws with the admonition that "prosecution is very different from persecution" and the complaint that "business success, no matter how honestly attained, is apparently regarded by the Democratic party as in itself a crime."[20] That division continued into the 1930s, when Democrats and liberals were especially vehement in their criticism of the "banksters" who were widely identified as responsible for the collapse of the financial system in 1929.[21]

In the late nineteenth and early twentieth centuries, there was a close connection between economic regulation and the procedural provisions of the Bill of Rights. The protections against unreasonable searches and seizures in the Fourth Amendment and against

18. L. Friedman (1993), 282.

19. Ross (1907). In that endorsement, Roosevelt referred to "the vast iniquities in modern business, finance," and other elite sectors. Ross, ix–x.

20. The platform text is at http://www.presidency.ucsb.edu/ws/index.php?pid=29634.

21. Gilbert King (2011).

compulsory self-incrimination in the Fifth Amendment were viewed and utilized primarily as tools to attack the use of criminal law in government regulation of economic activity.[22] Ken Kersch has shown that because the privacy rights protected by these constitutional provisions conflicted with efforts to regulate the economy, Progressives and other supporters of regulation opposed expansive interpretations of these provisions as well as the conceptions of privacy that underlay such interpretations.[23]

For the last several decades, the overall positions of political elites on criminal justice policy have fallen more clearly along ideological lines. The polarity of responses to criminal cases that developed in the Supreme Court appears in lower courts as well.[24] It is true that the strongly pro-prosecution tilt of the electorate often moves liberal candidates for office and elected officials to support pro-prosecution policies. Even so, clear ideological differences often appear in elected bodies. The divisions between liberals and conservatives in Congress are exemplified by the votes in the U.S. House on the 1996 legislation that limited habeas corpus actions by state prisoners in federal courts. On an amendment to eliminate the habeas corpus provisions from a broader bill, for instance, 73 percent of Northern Democrats and 5 percent of Republicans voted in favor.[25]

In the electoral arena, the national Republican and Democratic parties have taken different approaches to criminal justice questions, changes that have been quite visible since Republican presidential candidate Barry Goldwater emphasized law and order concerns in 1964.[26] In 1968, Republican candidate Richard Nixon (and third-party candidate George Wallace) took a strong pro-prosecution position on criminal justice questions and attacked the Supreme Court for its pro-defendant decisions.[27] In 1988, Republican candi-

22. Stuntz (2011), 125–27.
23. Kersch (2004), 27–66.
24. Nagel (1961), 844; Goldman (1975), 497; Carp, Manning, and Stidham (2009), 317; but see Sunstein et al. (2006), 48–50.
25. "House Votes" (1997), H-22.
26. Flamm (2005).
27. Stephenson (1999), 180–81.

date George H. W. Bush and his supporters strongly attacked Democratic candidate Michael Dukakis, governor of Massachusetts, for his opposition to the death penalty and especially for a Massachusetts program of furloughs for prisoners.[28]

Democratic candidates for national office, such as Bill Clinton, sometimes emphasize their own tough-on-crime credentials. But on the whole, they take more mixed positions on criminal justice questions than do Republicans. That difference is reflected in the national party platforms.[29] Democratic platforms do not offer strong endorsements of pro-defendant positions. But those platforms sometimes balance expressions of the party's commitment to attack crime with concern for fair treatment of defendants and sometimes point to means of crime prevention that lie outside the criminal justice system. In contrast, Republican platforms give a stronger emphasis to the need for pro-prosecution policies.

At least in part, the development of a clear conservative-liberal divide in the elite world has reflected change in the kinds of crimes on which debates over national policy focused. Supreme Court decisions applying the Bill of Rights to state prosecutions substantially increased the numbers of cases in the federal courts (including the Supreme Court itself) that involved "common" or "street" crimes. The growing reach of federal criminal statutes and growing concern about street crimes in some periods had a similar effect. In turn, both these developments made common crimes a more prominent federal issue. Meanwhile, business-related crime became a lower priority for federal law enforcement in the post-New Deal era. Thus, criminal justice as a national issue increasingly focused on what we might think of as ordinary crimes.

If conservative and liberal values make conservatives more favorable to the pro-prosecution side than liberals, the decline in the prominence of business crimes likely allowed those values to come more fully into play. That is because attitudes toward business

28. Dowd (1988).
29. This discussion of party platforms is based on relevant sections of Republican and Democratic platforms, archived at http://www.presidency.ucsb.edu/platforms.php.

potentially conflict with attitudes toward ordinary crimes in ideological terms. Similarly, values related to equality and affect toward social groups might have become more relevant as attention increasingly focused on crimes for which defendants are disproportionately people of lower economic status and members of racial minority groups.[30]

There is an important complication to that last point. Like defendants, victims of crimes are also disproportionately low in income and members of racial minority groups.[31] Moreover, crimes committed against minority-group members have not always been taken seriously by the criminal justice system.[32] For those reasons, people who are sympathetic toward those segments of society might favor stronger law enforcement and more severe criminal sanctions to protect them. Indeed, some members of the African American community take that position.[33] Thus the racial and class distribution of crime victims complicates the question of whether lenient or stringent enforcement of criminal law benefits disadvantaged groups.[34]

Nonetheless, liberals have focused on the poor and on members of racial minority groups as defendants rather than as targets of crime. This focus probably results in large part from perceptions of discrimination against suspects and defendants in the criminal justice system based on economic status and race.[35] Since the 1960s, liberals may also have reacted to the identification of racial minority groups with crime problems in some conservative commentaries and campaign appeals.[36] Perhaps the visible ideological divisions over constitutional criminal procedure in the Supreme Court also shaped ideological positions on criminal justice in other elite circles. Certainly, the Court's expansions of procedural rights in the 1950s and 1960s became a target for conservatives. In any event, a

30. Harlow (2000), 3, 5; Reaves (2013), 7.
31. Harrell et al. (2014); Truman and Langton (2014), 6, 9.
32. L. Miller (2010).
33. Flamm (2005), 5, 80, 127; Fortner (2015); see Murakawa (2014).
34. See Kennedy (1994).
35. See Cole (1999).
36. Flamm (2005), 5, 44, 182.

liberal-conservative division on criminal justice became firmly established among political elites.

Yet this ideological division does not apply to all types of crimes. It continues to be true that liberals typically favor stronger enforcement of laws against crimes committed on behalf of businesses than do conservatives, and the same is true of some other types of "white-collar" crimes.[37] Liberal complaints that these laws receive inadequate enforcement are symbolized by Ralph Nader's claim that "the more you steal, the less time you do, as long as you do it on the 20th floor."[38] This reversal of the ideological lines that exist on criminal justice as a whole is striking.[39]

There are other types of crimes that feature a similar reversal. These include "hate crimes" directed at certain groups,[40] violations of civil rights by public officials, possession and sale of firearms under some circumstances, domestic violence, and to a lesser degree sexual violence. The positions of conservative and liberal elites on some questions involving these crimes illustrate Stuntz's point that positions on criminal procedure are connected with attitudes toward offenses. On domestic and sexual violence, for instance, feminist groups that favor strong enforcement of the law have sought procedural changes specific to these offenses in order to facilitate that enforcement.[41]

These exceptions to the general tendencies of conservatives and liberals in the criminal justice field can be understood largely as a product of attitudes toward issues other than criminal justice. Gun policy is an obvious example. But affect toward the groups that are

37. Hagan (2010).

38. Taylor (1985).

39. The distinction between attitudes toward criminal justice generally and attitudes toward white-collar and business crime is symbolized by the work of legal scholar Brandon Garrett, whose books include *Convicting the Innocent: Where Criminal Prosecutions Go Wrong* (2011) and *Too Big to Jail: How Prosecutors Compromise with Corporations* (2014).

40. Adherents to critical race theory played a key role in developing the ideas that led to statutes directed at hate crimes. Delgado (1982); Matsuda et al. (1993); Jacobs and Potter (1998), ch. 5.

41. Michelle Anderson (2002).

perceived to be perpetrators and victims of those crimes undoubt-edly plays a part as well.

## CRIMINAL CASES IN THE COURT

The cases that the Supreme Court hears in criminal justice are more homogeneous than those on some other issues, in that every case involves contention between the defense and prosecution sides in some form. But the differences that do exist in the attributes of cases may contribute to an explanation of change in the Court's polarity. As on other issues, the identities of advocates for the two sides are also potentially relevant.

### Case Attributes

One significant case attribute is the distinction between substan-tive and procedural questions, which can be labeled *question type*. Although the offense with which a defendant is charged can influ-ence justices' responses to procedural questions, substantive and procedural questions might evoke somewhat different attitudes in general or in a particular context. In particular, as one legal scholar suggested, questions of statutory interpretation do not di-rectly raise the fundamental tradeoffs between competing values that exist on procedural questions in criminal justice.[42] For that reason, the ideological polarity of the Court might be weaker in substantive cases.

The second attribute is the distinction between federal and state prosecutions, which can be labeled *level of prosecution*. Justices might view their roles in overseeing criminal justice at the state and federal levels in different ways. Moreover, their attitudes toward the crimi-nal justice systems at the two levels could differ. Liberal justices, for instance, may view the system at the federal level as relatively benign while holding considerable suspicion of at least some state systems.

The third and fourth attributes relate to the offense (*white-collar* crime) and the offender (a *business* or someone acting on behalf

42. Farnsworth (2005), 97.

of a business). White-collar crime is difficult to define.[43] Various definitions have been offered, and different definitions encompass quite different sets of offenses.[44] One common definition, which I adopted, is that white-collar crime involves an effort to obtain financial gain without physical force or the threat of force, against either a victim or a victim's property.

On the whole, the socioeconomic status of white-collar offenders is higher than that of people who commit common crimes. That difference is a frequent theme in analyses of sentencing for white-collar crimes, which point to the empathy that judges feel for defendants whose backgrounds and situations are similar to their own.[45] But the extent of this empathy may differ along ideological lines, and that is true of Supreme Court justices as well as trial judges.

By no means, however, are all defendants in white-collar cases high in status. Moreover, white-collar crimes differ in the roles of those who commit them. A substantial proportion of these offenses are committed by businesses or by individuals who act on their behalf. But the white-collar label also encompasses wrongdoing by employees who act against their employers' interest and by people who stand outside the business world altogether, and together those categories account for a high proportion of white-collar offenses.[46]

Justices who act on their attitudes toward the business community might respond quite differently to the different types of white-collar crimes. For this reason I created a business-crime variable, which includes all offenses committed on behalf of the interests of a business. This definition captures the idea of corporate wrongdoing, the kind of white-collar crime that concerns people on the left such as Ralph Nader and Edwin Sutherland, the sociologist who coined the term white-collar crime.[47] As discussed earlier, business crime was a major concern of Progressives in an earlier era.

43. L. Friedman (1993), 290.
44. E.g., Edelhertz (1970), 3; Katz (1979), 435; Sutherland (1983), 7.
45. Wheeler, Mann, and Sarat (1988); Tillman and Pontell (1992).
46. Braithwaite (1993), 217, 219, 221.
47. Sutherland (1949).

Although question type and level of prosecution have some theoretical meaning, type of offense (white-collar) and type of offender (business) have a more substantial theoretical element. Differences in the Court's polarity on the basis of those two attributes could be interpreted in multiple ways, but the most likely source is affect toward different social groups.[48]

These four attributes are correlated with each other in the cases that the Supreme Court decides. The strongest correlation is between question type and level of prosecution. Since the Court does not hear cases to interpret state law, it reaches very few decisions on the basis of substantive questions in state prosecutions. In practice, then, these two attributes result in three types of cases: state procedural, federal procedural, and federal substantive. Because federal criminal statutes disproportionately cover white-collar and business offenses—although much less so today than a century ago—cases involving those offenses and defendants are considerably more common in federal prosecutions than in state prosecutions.[49] In turn, white-collar and business cases in the Court are more likely than other cases to raise substantive issues of statutory interpretation. Finally, as noted already, a substantial proportion of white-collar offenses are committed on behalf of businesses, and the great majority of business-crime cases in the Supreme Court are white-collar.[50]

The Court's criminal justice agenda can be compared across three periods: the 1910–36 Terms, the era of a muddled ideological

48. In addition to white-collar cases, other offenses in which attitudes among political elites diverge from the usual liberal-conservative divisions in criminal justice (such as prosecutions for violations of civil rights) might also affect the Court's polarity. But there were very few cases involving these offenses in the Supreme Court during the early twentieth century, so they could not have contributed much to the Court's muddled polarity of criminal justice in that period. In turn, because there was no room for a decline in the agenda shares of those cases, they could not help to account for the later shift in the Court's polarity. Cases involving gun offenses became more common late in the study period, and I will discuss the justices' responses to them later in this section.

49. See L. Hall (1937).

50. One exception, which I had not expected to encounter in the Supreme Court, is burning down one's own business for insurance money: *Russello v. United States* (1983); *United States v. Robinson* (1988).

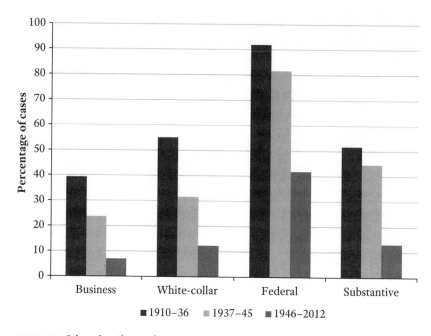

FIGURE 3.2. Selected attributes of criminal cases decided, 1910–2012 Terms.
*Notes*: As discussed in the text, cases for the first two periods are from a sample of Court terms.

polarity; the 1946–2012 Terms, the era of a clear polarity; and the transitional period between the two. Because only non-unanimous decisions were collected for the 1910–45 Terms, I gathered an additional sample of decisions that included all the criminal cases decided by the Court at five-term intervals from 1910 to 1940 as well as 1942. With that additional sample, the composition of the Court's agenda could be compared over time. The results are shown in figure 3.2.

The changes over time are striking but easy to understand. Once the Court began to oversee criminal procedure in state courts, its receptivity to state procedural cases reduced both the federal and substantive shares of the agenda. This change ensured that both business and white-collar cases would decline as well.

The declines in white-collar and business cases were less dramatic for decisions that divided the Court and thus defined its polarity, because those cases were more likely to elicit unanimous decisions than other cases in the 1910–36 Terms. Even in the non-unanimous cases, however, the change from the earlier period to the later one is quite substantial. Notably, in the 1946–2012 Terms there was a decline in the proportions of business and white-collar cases from each chief to the next. In the Roberts Court of the 2005–12 Terms, 3 percent of the non-unanimous decisions involved business defendants and 6 percent had white-collar defendants.

One potentially important attribute of criminal cases in the Court is the race of defendants. That attribute cannot be measured systematically, but it is clear that the proportion of defendants who were white declined considerably over time. From the 1930s on, the Court's opinions sometimes mentioned explicitly that the defendant was an African American.[51] There were substantial numbers of other cases in which minority racial status was evident from the question in the case, such as discrimination in jury selection, or the situation from which it arose, such as a civil rights protest.

### Advocates

Although there are no systematic data on the representation of criminal defendants in the Supreme Court, the dominant pattern appears to be one in which defendants' lawyers are inexperienced in Supreme Court advocacy—typically, the lawyers who have represented a defendant in lower courts. Even in the current era, a time when specialists and semi-specialists in Supreme Court advocacy argue a high proportion of the cases that the Court hears on the merits, as a group the lawyers who represent criminal defendants are relatively inexperienced.[52]

On the prosecution side, the federal government is the ultimate repeat player, represented by experienced advocates in the Office of the Solicitor General. Traditionally, representatives of state governments in criminal (and other) cases also tended to lack Supreme Court experience, and there were complaints about the quality of their advocacy. The creation of analogues to the federal solicitor general's office in most states since the 1990s has strengthened state advocacy in the

---

51. A Lexis search located eight such cases in the 1930s, fifteen in the 1940s, sixteen in the 1950s, and twenty in the 1960s.
52. Crespo (2016), 2005–17.

Court, but states probably had some advantage over criminal defendants in the quality of advocacy even before that time.[53]

Undoubtedly, the quality of advocacy for the two sides has had an impact on the Court's criminal justice decisions. But the key question for an understanding of the Court's polarity is whether the identities of attorneys on the two sides served as an ideological cue to the justices. In general, the answer has to be no: defendants and the prosecution were represented by the kinds of lawyers that the justices would expect. But there is an important exception: the role of the NAACP and its Legal and Educational Defense Fund (LDF) in sponsoring challenges to state criminal procedures and providing representation to defendants in those cases. I will discuss that role in examining the course of procedural rights in the Court later in this section.

Data on amicus participation in criminal cases were gathered for a sample of criminal cases that were decided in the 1946–2012 period. The sample included all orally argued cases involving white-collar crimes or business defendants and an equal number of cases with neither attribute, matched by time of decision, a total of 250 cases of each type. Amicus briefs have been relatively uncommon in criminal law, and their growth came later than in most other fields. In the Vinson Court, there were amicus briefs in only 11 percent of the cases in the sample. The Warren Court, with its major innovations in criminal procedure, still attracted amicus briefs in only 16 percent of the cases. Not until the Rehnquist Court did a majority of criminal cases have amicus briefs, and only in the Roberts Court was the mean number of briefs per case over two (at 3.04). The dearth of amicus briefs in criminal cases is largely a product of the relatively small number of interest groups that are concerned with criminal law.

Overall, there were twice as many briefs supporting defendants as briefs supporting the prosecution. Briefs on the defendant's side came primarily from legal groups. The ACLU was most prominent in the period as a whole, submitting briefs in 8 percent of the cases in the sample. The National Association of Criminal Defense Lawyers

53. B. Miller (2010).

was an active participant in the more recent part of the period. As expected, the federal and state governments were relatively frequent amici on the prosecution side, and groups with conservative positions on criminal justice and victims' rights groups increasingly submitted briefs over time.

The frequency of amicus participation in white-collar cases was about the same as in other criminal cases. The same was true of the smaller set of cases involving business crime. Business cases did not attract large numbers of amicus briefs from the business community, though there was a sprinkling of such cases beginning in the 1970s.

On the whole, like the identities of participating lawyers, amicus participation in criminal cases followed the lines that the justices would expect rather than providing them with new information about the interests on the two sides. However, the presence of briefs from large numbers of state governments, from the ACLU, or from the U.S. Chamber of Commerce might serve as a cue to the justices about the stakes in cases and thus make the justices' ideological stances more relevant to those cases and others like them.[54]

## THE JUSTICES' RESPONSES TO CASES

The substantial changes in the composition of the Court's criminal agenda over time might help to explain the change in its ideological polarity. For that reason, this examination of the justices' responses to criminal cases begins with the relationship between the attributes of cases and the Court's polarity over time. I then probe patterns in the voting behavior of individual justices. Finally, I take a different perspective on the Court's polarity over time by focusing on the Court's expansions of the procedural rights of criminal defendants.

54. The ACLU apparently played a critical role in *Mapp v. Ohio* (1961) with a brief passage in its amicus brief advocating that the Court apply the exclusionary rule for illegal searches and seizures to the states. In a case that everyone had assumed to be about state regulation of obscenity as late as the Court's conference, the Court ultimately adopted the ACLU's suggestion rather than deciding the obscenity issue. Stewart (1983), 1367–68; Long (2006), 67–69, 82–104.

### Case Attributes and the Court's Polarity

Table 3.2 depicts the bivariate relationships between the four case attributes and the polarity of decisions over time. For the most part, the differences in polarity between case categories are consistent with expectations. The one exception is white-collar cases in the 1910–36 Terms. Because of the small number of state cases in that period, the large difference in polarity between federal and state cases should not be given much weight.

The tendency for pro-defendant justices to be more liberal than pro-prosecution justices was relatively weak in the types of cases whose agenda shares declined over time. The only exception across all the periods shown in the table was white-collar cases in the 1910–36 Terms. However, the strength of these differences in polarity varied by time and case category. Most noteworthy are the sharp differences between case categories in the Court's polarity during the transitional 1937–45 Terms.

To probe the impact of the case attributes more deeply, I undertook multivariate analyses in which the dependent variables were the ideological orientation of the decision (using logistic regression) and the difference between the ideological scores of the pro-defendant and pro-prosecution justices (using linear regression). The periods analyzed were 1910–36, 1937–45, 1946–85, and 1986–2014.[55] Each equation included the variables for level of prosecution, question type, and, alternately, the white-collar or business variables.[56] Because there were few state substantive cases, the level of prosecution variable captured primarily the difference between state and federal procedural cases and the question-type variable captured primarily the difference between substantive and procedural federal cases.

---

55. The shorter periods in the 1946–2012 Terms defined by a chief justice's tenure were also analyzed. Those analyses identified some idiosyncratic relationships in particular periods, but there were no systematic patterns that did not appear in the longer periods used in the primary analyses.

56. As discussed in the appendix, I created three other variables related to the white-collar and business categories, such as whether a case involved both a white-collar crime and a business defendant. Analyses with those variables did not disclose any patterns beyond those that the white-collar and business variables identified.

TABLE 3.2. Percentages of non-unanimous decisions in which the pro-defendant side was more liberal, by period and selected case attributes

| Terms | White-collar | Non-WC | Business | Non-Bus. | Subst. | Proc. | Fed. | State |
|---|---|---|---|---|---|---|---|---|
| 1910–36 | 61.1 | 43.9 | 37.5 | 53.5 | 40.9 | 54.1 | 45.3 | (83.3) |
| 1937–45 | 51.9 | 85.0 | 44.4 | 81.6 | 63.3 | 78.4 | 67.3 | 91.7 |
| **1946–2012** | **82.4** | **95.1** | **85.5** | **94.1** | **74.0** | **96.2** | **88.2** | **97.2** |
| 1946–52 | 79.2 | 86.1 | 76.9 | 85.6 | 65.0 | 89.2 | 80.0 | 92.1 |
| 1953–68 | 89.4 | 93.3 | 88.0 | 93.1 | 83.9 | 93.8 | 90.5 | 95.2 |
| 1969–85 | 84.1 | 97.4 | 87.5 | 96.5 | 73.3 | 97.7 | 93.2 | 97.5 |
| 1986–2004 | 71.4 | 96.8 | 88.9 | 95.0 | 66.7 | 98.7 | 85.7 | 98.7 |
| 2005–12 | (80.0) | 92.3 | (66.7) | 92.4 | 81.5 | 94.7 | 81.4 | 97.5 |

*Notes*: Parentheses indicate fewer than ten cases in that category. The 1946–2012 Terms are in bold because the figures in that row are the totals for the five periods below it.

In the 1910–36 Terms, the bivariate effects for level of prosecution, white-collar offense, and business defendant largely held up in the estimates of changes in probabilities of liberal pro-defendant or conservative pro-defendant orientations for the those variables.[57] But caution in interpretation is needed of this result because there were only fifty-nine non-unanimous decisions.

The number of cases was only a little higher in the 1937–45 Terms (n=67), but the relationships between the business and white-collar variables and the Court's polarity were so strong that they are clearly meaningful. For substantive federal cases, the estimated probability that the pro-defendant side was more conservative than the other side increased from 26 percent to 61 percent (holding other variables constant) when there was a business defendant; for white-collar cases, the increase was from 22 percent to 56 percent. The estimated ideological difference between the two sides, measured by Martin-Quinn scores, changed by −2.05 when there was a white-collar defendant and −1.91 when there was a business defendant: relative to liberals, conservatives were considerably more likely to support defendants in these cases. When the white-collar and business variables were included in the same equation, the impact of a

57. Here and elsewhere, estimated probabilities were computed with the CLARIFY procedure. Gary King, Tomz, and Wittenberg (2000).

business defendant on the ideological difference between the two sides remained about the same, but the impact of a white-collar defendant declined considerably.[58] The level of prosecution had no meaningful impact on the Court's polarity; question type had a somewhat meaningful impact, but one that was considerably smaller than that of the business and white-collar variables.

The case attributes that shaped the Court's polarity in the 1937–45 Terms are illuminated by the cases that had the strongest polarity. Fourteen cases stood out in that respect, each with a median ideological difference between the two sides (measured by Martin-Quinn scores) of more than 2.90 in one direction or the other. The nine cases in which the pro-defendant justices were distinctly more liberal than the pro-prosecution justices were about evenly split between federal and state prosecutions. All involved procedural issues; three concerned the right to counsel for indigent defendants. Two were prosecutions for white-collar crimes, but there were no cases in which offenses were committed on behalf of businesses. In contrast, the five cases in which the pro-defendant justices were distinctly more conservative than their colleagues were all federal prosecutions of businesses and executives acting on behalf of businesses. Four were for regulatory offenses, three under the Sherman Antitrust Act and the fourth under the minimum wage law. These cases highlight the differential responses of the justices to different kinds of litigants and offenses during that period.

The impact of case attributes in the 1946–85 Terms and the 1986–2012 Terms is summarized in figure 3.3.[59] In both parts of the figure, the baseline is state procedural cases without white-collar defendants. In those cases, there was little chance that pro-defendant justices would be more conservative than their colleagues, and the

58. In the logit equation with both variables, the impact of each variable individually declined, but their joint impact on the probability that the pro-defendant side was more conservative in federal substantive cases was quite substantial—an increase from 22 percent to 64 percent.

59. The white-collar variable was included for the 1946–2012 Terms instead of the business variable because, as discussed shortly, that variable had a greater impact on the Court's polarity.

mean ideological difference between the two sides was quite high. The difference between state and federal cases, holding the other two attributes constant, was fairly small.

In contrast, shifting from procedural to substantive cases weakened the Court's ideological polarity considerably, and shifting from non-white-collar to white-collar cases did as well. There was a large cumulative difference between state procedural cases involving non-white-collar offenses and federal substantive cases with white-collar offenses, especially in the Rehnquist and Roberts Courts. In those Courts, the chances that the pro-defendant justices would be more conservative than their pro-prosecution colleagues went from nearly zero in the baseline category to nearly one-half, and the mean ideological difference between the two sides declined by 2.30.

At the bivariate level, the presence of a business defendant had considerable impact on the Court's polarity: across the whole period from the 1946 Term to the 2012 Term, cases in which the defendant acted on behalf of a business were nearly three times as likely as other cases to have pro-defendant justices who were more liberal than their colleagues. But in equations that included white-collar offenses, the impact of business defendants became quite weak. Thus, in contrast with the 1937–45 Terms, white-collar crimes had a more powerful impact on the justices than business status.

Just as the cases with strong polarity in either direction illuminate the Court's polarity in the transitional period of the 1937–45 Terms, the cases that depart most sharply from the Court's overall polarity in the period since then are also illuminating. As it happens, two legal scholars have discussed criminal cases in the Rehnquist and Roberts Courts in which the justices did not line up along the usual ideological lines. Ward Farnsworth analyzed what he called "dissents against type"—liberal justices dissenting from pro-defendant decisions, conservative justices from pro-prosecution decisions—in the Court's 1975 through 2007 Terms.[60] After examining dissents against type as a general phenomenon and the dissents of some specific justices, Farnsworth concluded that some of these dissents reflected

60. Farnsworth (2009).

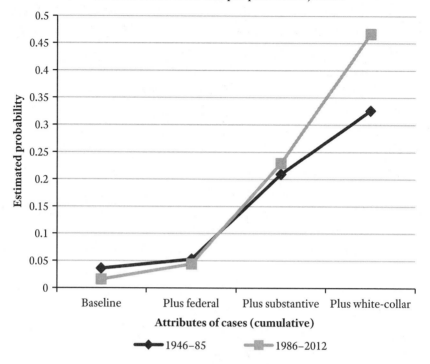

(a) Estimated probability that pro-defendant justices were more conservative than pro-prosecution justices

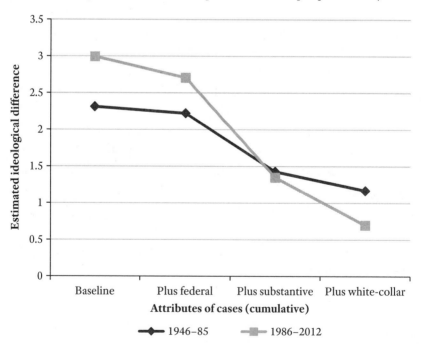

(b) Mean ideological difference between pro-defendant and pro-prosecution justices

FIGURE 3.3. Impact of case attributes on Court's ideological orientation, 1946–2012 Terms. *Notes*: The baseline is a state criminal prosecution with a procedural issue and a non-white-collar offense. Those three attributes were successively changed in the three analyses that followed. Thus, "Plus white-collar" refers to cases with federal prosecutions, substantive issues, and white-collar offenses.

The ideological difference for each case is the difference between the median Martin-Quinn scores of the pro-defendant and pro-prosecution justices. All values are positive: a positive value indicates that the pro-defendant justices were more liberal than their colleagues.

policy preferences that were not captured by ideology, especially attitudes toward white-collar crime. Others reflected interpretive methodologies or were largely idiosyncratic.

Rachel Barkow focused on conservative justices in the Rehnquist Court, comparing those she characterized as pragmatists (William Rehnquist, Sandra Day O'Connor, and Anthony Kennedy) with originalists (Antonin Scalia and Clarence Thomas).[61] She gave particular attention to the instances in which the conservatives disagreed with each other about case outcomes. The pattern of disagreements was mixed, but Barkow emphasized what she saw as the impact of originalist methodology in causing Justices Scalia and Thomas to take pro-defendant positions on questions such as the scope of the role of the jury under the Sixth Amendment.

To probe the sources of deviant cases further, I examined the Rehnquist and Roberts cases with the most negative median differences between pro-defendant and pro-prosecution justices—specifically, cases with difference scores more negative than −2.0. In the Rehnquist Court, nine cases met this criterion. All involved federal prosecutions and substantive questions. Defendants had been convicted of white-collar offenses in five of the nine cases, in one of which the defendant was acting for a business. In that case, *Moskal v. United States*, a car dealer who had been convicted of receiving vehicle titles with knowledge that they had fraudulent odometer

61. Barkow (2006).

readings was found to fall under the terms of a federal criminal statute.[62] Justices Scalia, O'Connor, and Kennedy dissented.

One of the white-collar cases, *Cheek v. United States*, is of particular interest.[63] Cheek was an airline pilot who stopped filing federal income tax returns and indicated on his W-4 forms for some years that he was exempt from income taxes. Charged with willfully failing to file federal tax returns and willfully attempting to evade income tax, Cheek argued that his actions had not been willful because they were based on a good-faith belief that he was not violating the law—a belief based on his involvement with a group that made legal arguments supporting non-payment of income taxes. Perhaps surprisingly, his position won support from six justices. Justice Blackmun dissented in a short and acerbic opinion that Justice Marshall joined.[64] While other considerations probably affected the justices' votes in the case, the justices' attitudes toward white-collar offenses, taxation, or both almost surely explain their positions.

Three other cases had attributes that worked against the Court's usual ideological polarity in criminal cases. *Caron v. United States*[65] and *Staples v. United States*[66] involved gun offenses. In both cases, liberal justices dissented from a statutory interpretation that favored the defendant. In *Koon v. United States*, the justices disagreed about application of the federal sentencing guidelines, with the Court's four liberal justices dissenting from a pro-defendant decision.[67] The defendants were two Los Angeles police officers who were charged with violating the civil rights of Rodney King in 1991 by using excessive force, an incident that received enormous national attention. This left only one case that cannot be understood in ideological terms, *Holloway v. United States*, which involved a statutory interpretation issue.[68]

---

62. *Moskal v. United States* (1990).
63. *Cheek v. United States* (1991).
64. Justice Souter did not participate in the decision.
65. *Caron v. United States* (1998).
66. *Staples v. United States* (1994).
67. *Koon v. United States* (1996).
68. *Holloway v. United States* (1999).

In the Roberts Court, which had very few non-unanimous decisions in white-collar and business cases, six decisions met the −2.0 criterion. Three arose from federal prosecutions, and two involved substantive issues. In only one of these six cases was there a countervailing ideological consideration. That case was *United States v. Hayes*, in which the defendant was charged with a gun possession offense in the context of domestic violence.[69] Of the other five cases, four had pro-prosecution decisions with dissents solely or primarily from conservative justices. One, *Oregon v. Ice*,[70] was one of the follow-ups to the Court's decisions striking down federal and state sentencing guidelines, decisions that had ideologically muddled divisions.[71] The others involved issues that might be considered technical but that could have broad application. Justice Scalia, Justice Thomas, or both dissented in all of these four cases, and their highly conservative Martin-Quinn scores were the primary reason for the strongly negative ideological differences between the two sides in these cases.[72] It may be that the interpretive methodologies emphasized by Barkow were the primary basis for these unusual alignments.[73]

The specific gun cases with unusual polarity raise the question whether the presence of a gun offense affected the Court's polarity in general. Because of the liberal-conservative division on gun policy questions in the elite world as a whole, a division reflected in the Court's two major decisions interpreting constitutional protections for gun rights,[74] we might expect the Court's polarity to weaken or even reverse in prosecutions under gun laws. This question is especially relevant because there was a relatively high proportion of prosecutions for gun offenses in the Court's criminal justice

69. *United States v. Hayes* (2009).

70. *Oregon v. Ice* (2009).

71. In those decisions, *Blakely v. Washington* (2004) and *United States v. Booker* (2005), the justices who voted to uphold the sentencing guidelines were Rehnquist, O'Connor, Kennedy, and Breyer.

72. In addition to *Ice*, the cases were *Day v. McDonough* (2006), *United States v. Resendiz-Ponce* (2007), and *Gonzales v. United States* (2008).

73. See Fischman (2015), S282–85.

74. *District of Columbia v. Heller* (2008); *McDonald v. City of Chicago* (2010).

decisions during the 1986–2012 Terms—7 percent in the Rehnquist Court, 14 percent in the Roberts Court.[75]

The picture is mixed. The presence of a gun offense had little effect on the ideological distance between the two sides when other case attributes are taken into account. But gun cases were four times as likely as other cases to have pro-defendant justices more conservative than their colleagues, and this relationship remained substantial with controls for other case attributes: gun cases were 17 percentage points more likely to have the reverse of the Court's usual polarity in criminal cases than were other cases. Altogether, five of the twenty cases with the most negative polarity were gun cases. Notably, all five cases involved interpretation of federal statutes relating to ownership and transfer of firearms. Thus, questions that relate directly to the ideological debates over gun policy affected the justices' responses to criminal cases.[76]

The patterns in the impact of case attributes provide evidence about the relationship between the Court's agenda and its polarity. In the 1937–45 Terms, the cases with different attributes began to evoke quite different ideological responses from justices, most notably by dividing them in opposite ways depending on the presence or absence of business defendants. Then, in the decades that followed, cases that were likely to evoke greater support for defendants from liberals than from conservatives became more dominant. Although the Court's polarity continued to differ with the attributes of cases, its overall polarity became more one-sided with the growing homogeneity of its criminal agenda.

The development of a more homogeneous criminal agenda may have had another effect as well. The growing dominance of cases whose attributes helped to make liberal justices more favorable to defendants than conservatives might color the justices' overall attitudes toward criminal justice, so that liberals tended to favor

75. These proportions and the analyses that are described here do not include armed robbery and other crimes for which use of a gun is part of the traditional definition of the offense.

76. One recent decision, *Abramski v. United States* (2014), fits the same pattern well. Another, *Voisine v. United States* (2016), fits it only in part.

defendants more than conservatives across cases of all types. An examination of voting by individual justices can probe that possibility along with other aspects of the Court's polarity.

## Justices

The transitional period of the 1937–45 Terms is a good place to start because there was such a substantial difference between the Court's polarity in white-collar and business cases, especially the latter, and its polarity in other criminal cases. I analyzed voting by the nine justices who participated in a majority of the non-unanimous criminal justice decisions in that period, comparing their responses to business and non-business cases. Because different justices participated in different sets of cases, comparisons among them are inexact. Still, patterns of voting support for defendants in different types of cases allow for meaningful comparison.

As part (a) of figure 3.4 shows, there was a strong rank-order correlation (+.967) between justices' liberalism across all issue areas and their pro-defendant voting in non-unanimous criminal cases with non-business defendants. In contrast, there was no relationship between overall liberalism and support for business defendants (−.033). The Pearson correlation between justices' support levels in business and non-business cases was positive but low (+.170). Three justices had differences of more than 30 percentage points in the relative levels of support they gave to business and non-business defendants. But it should be kept in mind that these data are limited to non-unanimous decisions, a limitation that exaggerates differences among justices.

Parts (b) and (c) of the figure each cover part of the period in which the Court's ideological polarity across all criminal cases was very strong, the Warren-Burger Courts and the Rehnquist-Roberts Courts. Because white-collar offenses had a stronger impact on the Court's polarity than business defendants, the comparison focuses on offense type. In contrast with the 1937–45 period, both unanimous and non-unanimous decisions are included.

In the Warren and Burger Courts, the wide variation in voting support for defendants is striking in light of the inclusion of

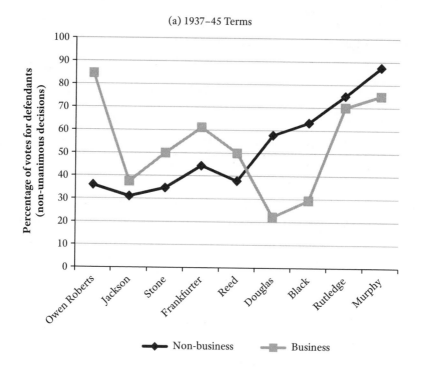

(a) 1937–45 Terms

Percentage of votes for defendants (non-unanimous decisions)

◆ Non-business   ■ Business

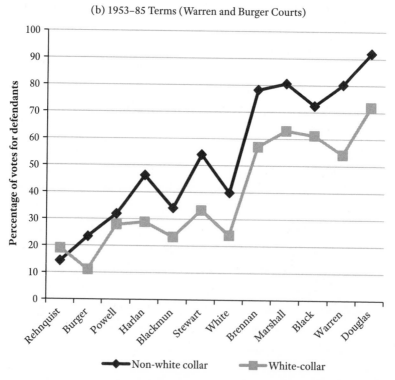

(b) 1953–85 Terms (Warren and Burger Courts)

Percentage of votes for defendants

◆ Non-white collar   ■ White-collar

(c) 1986–2012 Terms (Rehnquist and Roberts Courts)

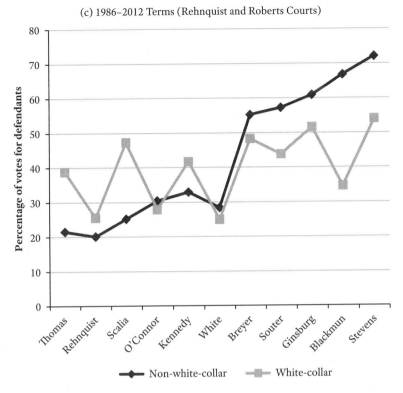

FIGURE 3.4. Justices' voting support for criminal defendants by case attributes.
Notes: In each chart, justices are listed in the order of their proportions of liberal and conservative votes in orally argued cases across all issues for the time period covered by the chart, based on the coding of votes in the Supreme Court Database. Justices were included in the chart for 1937–45 if they participated in a majority of the non-unanimous criminal decisions during that period; for 1953–85 if they were among the dozen justices who participated in the most criminal decisions; and for 1986–2012 if they participated in at least twenty decisions involving white-collar offenses.

unanimous decisions. What stands out, in contrast with the 1937–45 Terms, is the similarity in the patterns of support in white-collar and other cases. The rank-order correlations between justices' overall liberalism and their support for defendants were very high for both sets of cases, +.930 for non-white-collar cases and +.853 for white-collar cases. The Pearson correlation between support for the two sets of defendants was nearly perfect (+.962). This similarity suggests that justices responded to white-collar cases primarily on the basis of their general predispositions toward criminal cases. It is true that all of the Court's strong liberals voted for white-collar defendants at distinctly lower rates than for other defendants. But that was true of several conservative justices as well, and only William Rehnquist gave more support to white-collar defendants than to other defendants.

The Rehnquist and Roberts Courts featured a softening of that pattern. In non-white-collar cases the relationship between the justices' liberalism across all cases and their rates of voting for defendants was even higher than in the preceding period, with a rank-order correlation of +.964. Most noteworthy was a sharp difference between the Court's liberals and their more conservative colleagues. The justices' voting in cases with white-collar offenses did not follow ideological lines as sharply, with a rank-order correlation of +.500. Because there was some tendency for support for defendants to increase with the justices' liberalism even in white-collar cases, the Pearson correlation between the justices' voting in the two sets of cases was still high (+.597). But that correlation was distinctly lower than in the Warren-Burger period. At a time when white-collar cases were becoming relatively rare, they were also drawing a more distinctive pattern of responses from the justices.

The patterns in the justices' votes in substantive and procedural cases are also worth noting. There was a moderate correlation between the justices' proportions of pro-defendant votes in the two sets of cases (+.401) in the 1937–45 Terms and much higher correlations (+.744 and +.643, respectively) in the 1953–85 and 1986–2012 Terms. In both of the later periods the standard deviation of the justices' pro-defendant proportions was twice as high in procedural cases as in substantive cases. The rank-order correlation between the justices' liberalism across all issues and their proportions of pro-defendant votes was far higher for procedural cases than for substantive cases in the 1937–45 Terms and still distinctly higher in the two later periods.[77] These patterns support the conclusion that in the current era, liberal and conservative ideology is more directly reflected in criminal procedure than in criminal law. In part for this

---

77. The correlations for procedural and substantive cases, respectively, were .917 and .385 in 1937–45, .916 and .713 in 1953–85, and .965 and .618 in 1986–2012.

reason, the course of the Court's interpretations of procedural rights for defendants merits closer attention.

### The Course of Procedural Rights

The most prominent and most consequential element of the Supreme Court's work in criminal justice has been its decisions establishing principles for interpretation of constitutional provisions that protect defendants' procedural rights. Because of limited federal activity in criminal justice and the Court's limited power to review criminal cases, there were few major decisions involving defendants' rights before 1886. From that time on, the Court played a more active role in defining the procedural protections in the Bill of Rights. Although the Court's interpretations were mixed and variable over time, there was a strong movement toward expansion of the reach of those protections in two periods.

The first was the late nineteenth and early twentieth centuries. Decisions that advanced the procedural rights of defendants during this period occurred overwhelmingly in cases involving regulation of business practices (some of these cases civil rather than criminal), white-collar crime, or both.[78] In *Boyd v. United States*, the Court combined Fourth and Fifth Amendment protections and gave them a strikingly broad interpretation as protections of privacy.[79] *Boyd* was a civil forfeiture case that arose from suspected fraud by a business in paying an import tax. *Counselman v. Hitchcock*, which protected against compulsory testimony before a grand jury, arose from an investigation into railroad practices under the Interstate Commerce Act.[80] *Weems v. United States*, which held that a disproportionate prison sentence could violate the Eighth Amendment, arose from a prosecution for falsifying a public document.[81] In *Weeks v. United States*, which established the exclusionary rule

---

78. Stuntz (1995a), 1017–18. In addition to the cases discussed in this paragraph, examples include *Kepner v. United States* (1904) (mail fraud); *Hale v. Henkel* (1906) (antitrust); and *Burdeau v. McDowell* (1921) (mail fraud).

79. *Boyd v. United States* (1886).

80. *Counselman v. Hitchcock* (1892).

81. *Weems v. United States* (1910).

for illegal searches and seizures, the prosecution was for use of the mails in the operation of a lottery.[82] The extension of the exclusionary rule through the "fruit of the poisonous tree" doctrine came in *Silverthorne Lumber Company v. United States*, which arose from an investigation into business practices.[83] *Gouled v. United States*, which adopted the "mere evidence" rule limiting searches and seizures, involved a prosecution for mail fraud.[84]

There were multiple reasons for this pattern. One was the prominence of white-collar and business-related crimes in the limited range of federal criminal jurisdiction. Another was the skills of the attorneys who represented affluent people in the courts.[85] Third, some scholars have argued convincingly that the justices' favorable responses to certain constitutional claims in that era reflected their attitudes toward the offenses involved,[86] their sympathy for property rights,[87] or their opposition to regulation of business activities.[88] Whatever its sources were, the Court's expansion of procedural rights had considerable relevance to federal regulation of business activities.[89]

This pattern should not be oversimplified. The Court's decisions expanding the rights of white-collar and business defendants came alongside other decisions that interpreted those rights narrowly. Moreover, some of the white-collar cases had nothing to do with business practices. Finally, these expansive decisions constituted only a small portion of the Court's activity in criminal cases. But the single most prominent theme in the Court's decisions was protection of procedural rights in cases involving regulation of economic activity. That theme was consistent with the concern of most

82. *Weeks v. United States* (1914).
83. *Silverthorne Lumber Co. v. United States* (1920).
84. *Gouled v. United States* (1921).
85. Stuntz (2011), 127; see Twiss (1942). In *Counselman* and *Silverthorne*, the defendants were represented by prestigious attorneys who represented corporations in major constitutional cases during that era, James C. Carter and William D. Guthrie respectively. Twiss (1942), 143, 174–82, 191–95, 215–25.
86. Stuntz (1995b), 394.
87. Cloud (1996), 555–98.
88. Lillquist (1995).
89. Braeman (1988), 97; Stuntz (1995b), 423–25.

justices in that era about overreaching by government as economic regulator.

Most of the Court's major decisions protecting procedural rights in cases involving economic activity were unanimous. When the Court did divide, the divisions did not follow sharp or consistent ideological lines. In contrast, in the few cases in which the Court addressed major constitutional issues involving ordinary crime, the ideological lines were clear. *Frank v. Mangum*[90] and *Moore v. Dempsey*[91] involved murder cases in the South in which the defendants were members of religious and racial minorities, respectively. In each case, the trials fairly could be described as mob-dominated. In *Frank*, the relatively liberal Oliver Wendell Holmes and Charles Evans Hughes dissented from the Court's decision to uphold the conviction; in *Moore*, the conservatives James McReynolds and George Sutherland dissented from the decision to overturn the conviction.

In the 1920s and 1930s, the Court heard a number of cases that arose from prosecutions under federal and state Prohibition laws. Some of these cases raised questions of procedural rights under the Constitution in field that included search and seizure, self-incrimination, and double jeopardy. The Prohibition prosecutions helped to move the Court into the kinds of criminal cases that were more typical of state courts than federal courts.[92] They also played a role in the expansion of some procedural rights in the Supreme Court and other courts.[93]

The justices' responses to these cases were colored by their own attitudes toward Prohibition before its adoption and their assessments of the Prohibition laws in operation over the course of the 1920s.[94] In some respects, conservative justices who were unsympathetic to Prohibition were the most protective of procedural rights for the targets of Prohibition enforcement.[95] For instance, in *Carroll*

---

90. *Frank v. Mangum* (1915); see Dinnerstein (1968).
91. *Moore v. Dempsey* (1923).
92. Braeman (1988), 89–90.
93. Kersch (2004), 74, 80–81, 84.
94. Okrent (2010), 281–84.
95. Murchison (1994), 182–83; Kersch (2004), 32.

*v. United States*, a multifaceted case that effectively established the automobile exception to the requirement of a search warrant, McReynolds and Sutherland dissented from the Court's approval of a search aimed at intercepting illegal liquor.[96] But in *Olmstead v. United States*, in which wiretapping was used to gather evidence against a large-scale bootlegger, the four dissenters against the Court's admission of wiretapping evidence in Court included the three most liberal justices.[97]

*Moore v. Dempsey* represented an early indication of what became a second era of rights expansion. Beginning in the 1930s, the Court increasingly heard criminal cases that arose from state prosecutions of black defendants in the South. Notably, as the Court expanded the rights of defendants in cases involving common crimes, more often than not the defendants were black. Among these cases were *Powell v. Alabama*, arising from another mob-dominated trial, on the right to counsel;[98] and *Brown v. Mississippi*[99] and *Chambers v. Florida*,[100] on coerced confessions. Beginning in the 1930s, the Court also heard a long series of cases arising from the use of all-white grand juries and trial juries in Southern states. One legal scholar concluded that in the period from the mid-1930s to the early 1960s, "the Court's criminal procedure cases were thinly disguised race cases."[101]

When the Court began to incorporate specific guarantees of defendants' rights into the Fourteenth Amendment and expanded the scope of those rights, it frequently did so in cases that involved members of racial minority groups. Cases with black defendants included those incorporating the prohibition against cruel and unusual punishment,[102] the prohibition of illegal searches and seizures,[103] the

96. *Carroll v. United States* (1925).

97. *Olmstead v. United States* (1928). These were Holmes, Brandeis, and Harlan Fiske Stone. The fourth dissenter was Pierce Butler.

98. *Powell v. Alabama* (1932).

99. *Brown v. Mississippi* (1936).

100. *Chambers v. Florida* (1940).

101. Powe (2000), 492.

102. *Louisiana ex rel. Francis v. Resweber* (1947). The Court assumed, without deciding, that the prohibition of cruel and unusual punishment was incorporated into the Fourteenth Amendment. In *Robinson v. California* (1962), the Court implicitly affirmed that the right had been incorporated.

103. *Mapp v. Ohio* (1961), building on *Wolf v. Colorado* (1949).

right to a speedy trial,[104] and the right to a jury trial.[105] The speedy trial case grew out of civil rights activity, and the jury case arose from a confrontation between groups of black and white young men. The defendants in *Miranda v. Arizona*[106] and its precursor *Escobedo v. Illinois*[107] were Latino.

The identification of race as an important element in criminal procedure cases was strengthened by the participation of the NAACP and the NAACP LDF in some cases.[108] Thurgood Marshall was personally active in this field,[109] and he argued *Chambers* and *Lyons v. Oklahoma*, a coerced confession case, in the Supreme Court.[110] Marshall's 1949 rule that the LDF should take criminal cases only when "the man is innocent" may have helped to focus the justices' minds on defendants rather than the victims of crimes.[111] The LDF became increasingly involved in criminal justice over time, in part because of the use of criminal laws in Southern states to attack the civil rights movement and in part because of racial issues involving the death penalty.[112] The LDF sponsored the challenges to capital punishment in the key cases of *Furman v. Georgia*[113] and *McCleskey v. Kemp*,[114] among others. The cases that the NAACP brought and its advocacy in those cases helped to frame cases before the Court as conflicts between vulnerable defendants and an overbearing criminal justice system that was heavily infused with racial bias.

More broadly, these cases helped to establish the perception that broad interpretations of defendants' rights were favorable to racial minority groups. Ken Kersch has argued that the Court's growing support for criminal defendants can be understood as a part of its general commitment to attack racial discrimination.[115] Other schol-

104. *Klopfer v. North Carolina* (1967).
105. *Duncan v. Louisiana* (1968).
106. *Miranda v. Arizona* (1966).
107. *Escobedo v. Illinois* (1964).
108. See Gilbert King (2012).
109. Tushnet (1994), 56–66.
110. *Chambers v. Florida* (1940); *Lyons v. Oklahoma* (1944).
111. Gilbert King (2012), 48.
112. Meltsner (1973); Greenberg (1994), 440–48.
113. *Furman v. Georgia* (1972).
114. *McCleskey v. Kemp* (1987).
115. Ken Kersch (2004), 20, 88–89, 121–22.

ars have pointed to the importance of race in the Court's adoption of stronger protections for due process rights.[116]

Racial elements of criminal cases affected justices across the ideological spectrum: from the 1930s on, both liberal and conservative justices responded favorably to defendants who were subjected to blatant racial injustice. Among the early cases, *Brown* and *Chambers* were decided unanimously, and only two of the Court's conservatives (McReynolds and Pierce Butler) dissented in *Powell*. But in the longer run, liberal justices diverged from their colleagues in developing a broader sense of criminal defendants as people who were disadvantaged in the criminal justice system, in part because of their race. As one study shows, that image comes through clearly in opinions of the Warren Court.[117] In contrast, conservative justices sometimes emphasized the seriousness of the crimes of which defendants were convicted and the impact of these crimes on their victims and other people.[118]

The shift from an era in which the procedural rights of criminal defendants were identified largely with people who were well off to an era in which those rights were identified primarily with the disadvantaged was not a sharp break. During the 1930s and 1940s, there were still criminal and quasi-criminal cases in which litigants who were the subjects of economic regulation made significant procedural claims. Liberal justices sometimes resisted those claims.[119] But when prosecutions that grew out of government economic policy became scarce on the Court's agenda, the Court's liberals no longer had to sort out conflicts between defendants' rights and regulation of economic activity very often.

As William Stuntz pointed out, the Court's expansions of protections for ordinary criminal defendants under the Fourth and Fifth Amendments coexist with its acceptance of substantial governmental incursions on privacy in the economic arena, incursions

---

116. E.g., Klarman (2000).

117. Harcourt (1995), 1192–99; see Stuntz (1995b), 437–38.

118. Harcourt (1995), 1199–205. An especially vivid example is Justice Clarence Thomas's dissenting opinion in *Brumfield v. Cain* (2015).

119. Kersch (2004), 113–17.

that take forms such as regulatory searches and inspections of business premises.[120] Because of the conjunction of these developments, Stuntz concluded that "constitutional law is not bringing the politically powerless up to the level of the powerful; in this limited sense, the powerless do *better*."[121] Whether or not this conclusion is justified,[122] it suggests how perceptions of beneficiaries have shaped justices' application of their ideological stances to the rights of defendants.

From this perspective, it is understandable that in the current era, ideological differences between pro-defendant and pro-prosecution justices are relatively large on procedural questions and in cases that do not involve white-collar crimes. More than substantive questions, procedural questions feed into a perception of defendants as vulnerable underdogs. And even though white-collar defendants are a heterogeneous group, on the whole they seem less vulnerable than defendants in other cases.

Still, even in cases that departed sharply from the image that strengthened liberal support for criminal defendants—federal prosecutions of white-collar defendants with substantive issues—the justices who voted in favor of defendants in the Rehnquist and Roberts Courts were, on average, a little more liberal than those who voted for the prosecution. The movement toward a clear ideological polarity in criminal justice may have been spurred by a particular type of case, but if so, the effects on the Court's polarity were considerably broader than that.

## Conclusions

To many if not most observers, the current ideological polarity of criminal justice in the Supreme Court and in the larger elite world seems natural. But that view is challenged by the existence of a period in which the polarity of criminal justice was not nearly so clear.

120. Stuntz (1995a).
121. Stuntz, 1046. (Emphasis in original.)
122. See Seidman (1995).

Perhaps most striking is the fact that broad readings of constitutional protections of defendants' rights were once more of a conservative cause than a liberal one.

It could be argued that the current polarity *is* natural, that the more muddled polarity of the early twentieth century was an aberration. From this perspective, the prominence of white-collar crime and business defendants in that period skewed ideological responses to criminal cases in the Court and in other segments of the national elite. Once common crimes came to dominate the Court's agenda and the elite conversation about criminal justice, the polarity that we should expect emerged or reemerged.

This argument is reasonable. The values that some scholars have identified as connecting ideological camps with criminal justice might create a basic tendency for liberals to take positions that are more favorable to criminal defendants than those of conservatives. Similarly, the reality that defendants are disproportionately low in socioeconomic status and members of racial minority groups might connect criminal justice to the group affect of conservatives and liberals. Indeed, values and affect could reinforce each other in leading conservatives and liberals to adopt different perspectives on law and policy in criminal justice.

But in itself, the existence of a substantial change in the polarity of criminal justice raises doubts about how firmly the current polarity is rooted in general premises. Moreover, the strong shared understanding about conservative and liberal positions that now exists reflects a considerable element of historical contingency alongside deduction from broad premises. To the extent that liberal justices respond sympathetically to defendants, for instance, that sympathy is at least partly a product of the kinds of state criminal cases that the Court heard from the 1930s to the 1960s. Those cases confronted justices with evidence that many defendants were highly vulnerable people who were subjected to blatant racial discrimination. The Court as a whole, but especially liberal justices, responded positively to the procedural claims brought by those defendants. The Court's liberals also developed a broader sense of criminal defendants as people who needed protection. But this process was not inevitable. If the cases before the Court had instead highlighted the impact of crime on low-income people and members of racial minority groups, the justices might have responded differently.

Advocates before the Court played a key role in this process. As representatives of the black community before the Supreme Court, the NAACP and the LDF sponsored and supported challenges to the procedures used in state criminal proceedings and created a direct link between constitutional criminal procedure and racial equality. As a result, they helped to create an understanding that pro-defendant positions were favorable rather than unfavorable to racial minority groups.

This may be an issue on which the Court contributed substantially to the ideological understandings of other elite groups. The decisions of the 1950s and 1960s that expanded the procedural rights of criminal defendants usually evoked dissents from conservative justices. In the process, these decisions helped to connect those rights to liberalism and spurred conservatives to emphasize pro-prosecution positions. In this respect it is noteworthy that the Court's criminal justice decisions became the objects of attack for conservative presidential candidates in the 1960s.

In referring to the potential impact of values and group affect, I have not yet focused on the question of their relative importance. That question is more difficult to resolve in criminal justice than in freedom of expression, because plausible arguments can be made for the dominance of values that political psychologists have identified with liberalism and conservatism and for the dominance of attitudes toward criminal defendants as a whole.

I do think, however, that an explanation based solely on values can be ruled out. The reason is that since the 1930s, the Court's ideological polarity has differed with the types of defendants who appear in cases and the types of offenses for which they were convicted. The sharp differences in the justices' responses to business defendants and other defendants in the 1937–45 period might be explained by the connection between prosecutions of businesses and liberal economic programs, which in turn can be understood as a conflict of values. But it is unlikely that affect toward different types of defendants had no impact on the justices' responses to criminal cases in that period.

In the period since 1945, the difference in the Court's polarity between cases with white-collar offenses and other cases has not been as dramatic as the difference between business and non-business cases in the New Deal era. But with other case attributes held constant, the presence of a white-collar offense weakened the Court's polarity considerably in the Warren-Burger era and even more after that. That effect is telling. With the decline of federal prosecutions aimed at business practices, the white-collar cases that came to the Court connected less and less with the justices' attitudes toward economic regulation. Rather, the most prominent difference between white-collar cases and other criminal cases in the Court was the identity of the defendants. While both white-collar defendants and those charged with other crimes are heterogeneous in socioeconomic status, on the whole white-collar defendants are distinctly higher in status. Moreover, defendants who are accused of common crimes and white-collar offenses surely differ considerably in their racial composition. To a degree, those differences seem to pull justices away from their general ideological tendencies in criminal justice.

If values cannot explain everything about the polarity of criminal cases, almost surely they explain something. The values that political and social psychologists have identified as bases for liberal and conservative positions in criminal justice are meaningful, even if the application of those values (and perhaps the development of the values as well) has been influenced by the identities of defendants. The stronger polarity of procedural cases in the Court, compared with substantive cases, is consistent with a connection between liberalism and concern with procedural fairness—though here, the Court's major decisions on constitutional criminal procedure in the early twentieth century make it clear that we should not overstate the stability of that connection. And to a degree, the justices' differentiation between white-collar and common crimes arguably could be interpreted as a product of values related to equality rather than simply affect toward higher-status and lower-status groups.

If the evidence on criminal justice is more susceptible to alternative interpretations than the evidence on freedom of expression, it reinforces the evidence presented in chapter 2 in raising strong doubts about the dominance of values as a source of ideological polarity in the Court. There is considerable evidence that the perceptions of conservative and liberal justices were shaped by the most common attributes of the criminal defendants whose cases they reviewed after the New Deal period. During that period and the one that precede it, justices also differentiated among individual defendants on the basis of their attributes. In criminal justice, as in free expression, affect toward social groups has played a substantial part in defining liberal and conservative positions.

# 4

# Takings

In 1997, Susette Kelo bought a small house in New London, Connecticut.[1] A year later, the Pfizer pharmaceutical company announced its intention to build a large research facility near Kelo's neighborhood. A development corporation created by the city (NLDC) put together a plan to support and take advantage of the Pfizer facility by developing the land around it. Kelo's house was in a parcel that NLDC would use for one of several possible purposes related to a state park or marina.

After the city council approved the NLDC plan in 2000, Kelo and other property owners sued in state court. One of their claims was that the proposed taking of their property would violate the Fifth Amendment requirement that government could take property only for a "public use." After a mixed decision in the trial court, the Connecticut Supreme Court ruled in favor of the city in 2004.

Kelo and the other plaintiffs asked the U.S. Supreme Court to hear the case on the basis of the takings question, and the Court agreed. In June 2005, the Court affirmed the state supreme court

1. The facts of the *Kelo* case are taken from the Supreme Court's opinion in *Kelo v. City of New London* (2005, 472–77), and from Benedict (2009). On the decision and its context, see Schultz (2010) and Somin (2015).

ruling in *Kelo v. City of New London* by a 5–4 vote. The decision was greeted with widespread dismay and outrage, and one result was a wave of state legislation limiting government action to take private property.[2]

The decision split the Court along ideological lines: the four liberal justices voted in favor of the city, and its three strong conservatives voted in favor of Kelo. The city won by gaining the vote of Justice Anthony Kennedy, one of the two moderate conservatives on the Court. That lineup might have surprised an observer who was familiar with the Court and the case but not with the Court's takings decisions. Opinion on urban redevelopment has never fallen neatly along ideological lines, and disillusionment with urban renewal programs was widely shared among both liberals and conservatives.[3] But that sentiment was especially strong among liberals because of the perception that urban renewal served business interests at the expense of low-income residents and African American communities.[4] It became common to say, as writer James Baldwin did in 1963, that "urban renewal means Negro removal."[5] Indeed, the NAACP submitted an amicus curiae brief in support of Susette Kelo, and one cosigner was another civil rights group, the Southern Christian Leadership Conference. Thus, liberals with a commitment to social and economic equality would seem likely to be troubled by New London's version of urban renewal.

As for the litigants in *Kelo*, conservative justices might be expected to sympathize with an economically troubled city that sought to spur development in conjunction with the initiative of a business corporation. For their part, liberal justices might be expected to sympathize with a woman who was far from wealthy and who was in danger of losing a home that she loved, especially when a large company implicitly stood on the other side.

2. Nadler and Diamond (2008); Wolf (2008); Somin (2015), chs. 5–6.
3. See Martin Anderson (1964).
4. Gelfand (1975), 208–13; Judd and Swanstrom (1998), 181–94; Teaford (2000); Lavine (2010), 469–73.
5. Dickinson (1963).

For those who did follow the Court's takings decisions, however, the actual division among the justices in *Kelo* was no surprise. For more than two decades, conservative justices had been considerably more favorable to takings claims than the Court's liberals. Whatever set of forces created this polarity, they were strong enough to overcome the attributes of the *Kelo* case that seemed to work in the opposite direction.

Thus the Court's decision in *Kelo* makes takings an interesting issue in which to explore the Court's ideological polarity, and takings qualified for inclusion in this study because the Court's polarity on the issue shifted twice during the twentieth century. In this chapter, I analyze the sources of those shifts, with particular attention to the second shift that produced the Court's current line of division.

The basic approach that I take is the same as the one used to analyze free expression and criminal justice. Because takings is a relatively obscure issue, however, I discuss the substance of the issue at greater length.[6] And because the numbers of takings decisions are relatively small, I give more attention to individual cases than I did in the preceding chapters.

## Interpreting the Takings Clause

The Fifth Amendment to the U.S. Constitution concludes with the takings clause: "nor shall private property be taken for public use, without just compensation."[7] The Court has incorporated the takings clause into the due process clause of the Fourteenth Amendment. *Chicago, Burlington and Quincy Railroad Co. v. Chicago*, decided in 1897, is generally regarded as making that incorporation, although the Court's opinion was somewhat ambiguous on that point.[8]

For the most part, the questions that the Court addresses on takings concern three terms in the takings clause.[9] Logically, the first

---

6. As indicated by this sentence, I treat "takings" as singular rather than plural.

7. See Treanor (1985).

8. *Chicago, Burlington & Quincy Railroad Co. v. Chicago* (1897).

9. In this discussion I draw from several useful summaries of takings law: Meltz (1991, 2007, 2015), Meltz, Merriam, and Frank (1999), Schultz (2010, chs. 4–6), and the Congressional Research Service (2016, 1572–603).

question is whether government has taken property. Because that is the most important and most complex question, I take up the other two before returning to it.

The second question is whether a government taking is for a public use. Although the language of the takings clause is not entirely clear on this matter, the Court has consistently held that government can take property only for a public rather than a private use. There was a period when courts sometimes equated public use with "use by the public," a narrow reading. But since the early twentieth century, the Supreme Court consistently has adhered to the broader meaning of serving the public good. It has also given strong deference to legislative judgments about public use. The majority opinion in *Kelo* expressed that deference, and arguably the Court's decision was simply reaffirming its long-standing doctrinal position on this question.[10]

The third question is what constitutes just compensation for a taking. The Court generally has equated just compensation with the market value of property that government takes. The Court has decided many cases about the calculation of just compensation, largely because of difficulties in determining market value. But this question has aroused less concern and controversy than the other two.

The first question—whether a taking of property has occurred—is easy to answer when government directly and permanently takes a parcel of physical property. The question is more difficult under other circumstances, such as when government takes something that may or may not be definable as property.[11] The most controversial aspect of this question concerns regulatory takings, in which government limits the use of property and thereby reduces its value. In *Pennsylvania Coal Co. v. Mahon*, the Court made explicit what earlier decisions had suggested by holding that government regulation

10. In *Berman v. Parker* (1954), the Court had rejected a challenge to use of eminent domain power for urban redevelopment. Lavine (2010). The Court also interpreted "public use" broadly in *Hawaii Housing Authority v. Midkiff* (1984).

11. Some commentators treat the definition of property and the definition of a taking as separate questions, so that they list four questions in takings law rather than three. Schultz (2010), 60–61; Avery and McLaughlin (2013), 50–51.

sometimes constitutes a taking for which compensation is required.[12] Because a great many government actions reduce the value of property, a rule that any such actions violate the takings clause would have a radical effect on the scope of government power.[13] Because the Court has rejected such a rule, the justices have had to take on the difficult task of drawing the line between regulations that require compensation to property owners and those that do not.

Commentators regularly refer to the Court's jurisprudence on the takings clause as confused, sometimes describing it as "a muddle."[14] As one legal scholar put it, the Court's takings clause jurisprudence "is a top contender for the dubious title of 'most incoherent area of American law.'"[15] Citing the effects of divisions among the justices, another scholar referred to "the futility of reconciling what may be, at bottom, irreconcilable rulings."[16] But one leading commentator has argued that in the area of regulatory takings, where the Court has had the greatest difficulty, decisions such as *Penn Central v. New York City* have produced greater clarity.[17]

In the cases that the Court decides, the takings clause is sometimes connected to other legal provisions. In the late nineteenth and early twentieth centuries, the protection against takings by state governments and substantive due process were intertwined under the Fourteenth Amendment, an intertwining that arguably still exists.[18] Cryptic opinions were common in that era, and it is often quite uncertain whether the Court was ruling on takings or on substantive due process. Indeed, Justice John Paul Stevens asserted after his retirement that the Court did not actually incorporate the takings clause into the Fourteenth Amendment in 1897, despite the general assumption that it did so, because its *Chicago, Burlington, and Quincy* decision was instead based on substantive due process.[19]

12. Fischel (1995), ch. 1.
13. See R. Epstein (1985).
14. Rose (1984), 561; Gaba (2007), 569.
15. Schroeder (1996), 1531.
16. Lazarus (1997), 1101.
17. *Penn Central Transportation Co. v. New York City* (1978); Meltz (2007), 370–71.
18. Davis and Glicksman (1989); Berger (1995); Ely (1996), 122.
19. Stevens (2012), 946–47.

## The Ideological Polarity of Takings Decisions

For the analysis of takings, Supreme Court decisions were taken from the 1910 through 2012 Terms of the Court: all takings decisions from the 1937–2012 Terms and non-unanimous decisions from the 1910–36 Terms. The limitation to non-unanimous decisions in the early period was based on the difficulty of distinguishing takings cases from other cases in that period, a difficulty that made it useful to focus on the subset of decisions that established the Court's ideological polarity.

It is common for the Court to address takings claims alongside other legal issues in a case, and that overlap complicates the analysis of justices' votes. Even when the Court decides a takings question, some justices may not address that question. And in some cases, a justice agrees with a takings claim but votes against the claimant on other grounds, or votes for the claimant despite rejecting the takings claim. To capture the justices' positions on takings most accurately, I analyzed their votes on the takings claim rather than their votes on the overall case outcome. Based on this criterion, the votes of some justices in some cases were not counted.

As in chapters 2 and 3, the ideological polarity of non-unanimous decisions was determined by comparing the median ideological scores of the justices on the two sides in each decision. Table 4.1 summarizes the ideological polarity of the justices' votes on takings claims, dividing the 1910–2012 Terms into three periods. The results are striking: there were two periods in which the justices on the pro-claimant side were nearly always more conservative than their colleagues opposing the takings claim, with a period in between in which there was a weaker tendency for pro-claimant justices to be more liberal than justices on the other side.

The dividing lines were drawn at the points that maximized the differences between adjacent periods. Although that rule is appropriate for identification of break points, it may also exaggerate the actual differences between periods. If the first line were drawn after the 1936 Term, the percentage for the first period would change little (90.9%). But the Court's polarity in the second period would

TABLE 4.1. Ideological patterns of justices' votes in non-unanimous takings decisions, 1910–2012 Terms

| Terms | Side with more conservative ideology score | | Percent with pro-claimant side more conservative |
|---|---|---|---|
| | Pro-claimant | Anti-claimant | |
| 1910–44 | 25 | 2 | 92.6 |
| 1945–79 | 9 | 16 | 36.0 |
| 1980–2012 | 21 | 1 | 95.5 |

*Notes*: Cases are included if some justices voted for a takings claim and other justices voted against the claim. Justices are treated as pro-claimant or anti-claimant based on their votes on the takings claim in a case rather than on the overall outcome for the takings claimant.

be almost evenly split, with fourteen decisions in which the pro-claimant side was more liberal and sixteen in which the pro-claimant justices were more conservative. However, there would still be a sharp difference between the second period and the periods that preceded and followed it. In any event, moving the line between the second and third periods forward or backward has little effect.[20]

To probe the polarity of the justices' votes in more detail, the magnitude of ideological differences between the justices on the two sides can be described.[21] Within the first period, the tendency for pro-claimant justices to be more conservative than their colleagues on the other side became even more pronounced in the 1930s. The cases in the 1920–36 Terms are a mix of some with substantial ideological differences between the two sides and others in which the differences were only marginal. In each of the last four cases in that period, decided in the New Deal era, the Court's four strong conservatives all favored the takings claimant and its three liberals were all on the other side.[22] Of course, that was also true of many

20. If the line is moved three years earlier, 32 percent of the decisions in the 1945–76 Terms and 92 percent of the decisions in the 1977–2012 Terms had a pro-claimant side that was more conservative than the anti-claimant side. If the line is moved three years later, the corresponding percentages were 43 percent and 95 percent.

21. As noted in chapter 3, because the two sets of scores used prior to 1937 are not comparable with the Martin-Quinn scores or with each other, it is possible to speak of the magnitude of ideological differences only in general terms.

22. The cases were *Interstate Commerce Commission v. Oregon-Washington R. & Nav. Co.* (1933); *Norman v. B & O Railroad Co.* (1935); *Railroad Retirement Board v.*

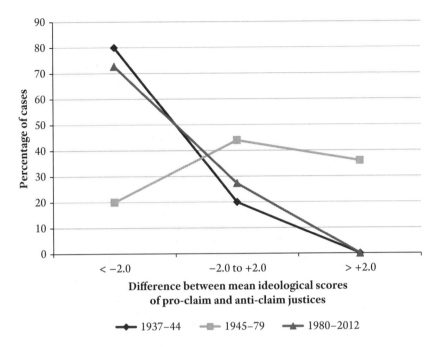

FIGURE 4.1. Magnitude of ideological differences between pro-claimant and anti-claimant justices by category, non-unanimous decisions, 1937–2012 Terms.
*Notes*: Years shown are Court terms. The differences in scores are positive if pro-claim justices were more liberal than anti-claim justices.

decisions on the validity of New Deal programs under other constitutional provisions.

In the five non-unanimous decisions in the 1937–44 Terms, a period when Martin-Quinn scores were available, the mean ideological difference between justices on the two sides was −2.80, a strong tendency for pro-claimant justices to be more conservative than their colleagues who voted against the takings claim. The mean for the 1945–79 Terms was +1.08; in the 1980–2012 Terms, it was −2.65.

Figure 4.1 provides a different perspective on the magnitude of the difference between the median Martin-Quinn scores of the

<hr />

*Alton Railroad Co.* (1935); and *West v. Chesapeake & Potomac Telephone Co.* (1935). In *Norman* and *Alton*, two important decisions on New Deal policies, the takings question played only a secondary role in the Court's decisions.

justices on the two sides for the periods for which they were available. In interpreting the percentages for the 1937–44 Terms, it must be kept in mind that there were only five non-unanimous decisions in that period. Still, the similarity between the distributions for the first and third periods and the difference between both those periods and the second period are striking.

In the comparison between the second and third periods, each of which had enough decisions for the percentages to be quite meaningful, two changes stand out. First, the proportion of decisions without strong polarity in either direction fell substantially. Second, in the decisions that did have a strong polarity, the Court went from a period in which the pro-claimant side was more liberal than the anti-claimant side in most cases to a period in which the pro-claimant side was more conservative in nearly all cases. The Court's polarity was especially strong in the 1987–2012 Terms, in which all but one of the thirteen cases in which justices disagreed about the takings question had difference scores below −2.0. This pattern is illustrated by *Kelo* and by the last takings decision in that period, *Koontz v. St. Johns River Water Management District*, in which all five of the Court's Republican appointees supported the claimant and all four Democrats opposed him.[23]

The next two sections probe the sources of the two changes in the Court's polarity in takings. I give particular attention to the second change, for which relevant information is more abundant.

## Explaining the First Shift in Polarity

As in chapters 2 and 3, the first question in examining possible sources of shifts in polarity is how values associated with conservatism and liberalism might translate into positions on takings. It is difficult to define values with a direct relevance to takings in the abstract, although it could be argued that government takings of

---

23. *Koontz v. St. Johns River Water Management District* (2013). A similar lineup appeared in *Horne v. Department of Agriculture* (2015), a decision relating to federal regulation of agricultural production, although only Justice Sotomayor fully dissented from the Court's decision.

property conflict with the preference for market outcomes that Feldman identified as a basic conservative value. In practice, possible linkages between takings and broad values have been situational, based on policies that government takings are intended to further.

These possible linkages were clear in the period from the 1910 Term through the 1944 Term. The liberal-conservative divide in takings cases in that period can be put in the context of the debate over the constitutional power of government in the economic arena, a debate in which there were strong divisions along ideological lines. To provide the full context of that debate, it is necessary to start with the late nineteenth century.[24]

The Supreme Court began to give meaningful attention to takings in the 1870s, and it issued some important takings decisions in that decade and the remainder of the nineteenth century.[25] The invigoration of the takings clause as a protection of private property from the 1870s on was part of the broader movement to strengthen constitutional protections against government intervention in the economy. That connection is made clear by the intermingling of takings and substantive due process, the constitutional doctrine that played the largest role in court decisions limiting economic regulation.[26] Divisions within the Supreme Court on government economic power were usually along liberal-conservative lines, and it seems inevitable that this general pattern would be reproduced in takings cases.

The strength of the ideological polarity in takings cases is striking. During the 1910–36 Terms, Louis Brandeis voted against takings claims in fifteen of the eighteen non-unanimous decisions in which he participated, Oliver Wendell Holmes in eleven of eighteen, Harlan Fiske Stone in eight of ten. The "Four Horsemen" who voted to strike down New Deal policies more often than their colleagues showed the opposite tendency: Willis Van Devanter voted

24. This discussion draws from several histories and commentaries on takings in the era from the 1870s to the 1930s, including L. Friedman (1986), Scheiber (1989), Fischel (1995, ch. 1), and Ely (1996; 2008, chs. 5–6).

25. Two decisions that stand out are *Pumpelly v. Green Bay Company* (1872) and *Mugler v. Kansas* (1887).

26. See Corwin (1909), 658–62.

for claimants in nineteen of twenty-two non-unanimous decisions, James McReynolds in fifteen of nineteen, George Sutherland in eleven of thirteen, and Pierce Butler in twelve of twelve.

Of the fourteen non-unanimous takings decisions in the 1921–36 Terms, six involved a regulatory takings question. The average ideological difference between the justices on the two sides was greater in this set of cases than in cases involving other types of takings questions. Except for one ambiguous case, all of the takings decisions in which the Court divided in the 1910–36 Terms involved claims by businesses. In three-quarters of those cases the business was a named company rather than an individual acting in a business capacity. And most of the companies were large, including several railroads, energy producers, and public utilities.[27]

One link between takings and the broader issue of government economic power in that era was the presence of John W. Davis as the attorney arguing several takings cases.[28] Davis was solicitor general in the Woodrow Wilson administration. He later became a private attorney who represented primarily businesses, and he was a frequent participant in Supreme Court litigation.[29] In the 1930s, he was an organizer of the American Liberty League, an anti-New Deal group that gave some emphasis to economic rights under the Constitution.[30] In the 1920s and 1930s, he frequently argued in the Supreme Court on behalf of challenges to government regulation of business. Among these challenges were half a dozen takings cases, including four of the fourteen cases with non-unanimous decisions in the 1921–36 Terms. He argued for the claimants in *Pennsylvania*

27. Railroads were frequent participants in litigation challenging government regulation of economic activity, including takings cases. See Ely (2001), 199–200. Between 1910 and 1919, the Supreme Court struck down forty-one state laws in cases brought by railroads. Baum (2016), 168. The role of railroads in takings litigation is ironic in the sense that they benefited considerably from the delegation of eminent domain power to them by state governments. Ely (2001), 35–39, 189–98.

28. See Harbaugh (1973).

29. Readers may recall that he also represented the state of South Carolina in *Briggs v. Elliott*, a companion case to *Brown v. Board of Education* (1954) that was decided under the *Brown* title. That was Davis's last oral argument in the Supreme Court.

30. Wolfskill (1962).

*Coal Co. v. Mahon*, the case in which the Court established the doctrine of regulatory takings, and *Louisville Joint Stock Land Bank v. Radford*, in which the Court unanimously struck down a federal statute amending the federal bankruptcy law to give farmers greater protection against repossession of their farms.[31]

Thus there is nothing surprising about the way that the justices divided in takings cases in that era. Takings was perceived as a species of government constraints on property rights and business activity, constraints that aroused strong conservative opposition. When the justices disagreed in a takings case, it was natural that their division would usually be along the same conservative-liberal lines as other economic cases—the same lines on which people outside the Court divided on economic issues. The question, then, is why that alignment did not continue.

The answer seems to lie in two connected developments in the late 1930s and 1940s. The first was a substantial change in the legal and political context of takings. Between 1937 and 1942 the Supreme Court largely wiped out constitutional limits on government power to regulate the economy, with the exception of limits on state actions that conflicted with federal power. Substantive due process was no longer an important constitutional concept. In the political arena too, the debate over government regulatory power died down. There remained takings questions to resolve, but those questions were no longer closely connected with debates over the government's role in regulating the economy.[32]

The second development was a change in the types of claims that the Court resolved. In the 1937–49 Terms, companies continued to dominate the cases in which the justices divided on takings questions, appearing in eleven of the thirteen non-unanimous decisions. But regulatory takings faded from the Court's agenda, appearing in only two of the Court's twenty-seven takings decisions in the 1937–49 Terms. The most common question, which arose in

---

31. *Louisville Joint Stock Land Bank v. Radford* (1935).

32. The decline in substantive due process also made it easier to identify which cases were actually decided on the basis of the takings clause.

a slight majority of all cases and two-thirds of the divided decisions, was the level of compensation that a property owner was owed. If regulatory takings is the most consequential category of cases in this field, compensation is the least consequential. Overall, compared with the preceding era, the post-1937 cases raised relatively narrow questions. There were no takings claimants who challenged major government programs.

The change in the Court's takings agenda reflected a wider change in the social and political context of takings. The Court itself contributed to that change in the late 1930s and early 1940s by adopting a strong position favoring government power over the economy. For proponents and opponents of government activism, there was no longer a big legal battle to fight, and they turned their attention away from constitutional litigation. John W. Davis argued no more takings cases in the Court.[33] Thus, justices had less reason to perceive the combatants in takings disputes as representing liberal and conservative political forces.

This shift from broad to narrower questions followed the general pattern in the Court's work on federal regulation of the economy in the 1940s.[34] But in contrast with other constitutional questions such as the scope of the commerce power, the Court continued to give steady attention to takings questions under the Fifth Amendment. There was another difference. The Court signaled its newfound acceptance of broad commerce and taxing and spending powers with landmark decisions that made major doctrinal changes.[35] There were no such landmarks in takings law. At least in non-unanimous decisions, the Court became far less favorable to claimants, who secured

33. Based on the non-unanimous decisions of the 1920–36 Terms and a larger (but not comprehensive) set of takings decisions from that period identified by Meltz (2015), it also appears that takings claimants after 1937 were distinctly less likely to hire lawyers from New York City and Washington, DC, to argue their cases in the Court. But because these cases were not fully representative of all takings cases in the Court during that period, this comparison may exaggerate the differences between the two eras.

34. Pacelle (1991), 110.

35. On the commerce power, the key decision was *National Labor Relations Board v. Jones & Laughlin Steel Corp.* (1937). On the taxing and spending power, the key decisions were *Helvering v. Davis* (1937) and *United States v. Butler* (1937).

majorities on their takings claims in 86 percent of those decisions in the 1921–36 Terms but only 31 percent in the 1937–49 Terms. (Claimants did considerably worse in unanimous decisions in the latter period, winning 14 percent of the time.) But the Court made no dramatic changes in the law. Rather, it simply ruled against claimants in a series of mostly narrow decisions.

As noted earlier, the non-unanimous decisions in the 1937–44 Terms followed the earlier pattern in which pro-claimant justices were far more conservative than their anti-claimant colleagues. The most likely explanation for this lag is that it took some time for the established ideological meaning of takings to erode. With time the change in takings as an issue must have become apparent to the justices, so that they started to perceive the issue in a different way. In the 1945–49 Terms, five of the eight non-unanimous decisions found the pro-claimant side more liberal than the anti-claimant side, albeit usually by a small margin. In the three decades that followed, this pattern of mixed polarity with a leaning toward liberal support for takings claimants continued.

In the progression from one era to the next, then, the justices' perceptions of the ideological meaning of takings changed. Indeed, takings as an entity seemed to become disengaged from ideology. Justices might respond to individual cases in ideological terms, but not on the basis of a strong orientation toward takings as a whole.

The analysis of the Court's second shift in polarity in the next section sheds additional light on the ideological meaning of takings between the 1940s and 1970s. Following that section, it will be possible to consider the mechanisms and sources of the two shifts together.

## Explaining the Second Shift in Polarity

In the 1940s, what had been a clear ideological polarity to takings cases in the Supreme Court disappeared. What caused that polarity to reappear in the 1980s? As in the analyses of free expression and criminal justice, I consider developments outside the Court, the cases that the Court heard, and the justices' responses to those events and cases.

## *TAKINGS OUTSIDE THE COURT*

In the years from the late 1930s through the early 1970s, takings law and policy was not a significant public issue. National party platforms never referred to takings even indirectly.[36] There were only occasional references to takings-related matters in the *New York Times*, none of them treating takings as a matter of national debate or importance.

Takings began to break free from obscurity in the 1970s as a result of responses by political conservatives to unfavorable political and legal developments. One of those conditions was the success of the environmental movement in shaping public policy. The other was the perceived liberalism of the federal courts and elite segments of the legal profession and the success of liberal interest groups as legal advocates.

Historically, what was then called conservation had received at least as much support from conservatives as from liberals. Early in the 1970s, when a new concern with environmental protection developed, there was a degree of consensus across ideological lines on the need to protect the physical environment. But this consensus declined with a growing perception of the tradeoffs involved in environmental protection.[37] People in the business community, farmers and ranchers, and other landowners increasingly resented the economic costs and restrictions on business practices that resulted from environmental regulation. One result was a "property rights" movement that arose primarily in opposition to the environmental movement.[38] The property rights movement was especially strong in the West, where opposition to federal control of public lands helped to spur what was called the Sagebrush Rebellion.[39] The decline in consensus was re-

36. Discussions of party platforms in this section are based on searches of the Republican and Democratic platforms, archived at http://www.presidency.ucsb.edu/platforms.php.

37. Kraft and Vig (2000).

38. Marzulla (1995); Meltz (1995), 1–7; Pralle and McCann (2000); Olivetti and Worsham (2003), ch. 3.

39. Cawley (1993).

flected in national Republican Party platforms, which moved from enthusiastic support for environmental protection to considerable skepticism about environmentalism between 1972 and 1980.

Meanwhile, a new conservative legal movement emerged.[40] One facet of that movement was an effort by legal scholars and others to establish and articulate conservative positions on constitutional issues, an effort that helped to spur development of the Federalist Society as a national organization of lawyers.[41] As part of this effort, some conservative legal theorists developed arguments for broad interpretations of the takings clause, especially in the area of regulatory takings. Most prominent was Richard Epstein of the University of Chicago Law School, whose arguments for a sweeping invalidation of economic regulations through the takings clause were widely circulated over several years and then presented in his book *Takings* in 1985. A strengthened takings clause was attractive to some conservatives as a means to raise the costs of government action and thus to limit regulation and economic redistribution.[42]

Another facet of the conservative legal movement was the creation and growth of conservative public interest law firms that were intended to counter their liberal counterparts by pressing conservative legal positions on the courts. Like free speech, takings has had a prominent place on the agendas of some of these firms. Takings was especially important to the Pacific Legal Foundation (PLF), one of the earliest and most active firms. The founding of the PLF in 1973 was driven in part by concern about the success of liberal litigating groups on environmental questions.[43] The Institute for Justice, a conservative and libertarian public interest law firm founded in 1991, later became the key litigator seeking a broad reading of the takings clause.

The Reagan administration supported that broad reading. During President Reagan's second term, lawyers in the Justice Department

40. Southworth (2008); Teles (2008).
41. Southworth (2008), 130–41; Teles (2008); Hollis-Brusky (2015).
42. Norton (1990), 85.
43. Teles (2008), 60–61.

joined the effort to expand protections of property through the takings clause.[44] One reflection of that effort was Executive Order 12630, issued in 1988, which increased the obligation of federal agencies to provide compensation for regulatory takings. The Reagan administration also appointed judges who favored a broad reading of the takings clause to the lower courts that have the greatest impact on takings law, the Claims Court (now the Court of Federal Claims) and the Court of Appeals for the Federal Circuit. One of those judges, Chief Judge Loren Smith of the Claims Court, spearheaded his court's movement toward a strong pro-claimant position. The Federal Circuit, which reviewed Claims Court decisions, shifted in the same direction.[45]

Many of the participants in these developments, both within and outside government, are lawyers who belong to the Federalist Society.[46] The Society gives attention to property rights, and the activities of its members on takings questions reflect the growth of conservative intellectual and advocacy networks that the Society has helped to foster.

Those networks extend beyond the legal community. The 1992 Republican platform included long discussions of property rights and takings, and every Republican platform since then has referred to takings. The "Contract with America," announced on behalf of Republican candidates for the House of Representatives in 1994, included a provision allowing private property owners to recover money from the federal government for federal action that reduced the value of their property. A version of that proposal passed the

44. Fried (1991), 182–86; Kmiec (1992), 115–28.
45. Castleton (1992); Moore (1992); Huffman (1995); Kendall and Lord (1998), 533–38. The Court of Federal Claims can award money to claimants in takings cases, but it does not have jurisdiction to rule on the constitutional validity of federal statutes and regulations. Cases raising that question must go to the federal district courts. In 1998, the House approved a bill to allow both courts to hear both monetary and constitutional questions. Advocates for the bill presented it as a way to eliminate a practical problem for claimants. But their primary motivation was to give the Court of Federal Claims the power to invalidate federal laws, and the House split largely along party lines. Coyle (1997); US House of Representatives (1997).
46. Avery and McLaughlin (2013), ch. 2.

House in 1995. The vote on that bill and other congressional votes on property rights proposals in the years that followed generally split along partisan and ideological lines.[47]

## TAKINGS CASES IN THE COURT

The renewed concern with takings in the 1970s was reflected in litigation activity. Conservative public interest groups began to submit amicus briefs on the merits of takings cases to the Supreme Court in 1978. The Reagan administration took the unusual position of supporting a legal challenge to government takings power by submitting an amicus brief on behalf of the takings claimant in *Nollan v. California Coastal Commission*, a major case on regulatory takings.[48] The Pacific Legal Foundation sponsored the *Nollan* case, and the Washington Legal Foundation brought two later takings cases.[49] The lawyers who presented oral arguments on behalf of claimants in takings cases since the 1970s included counsel for those two groups as well as Rex Lee and Charles Fried, each of whom had been solicitor general in the Reagan administration.

In this new wave of takings litigation, cases brought to the Court increasingly involved regulatory takings, environmental policy, and broad legal and policy issues. In a sample of certiorari petitions submitted in the 1996–2011 Terms, 27 percent concerned regulatory takings and 28 percent related to environmental laws or other liberal policies. Beginning in the late 1970s, when takings began to change as a legal and policy issue, those attributes were even more common in the cases that the Court accepted and decided. Table 4.2 summarizes these and other attributes of takings cases in the Court before and after that time.

47. The 1995 vote in the House was 205–23 in favor among Republicans, 39–21 among Southern Democrats, and 33–103 among Northern Democrats. In an exception to the overall pattern, some of the votes responding to the *Kelo* decision did unite Democrats and Republicans.

48. *Nollan v. California Coastal Commission* (1987).

49. The cases were *Phillips v. Washington Legal Foundation* (1998) and *Brown v. Legal Foundation of Washington* (2003).

TABLE 4.2. Selected attributes of takings cases, 1937–76 and 1977–2012 Terms, in percentages

| Attribute | Terms | | Change (inpct. points) |
|---|---|---|---|
| | 1937–76 | 1977–2012 | |
| Claimant | | | |
| Indian tribe or Native American | 5.3 | 6.7 | +1.4 |
| Other individual | 12.3 | 8.3 | −3.9 |
| Individual or business (uncertain) | 14.0 | 10.0 | −4.0 |
| Business | 8.8 | 18.3 | +9.6 |
| Company | 56.1 | 43.3 | −12.8 |
| Other | 3.5 | 13.3 | +9.8 |
| Legal Question | | | |
| Regulatory taking | 17.5 | 51.7 | +34.1 |
| Other taking | 29.8 | 23.3 | −6.5 |
| Public use | 3.5 | 3.3 | −0.2 |
| Compensation | 36.8 | 8.3 | −28.5 |
| Other or mixed | 12.3 | 13.3 | +1.2 |
| Political Issue | | | |
| Environmental policy | 0.0 | 36.7 | +36.7 |
| Other liberal policy | 7.0 | 18.3 | +11.3 |
| Neither | 93.0 | 45.0 | −48.0 |
| Salient Case | | | |
| Yes | 10.5 | 16.7 | +6.1 |

*Sources*: Front-page coverage in the *New York Times* for the 1946–2004 Terms was taken from L. Epstein et al. (2007, 153–74); for other Terms, archives of the *Times* were consulted.

*Notes*: "Change" is the increase or decrease in that attribute, in percentage points, from the 1937–76 period to the 1977–2012 period. The claimant is the party asserting a takings claim. "Business" is a business, defined broadly, without a company name; "company" is a business with a company name. "Other taking" refers to the question of whether a taking had occurred, with the exception of regulatory takings cases. "Other liberal policy" refers to cases in which a claimant directly challenged a government policy that would generally be perceived as politically liberal, such as assistance to low-income people. A salient case is one that received front-page coverage in the *New York Times* on the following day.

The takings cases that the Court decided in the 1937–76 Terms involved a mix of legal questions that varied considerably in their breadth. On the whole, however, those questions were relatively narrow, and few decisions would be regarded as landmarks. That pattern is underlined by the high proportion of cases that involved the amount of compensation to be paid for a taking. By one common measure of salience for Court decisions, whether a decision was reported on the front page of the *New York Times*,[50] only six

50. L. Epstein and Segal (2000).

takings decisions in that era were salient. In one of those six cases, the takings question was a sidelight rather than the source of public interest in the case.

As the table shows, the cases that the Court decided in its 1977–2012 Terms were similar to those in the preceding era in some respects. But there were also some significant changes. Compensation cases declined substantially, and regulatory takings grew even more substantially. Challenges to environmental policies emerged for the first time and occupied a large share of the takings agenda. There was also an increase in challenges to other liberal government policies on matters such as rent control and labor-management relations. More cases involved questions with potentially broad impact, especially on the question of when regulation of property constitutes a taking.[51] As a result, there was a somewhat higher rate of salient decisions by the *New York Times* measure.[52]

The growing political and legal salience of takings cases in the Court was reflected in amicus activity.[53] As figure 4.2 shows, until the mid-1970s the average numbers of amicus briefs per case were at about the same level as the proportions across all issues. From then on, briefs in takings cases proliferated even more rapidly than amicus briefs across all issues. By the decade from 1986 through 1995, the mean number of briefs per takings cases was more than double the average across all cases, and the mean continued to increase after that decade. Every takings case in the 1987–2012 Terms had at least

---

51. Among these cases were *Penn Central Transportation Company v. New York City* (1978); *Nollan v. California Coastal Commission* (1987); *Lucas v. South Carolina Coastal Council* (1992); and *Dolan v. City of Tigard* (1994).

52. The proportion of cases in which takings claims were brought against the federal government was far lower in the post-1980 period (48 percent, down from 79 percent in the pre-1980 period). In the post-1980 period, the Court was more polarized ideologically in the cases involving state and local governments than in cases involving the federal government. (There were too few divided decisions involving state and local governments in the pre-1980 period to make that comparison.) It appears that both these patterns result primarily from the types of questions that the Court addressed rather than the level of government involved; one reason is that conservative justices seem unlikely to take a more negative view of government action when it comes from the state and local levels.

53. See Thorpe et al. (2010).

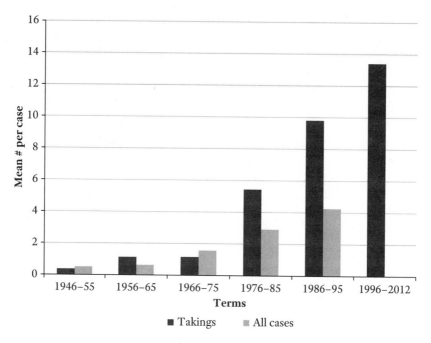

FIGURE 4.2. Rates of amicus briefs in takings cases and all cases, by period.
*Notes*: The mean for takings cases in the 1956–65 Terms is artificially high because one case in which takings was not the central issue had several amicus briefs. If that case is excluded, the mean is 0.50 rather than 1.00.
*Sources*: Data on all cases are from Kearney and Merrill (2000), 752–53. Those data extend only through the 1995 Term. The counting methods used in that study are not fully comparable with those used for the takings cases.

one amicus brief; across all policy issues in that period, 85 percent had amicus briefs.[54]

There are some general patterns to the lineup of amici in takings cases since the mid-1970s. Opponents of takings claims typically include governments defending their powers, frequently with briefs signed by multiple states. These governments are usually joined by private liberal groups, most often groups with environmental interests. Takings claimants receive the preponderance of their support from conservative interests, with business groups and ideological groups (including public interest law firms) the most prominent.

54. The 85 percent rate was calculated from data in L. Epstein et al. (2015, 703).

## JUSTICES' RESPONSES TO CASES

As in the preceding two chapters, patterns in the justices' responses to the takings cases they decided provide significant information about the sources of the changes in the Court's polarity between the two periods. The relatively small numbers of cases that the Court decided in each period make it more difficult to identify patterns in some respects, but they also allow a closer look at individual decisions.

### Case Attributes and the Court's Polarity

In the 1945–79 Terms the Court's polarity was mixed, with the pro-claimant justices more liberal than their colleagues in sixteen of twenty-five cases. What distinguishes the two sets of cases from each other?

Among the attributes of cases that are summarized in table 4.2, the presence of a named company as a claimant and of a regulatory takings issue were both associated with substantial differences in the Court's polarity. There were no non-unanimous regulatory decisions with claimants other than companies. Table 4.3 shows the polarity for the other three combinations of those two case attributes.

The small number of regulatory takings cases should be kept in mind in interpreting the patterns in the table. Still, the table indicates that both the claimant and the issue made considerable difference.

TABLE 4.3. Ideological polarity of decisions with different combinations of case attributes, 1945–79 Terms

| Company claimant? | Regulatory takings? | N | Percent with more conservative pro-claimant side | Mean difference in polarity | Median difference in polarity |
|---|---|---|---|---|---|
| No | No | 9 | 22.2 | +2.15 | +2.75 |
| Yes | No | 12 | 33.3 | +0.60 | +0.56 |
| Yes | Yes | 4 | 75.0 | +0.10 | −1.86 |

*Notes*: For differences in polarity, positive signs indicate that the pro-claimant side was more liberal than the anti-claimant side. There were no regulatory takings cases with claimants other than companies. The difference between the mean and median for regulatory cases reflects the presence of one outlier decision. In that decision Justice William O. Douglas, with a highly liberal Martin-Quinn score, was the sole pro-claimant dissenter on the takings issue.

The Court's relatively weak polarity across all cases obscured a strong tendency for liberal justices to favor takings claims more than their conservative colleagues when the claimants were not companies. That strong tendency accounts for the fact that the mean ideological difference between pro-claimant and anti-claimant justices during the 1945–79 Terms was over +1.0 (+1.08).

As takings litigation changed in the 1970s and 1980s, regulatory takings came to occupy a much larger portion of the agenda. Of all the cases decided in the 1945–79 Terms, 26 percent were based on regulatory takings; the proportion in 1980–2012 was 51 percent. Moreover, beginning in the late 1970s the Court's regulatory takings agenda included cases that raised broad and consequential questions about when regulation of land use implicated the takings clause. A majority of the regulatory cases directly implicated environmental policy.

Not surprisingly, regulatory cases became more contentious. Decisions on regulatory takings in 1945–79 were unanimous 71 percent of the time, compared with 42 percent in 1980–2012. Moreover, even in a period when the pro-claimant justices were more conservative than their colleagues in all but one non-unanimous decision, the polarity of the regulatory cases was especially strong. The mean ideological difference between the two sides was −2.82 in cases involving regulatory takings, compared with −2.29 in other cases. Even more important, however, those two figures show that the growth in non-unanimous regulatory takings decisions was far from the whole story: the Court's shift in polarity was quite substantial in both types of cases.[55]

In terms of policy issues, the non-unanimous decisions can be put in three categories, based on the presence or absence of environmental questions and other liberal policies. In the six decisions that involved neither type of policy, the mean difference between the two sides was −2.27. In the twelve decisions involving environmental

55. In the 1980–2012 Terms, several regulatory takings cases were brought by claimants other than companies, so the two categories were more independent of each other. The mean ideological differences between the two sides were almost identical in company (−2.41) and non-company (−2.37) cases.

policy, the mean difference was −2.71. In the four decisions involving other liberal policies, the mean difference was −3.03. Among the liberal policy cases, *Phillips v. Washington Legal Foundation* and *Brown v. Legal Foundation of Washington* involved challenges to state programs under which interest on lawyers' trust accounts went to programs providing legal assistance to low-income litigants and serving other purposes.[56] *Pennell v. City of San Jose* challenged a rent-control program.[57] And *Eastern Enterprises v. Appel* concerned a statute that required a coal company to pay medical benefits to former employees.[58] The Court's strong polarity in those decisions is not surprising—though there were six other cases with challenges to liberal policies on which the Court was unanimous.

There were two takings cases in the 1980–2012 Terms in which the difference between the median Martin-Quinn scores of the two sides was between −1.0 and +1.0, an indication that the lines of division had a weak ideological polarity. One of the decisions with a weak polarity, *Dames & Moore v. Regan*, involved a challenge to President Carter's action freezing property of the Iranian government that was subject to U.S. jurisdiction.[59] The takings question in the case was clearly secondary to a question of presidential power. The only dissenter was the moderate conservative Lewis Powell.

The other decision of this type was *United States v. Locke*, which resulted from an apparent drafting error.[60] A statutory provision required that owners of mining claims on federal land must file a document each year "prior to December 31" to maintain their claims. The Bureau of Land Management ruled that a person who filed the document *on* December 31st had failed to meet this requirement. The Court ruled that the statute must be construed on the basis of its literal language and that the filing requirement did not violate the takings clause. John Paul Stevens, joined by William Brennan, dissented

---

56. *Phillips v. Washington Legal Foundation* (1998); *Brown v. Legal Foundation of Washington* (2003).

57. *Pennell v. City of San Jose* (1988).

58. *Eastern Enterprises v. Appel* (1998).

59. *Dames & Moore v. Regan* (1981).

60. *United States v. Locke* (1985).

on the ground that the statute should not be read literally, so he did not reach the takings claim. Justice Powell dissented on the ground that the statute did violate the takings clause, in conjunction with due process. In this case, unlike *Dames & Moore*, the pro-claimant side was slightly more liberal than the anti-claimant side. Although twenty-two cases is not an enormous number, it is nonetheless striking that only in one non-unanimous decision in the 1980–2012 Terms were the pro-claimant justices more liberal than their colleagues, and that was by only a small margin on an idiosyncratic question.[61]

### Justices

Voting patterns of individual justices provide additional evidence about the mixed polarity of the second period and the transition to the strong polarity of the third period. Table 4.3 indicated that during the 1945–79 Terms, the Court's polarity in individual cases varied with the presence or absence of a company as claimant. The table suggests that the presence of a regulatory takings question also made a substantial difference. The same relationships can be analyzed at the individual level.

Figure 4.3 shows the impact of companies as claimants on the votes of justices who ruled on at least eight claims by both company and non-company claimants during that period. The justices are placed in order of their ideological stances across all issues during the 1945–79 period. The figure shows that the relationship between the justices' ideological stances and the impact of company claimants was imperfect but substantial: the rank-order correlation

---

61. There was one takings-related case, *Wilkie v. Robbins* (2007), in which the pro-claimant dissenters (John Paul Stevens and Ruth Bader Ginsburg) were far more liberal than the anti-claimant justices in the majority. But the majority never addressed the takings issue raised in the case. Rather, the majority opinion focused on the scope of the remedy for violations of constitutional rights established in *Bivens v. Six Unknown Federal Narcotics Agents* (1971). Most "*Bivens* actions" are brought on behalf of rights that liberals favor more than conservatives (see Reinert 2010), and most conservative justices opposed the *Bivens* remedy from the start and later favored narrow interpretations of *Bivens*. This position outweighed any sympathy that the conservative justices might have felt for a claimant whose allegations against federal officials fit quite well the emotions connected with the Sagebrush Rebellion and the narrative of the rebels.

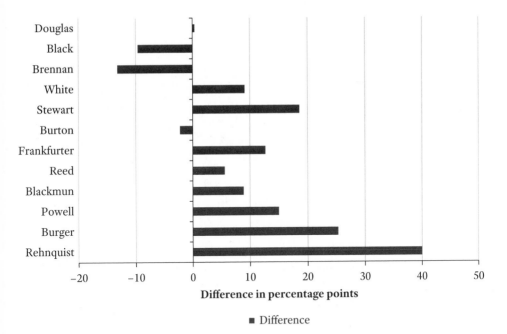

FIGURE 4.3. Differences in justices' voting support for claimants between cases with companies and other claimants, 1945–79 Terms.

*Notes*: Justices are included if they voted on takings claims in at least eight cases with companies as claimants and eight cases with non-company claimants. The justices are listed in order of their proportions of liberal votes in orally argued cases across all issues for the 1945-1979 Terms, as coded in the Supreme Court Database.

between overall conservatism and the difference between a justice's support for companies and support for other claimants was +.734.[62]

In contrast with the non-unanimous cases during that period, there were a few unanimous decisions with non-company claimants and regulatory questions, so it is possible to look at the relationship between regulatory cases and justices' voting patterns as well. There were nine justices who voted on at least five regulatory takings claims. For those justices, the rank-order correlation between their overall conservatism and the difference in their voting

62. The differences in the figure suggest that companies did substantially better in getting a favorable ruling on their claims than other types of litigants during that period, but that suggestion reflects which justices did and did not appear in the figure. Overall, non-company claimants did slightly better than company claimants, a 29.2 percent win rate versus 27.6 percent.

support for claimants in regulatory and non-regulatory cases was +.833, even higher than the analogous correlation for company and non-company claimants. The three most liberal justices—all substantially more liberal than any of the other justices included in the analysis—all voted for the claimant in non-regulatory cases at a rate more than 30 percentage points higher than regulatory claimants.[63]

Primarily because of the relatively small numbers of cases in which most justices participated during the 1945–79 Terms, logistic regression equations for individual justices' votes with company claimants and regulatory takings as independent variables did not produce clear results. However, the equations suggest that the identity of the claimant had a more powerful impact on some justices and that the type of takings issue had a more powerful impact on others. In any event, the voting patterns of individual justices reinforce the Court-level evidence that the mixed polarity of the 1945–79 Terms was not a random pattern.

In light of the Court's strong polarity in the 1980–2012 Terms, we would not expect case attributes to have as strong an impact on the justices' voting in ideological terms as they did in the preceding period. Indeed, that is the case. The rank-order correlations between justices' ideological stances and the differences in justices' voting based on a company claimant and a regulatory issue were much weaker. However, the correlation for regulatory questions was both meaningful (+.560) and considerably higher than the correlation for company claimants. This result suggests that regulatory takings questions elicited a stronger reaction along ideological lines in the recent period than did companies as takings claimants.

### RETURNING TO KELO

A strong ideological polarity to takings was reestablished in the 1980s and maintained in the decades that followed. These changes reflected the combined effects of developments outside the Court, changes

---

63. Those justices were Thurgood Marshall (36 percentage points), William Brennan (35 percentage points), and William O. Douglas (32 percentage points).

in the mix of cases that the Court heard, and the justices' responses to those cases. As in other issue areas, the Court has continued to reach unanimity in a high proportion of cases. But when the justices do disagree, the ideological sides once again are well defined.

Still, it is not obvious why the ideological lines on the Court should be so consistent in the current era, extending across all types of takings cases—and, notably, across all types of claimants. The proportion of claimants that fell in the two business categories together was actually a little lower in the 1980–2012 Terms than in the 1945–79 Terms, and fewer claimants were companies.[64] In the cases that divided the Court in the 1980–2012 Terms, some of the businesses with takings claims were small enterprises that were barely distinguishable from individuals. Why were liberal justices less favorable than conservatives to these claimants, parties that generally can be characterized as underdogs in relation to the governments that opposed them?

More specifically, to return to the chapter's original question, why was it that the Court's strong conservatives rather than its liberals supported Susette Kelo? As noted at the beginning of the chapter, both the identities of the two sides and the content of the city policy that was challenged would seem to make Kelo's case especially appealing to liberal justices. Moreover, *Kelo* was about the public use requirement of the takings clause, and a ruling in Kelo's favor would not have affected the regulatory takings questions that were at the heart of the battles over takings law and policy. Nor was the case about environmental policy, which had become a key driving force in those battles.

The best answer is that developments in takings debates and litigation created a context for cases such as *Kelo*, a context that shaped justices' perceptions of these cases. Regardless of their attitudes toward the claimants in specific cases or the stakes of cases for public policy, the justices connected those cases with broader tides in the

---

64. In the 1945–79 Terms, 55 percent of the claimants had company names, and another 11 percent were classified as businesses. In the 1980–2012 Terms, the corresponding figures were 43 percent and 18 percent.

takings field, tides that had moved their attitudes about takings law toward one side or the other.

Indeed, that redefinition of the ideological meaning of takings was reinforced by the participants in *Kelo* other than the litigants themselves.[65] Kelo's challenge to the taking of her home was sponsored by the conservative Institute for Justice as part of its takings agenda. She received amicus support from a long list of conservative political groups (though not from the business community). The presence of these participants provided a clear indication that *Kelo* was connected with the general conservative drive for a more expansive interpretation of the takings clause.[66] Both conservative and liberal justices seemed to focus on the long-term goals and interests of groups in the takings field rather than the specific interests of the litigants in *Kelo*. Thus the lineup of the justices in *Kelo* provides strong evidence of the justices' ideologically based commitments to the two sides in takings during the current era.

## Conclusions

In the early twentieth century, pro-claimant justices in non-unanimous takings cases were almost always more conservative than their colleagues. That polarity disappeared and was even reversed somewhat in the period from the late 1940s through the late 1970s. It then reappeared in as strong a form as it had taken a half century earlier. If the line between the first two periods had been drawn differently, the contrasts between periods would not be quite as stark. But it is clear that the Court's polarity underwent two fundamental shifts.

A case can be made for the primacy of values in these shifts. Takings has had a strong polarity at times when it is clearly connected

---

65. See Wilkerson (2010).

66. Liberal justices might also have perceived that conservative groups deliberately brought cases involving sympathetic claimants that were individuals or small businesses. See Echeverria (1997), 354–56. Certainly the property rights movement has sought to identify its goals with individuals such as homeowners rather than with large businesses. Pralle and McCann (2000), 60–68.

with government regulation of economic activity. Because liberals and conservatives differ in their support for government policies that modify market outcomes in the service of equality, a connection between takings and regulation brings those values into play. In contrast, during the period when that connection had atrophied, the polarity of takings in the Court weakened. In the period that began around 1980, the revival of this connection was reinforced by the growing number of takings-based challenges to other policies that were generally identified as liberal and that could be connected to liberal values such as equality.

This two-step relationship between takings and broad ideological values surely provides a substantial part of the explanation for the strong polarity to takings during two periods and the absence of that polarity in between. But group affect played a substantial role as well, in two respects.

The first concerns the direct and indirect beneficiaries of decisions favoring takings claimants. Until the 1940s the cases that divided the Court were most often brought by large businesses, a pattern that likely engaged the justices' attitudes toward the business community. And during the subsequent period in which ideological lines in takings cases were muddled, the pro-claimant justices were considerably more liberal relative to their colleagues when the claimant was someone other than a company.

The second concerns advocates, both in and outside the Court. During the periods of clear ideological lines on takings, the most visible advocates for expansive interpretations of the takings clause have come from the conservative side of the political spectrum. Takings was a conservative cause in the period that culminated in the New Deal. The same has been true since the late 1970s, as conservative thinkers, public interest groups, and the Republican Party have argued for revitalization of the takings clause.

These broader movements were reflected in the identities of the lawyers arguing for claimants and, in the recent period, the amici who supported them. The fact that the Court's strong polarity in the recent period extended to cases that lacked a direct relationship with regulatory policy, such as *Kelo*, suggests that justices responded in part to conservative advocacy on behalf of takings claimants in those cases. In the period between those two eras, in contrast, advocates for takings claimants lacked that ideological coloration, and there was no visible conservative takings movement outside the Court.

As in criminal justice, the best reading of the evidence is that both values and group affect played a significant part in the shifting linkage between ideology and takings in the Court. Here too, the two have reinforced each other. When government regulation and big business became less relevant to takings cases, justices stopped responding to those cases along consistent ideological lines. When regulation once again played a substantial part in the takings cases that the Court heard and conservative advocacy became prominent, those ideological lines reemerged.

Takings illuminates the process by which shared understandings of linkages between ideology and issues develop and shape justices' responses to cases. During two eras, advocacy for a broad reading of the takings clause by people who were identified with conservative interests helped to stamp takings as a conservative clause. The importance of environmental policy as a spur for conservative advocacy in the recent era is especially intriguing, because it took a while for the new wave of environmental regulation in the 1970s to be identified as a liberal policy; the connection between ideology and environmental policy was not self-evident.

Although the justices' responses to small numbers of cases should be interpreted cautiously, it is noteworthy that there was something of a lag in both of the Court's shifts in polarity. After takings as an issue and takings cases became disengaged from big questions about economic regulation, for a few years the justices continued to divide consistently along ideological lines. After takings cases started to reflect conservative causes once again, it took a few years for a clear ideological polarity to reappear. Where conditions that shape the ideological meaning of an issue are changing, such a lag seems likely.

This chronology does not mean that the understandings of ideological positions in takings were simply arbitrary. As on other issues, broad premises based on values and affect toward social groups were important in shaping these understandings in each era. But these premises were filtered through the perceptions of political elites about which positions were liberal and conservative, perceptions that were reflected in the responses of justices to the takings cases they decided.

# 5

# Inquiries into Other Issues

The preceding three chapters analyzed three issues on which the ideological polarity of the Supreme Court shifted over time. These case studies provide considerable evidence about the sources of linkages between ideology and issues. This chapter adds to the body of evidence by analyzing several other issues more briefly.

The primary reason for this extension of the study is that the three issues analyzed so far are necessarily a sample of the Court's work. Moreover, those issues might be unrepresentative because each issue featured a substantial change in the Court's ideological polarity. For these reasons, even less extensive studies of other issues provide a firmer basis for conclusions about the mechanisms and sources of linkages between ideology to issues.

I used the broad and narrow issue categories in the Supreme Court Database as a starting point in identifying additional issues to examine. As in the selection of issues for the primary case studies, I left aside structural issues such as federalism. One important criterion for inclusion was that the Court had decided substantial numbers of cases on an issue over time, and several issues that had seemed promising failed to meet that criterion. Ultimately, I ended up with a range of issues that varied in their breadth. Those issues, like most others, fall into the general categories of civil liberties and economics.

Analysis of these issues followed the same general methods as the more extensive case studies in earlier chapters. Potential cases were identified primarily from relevant issues in the Supreme Court Database; I then read the opinions in those cases to determine whether they actually included and were decided on the basis of the issue identified by the Database. The ideological polarity of the Court's decisions was calculated from the same sources and in the same way as in the earlier studies. The time periods for the studies varied, always covering the 1946–2012 Terms but some extending back further in time.

## Civil Liberties

Freedom of expression and criminal justice are among the non-economic civil liberties issues that collectively have occupied a large share of the Supreme Court's attention over the past several decades. Because of the centrality of this field to the Court's work, other civil liberties issues should be examined as well. In this section I consider discrimination along racial and gender lines as well as religious freedom and the establishment of religion.

### RACIAL DISCRIMINATION

Like criminal justice, racial discrimination is an issue on which there initially seems to be little to say, because the Court's polarity in the current era is so clear: when the Court divides, liberal justices are more favorable to claims of discrimination by members of racial minority groups than are their conservative colleagues. However, it is worthwhile to document just what the Court's polarity looks like and how long it has taken its current form. Moreover, differences between the justices' responses to "ordinary" discrimination cases and their responses to affirmative action, another well-known feature of this issue, should be documented and considered.

In the long period from the 1910 Term through the 1945 Term, I identified only eleven racial discrimination cases in which the Court divided. In five of those cases, the pro-equality justices were more conservative than the justices who rejected a discrimination claim. Four of those cases came in the first decade of the period. To a degree, the divisions in those cases may have reflected the existence of multiple dimensions to ideology in that period. The other case was *Korematsu v. United States*, in which the Court upheld the government's policies toward Japanese Americans during World War II.[67] The Court divided along non-ideological lines, but the dissenters as a group were somewhat more conservative than justices in the majority.

Starting with the Vinson Court in 1946, the Court heard increasing numbers of cases involving racial discrimination. In the cases that divided the Court, the ideological polarity took the form that we would expect. Of the fifty-nine non-unanimous decisions in the 1946–76 Terms, in all but three the justices who favored the discrimination claimant were more liberal than the justices on the other side. Of the three exceptions, two resulted from Hugo Black's dissents late in his career, when he had become more conservative on some kinds of racial issues than he was overall.[68] The third case was *United Jewish Organizations v. Carey*, in which Warren Burger dissented from a decision upholding an apportionment plan that had been challenged under the Constitution as discriminating in favor of black representation.[69]

The *Carey* case was the harbinger of a period in which the Court addressed significant numbers of discrimination cases brought by whites, primarily challenges to affirmative action programs and to election districting that was perceived as favoring black voters over whites. At the same time, cases involving allegations of discrimination against racial minority groups remained abundant. With growing dissensus in the Court over racial questions, there were 105 non-unanimous decisions on this issue in the 1977–2012 Terms.

Not surprisingly, there was a sharp difference in polarity between sets of cases that were distinguished by the claimant's racial identity. Of the eighty-three cases involving claims of discrimination against

67. *Korematsu v. United States* (1944).
68. The decisions were *South Carolina v. Katzenbach* (1966) and *Perkins v. Matthews* (1971). In *Perkins,* John Harlan also dissented in part.
69. *United Jewish Organizations v. Carey* (1977).

members of racial minority groups, in only one case was the pro-claimant side more conservative than the anti-claimant side, and that case involved a procedural dispute between an employer and the Equal Employment Opportunity Commission that did not directly relate to the discrimination claim.[70] In contrast, in all of the twenty-two cases with discrimination claims by whites, the pro-claimant justices were more conservative than the justices on the other side. The mean ideological difference between the justices favoring and opposing the claimant was +2.83 in the discrimination cases brought by members of racial minority groups, compared with −2.89 in the cases with white claimants. (A positive difference score means that pro-claimant justices were more liberal than justices who voted against the claimant.)

If these findings are unsurprising, their interpretation is not necessarily obvious. Perhaps the most straightforward interpretation is that the justices were acting on their affect toward communities of racial minority groups: the more liberal they were, the more they were inclined to take the position that favored the interests of those communities. Alternatively, they were acting on their attitudes toward equality: for justices who have a strong commitment to equality, it advances that goal to rule in favor of minority groups even where doing so requires rejection of a claim that government or a private institution is discriminating.

In either instance, there is no inexorable logic leading to the pattern of ideological polarity that occurred in the Court. After all, it could be argued that equality and the interests of racial minority groups are best fostered by strictly equal treatment of different racial groups. That argument is reflected in Chief Justice John Roberts's aphorism that "the way to stop discrimination on the basis of race is to stop discriminating on the basis of race."[71] Justice Clarence Thomas's opinions and other writings express a similar position.[72]

---

70. The case was *Equal Employment Opportunity Commission v. Associated Dry Goods Corp.* (1981), in which Justice Stevens filed a lone dissent.

71. *Parents Involved in Community Schools v. Seattle School District No. 1,* at 748 (2007).

72. Gerber (1999), 69–112; Rossum (2014), 184–213.

Although the logic is uncertain, there is a clear shared understanding in the world of political elites: support for affirmative action and similar programs is seen as a liberal position. On the whole, liberal interest groups and policy makers are considerably more favorable to those programs than are conservatives. In the Supreme Court, the lineups of amicus briefs in cases involving claims of discrimination against whites generally follow ideological lines, with conservative groups supporting those claims.[73] Most important, civil rights groups support affirmative action as a means to advance equality. In light of this consensus, it is almost inevitable that the justices' positions fall along the lines they do.

### SEX DISCRIMINATION

Sex discrimination provides a useful counterpart to racial discrimination. In the first four decades of the twentieth century, most Supreme Court cases involving differential treatment of women and men arose from challenges to government regulations of employment conditions for women, such as minimum-wage and maximum-hour rules. Outside the Court, it was generally liberals who favored such provisions, both because they were part of a broader program of regulation of business practices and because of a perception that they benefited women.[74]

Most of the Court's decisions in these cases were unanimous. The justices did disagree about whether the minimum wage statutes passed constitutional muster, and for the most part liberals voted to uphold those statutes and conservatives to strike them down.[75] In two early twentieth-century cases that involved other kinds of legal distinctions between men and women, the Court did not divide along ideological lines.[76] The Vinson Court split on the exclusion of

73. The major exception is businesses and business groups that support affirmative action programs, such as the "65 Leading American Businesses" that submitted an amicus brief in support of the programs at the University of Michigan in *Gratz v. Bollinger* (2003) and *Grutter v. Bollinger* (2003).

74. Baer (1978); Novkov (2001).

75. *Adkins v. Children's Hospital* (1923); *Morehead v. New York ex rel. Tipaldo*, (1936); *West Coast Hotel Co. v. Parrish*, (1937).

76. *Thompson v. Thompson* (1910); *Quong Wing v. Kirkendall* (1912).

women from juries in a federal court and on a statute that prohibited nearly all women from working as bartenders. In those cases, the justices who upheld the practices were considerably more conservative than those who voted to strike them down.[77]

In 1971 the Court began to hear substantial numbers of sex discrimination cases. These included constitutional challenges to government policies that differentiated by sex, primarily under equal protection, and interpretation of federal statutes that prohibited discrimination. In all but one of the forty-three non-unanimous decisions during the 1971–2012 Terms, the justices who favored a sex discrimination claimant were more liberal than their colleagues, generally by a large margin.

The noteworthy feature of this record is that many of these cases arose from claims that laws or practices discriminated against men.[78] Among the constitutional cases, most involved such claims. In several of these cases, governments defended the challenged policies on the ground that they were efforts to ameliorate women's economic disadvantages.

The Court's pattern of polarity in these cases was very different from the pattern in cases involving racial discrimination claims by white litigants. In all twenty-five non-unanimous decisions in constitutional cases during the 1970–2012 Terms, the justices who favored the challenge to sex discrimination had a median Martin-Quinn score more than 1.0 lower (and thus were considerably more liberal) than the justices who voted to uphold the law under challenge. The mean difference score in cases involving discrimination against women (+3.14) was even stronger than the mean for those involving discrimination against men (+2.41), but that difference is less noteworthy than the similarity. (As in racial discrimination, a positive difference score means that the pro-claimant justices were more liberal than their colleagues on the other side.)

The best and perhaps only explanation for this pattern concerns the advocates of challenges to sex discrimination. During the 1970–82

---

77. The cases were, respectively, *Ballard v. United States* (1946) and *Goesaert v. Cleary* (1948).

78. There were also some cases in which the discrimination could be defined either as working against women or as working against men.

Terms—when the Court heard the preponderance of the constitutional challenges to sex discrimination that it has addressed—the primary litigator against sex discrimination was the Women's Rights Project (WRP) of the ACLU. The WRP took the position that virtually all laws and practices that discriminated by sex ultimately worked to the disadvantage of women. As head of the WRP during most of that period, Ruth Bader Ginsburg deliberately sought out challenges to laws that discriminated against men in the belief that the all-male Court would be sympathetic to such challenges.[79] The message to the Court was clear.

The one post-1970 sex discrimination case in which the Court's polarity was reversed was *Johnson v. Transportation Agency*.[80] In *Johnson*, a man challenged a government agency's affirmative action program under which a woman had received a promotion that he sought. His challenge was under Title 7 of the Civil Rights Act of 1964, which prohibits discrimination in employment by sex. In this case, in contrast with the discrimination cases brought by the Women's Rights Project, the ACLU and an array of women's groups joined in an amicus brief in favor of the program. The dissenters from the Court's decision upholding the affirmative action program were distinctly more conservative than the majority. Like women's rights groups, the justices differentiated in ideological terms between this employment practice and traditional laws that favored women. This decision underlines the importance of the way that other laws and practices favoring women were portrayed by the litigants. If supporters of women's rights had argued that the traditional laws were desirable and constitutionally valid, the ideological lines on the Court in those cases probably would have been quite different.

Even more than the racial discrimination cases, then, voting patterns in sex discrimination cases provide evidence that ideological lines on issues are defined by shared understandings that do not necessarily reflect a deductive logic. As with race, the ways that these lines were defined could be understood as a product of either values

---

79. Amy Campbell (2002); Strebeigh (2009), chs. 1, 4.
80. *Johnson v. Transportation Agency* (1987).

relating to equality or affect toward a disadvantaged group. But the justices' responses to the cases brought by the WRP strongly suggest that the Court's liberals reacted primarily to the interests of women as defined by advocates for them rather than to an abstract conception of equality.[81]

## *RELIGION*

The other (mostly) civil liberties issue that I analyzed was religion, defined broadly to include cases involving the religion clauses of the First Amendment, two federal statutes that were designed to protect religious freedom,[82] and other claims made by litigants who were identified in the Supreme Court Database as religious actors. I analyzed constitutional cases based on the free exercise clause, statutory religious freedom cases, and religious actor cases together; establishment clause cases were analyzed separately.

The polarity of cases in the first, broader set of cases was mixed. Of the thirty-three non-unanimous decisions in this category in the 1946–2012 Terms, in 73 percent the justices who favored the religious claimant were more liberal than their colleagues. The scores for the ideological difference between justices voting for the religious claim and anti-claimant justices had a wide range and a high standard deviation. The question was what accounted for this variation.

One possibility is that justices responded differentially to claims based on the religious affiliation of the claimant. In their analysis of Supreme Court decisions on the free exercise clause, Frank Way and Barbara Burt found differences in the Court's response to free exercise claims based on religious affiliation, which they trichotomized as "established" (mainline Protestant, Roman Catholic, and Jewish), "marginal" (such as Seventh Day Adventists and Muslim), and "other"

---

81. As discussed in chapter 1, something similar may have happened in *Coker v. Georgia* (1977), which raised the question of whether a state could impose the death penalty for sexual assault when the victim was an adult: the ACLU amicus brief co-authored by Ginsburg provided a cue about which decision favored the interests of women.

82. These are the Religious Freedom Restoration Act of 1993 and the Religious Land Use and Institutionalized Persons Act of 2000.

(such as Christian Scientist and prisoner churches).[83] These distinctions are potentially relevant to the Court's ideological polarity, in that conservative justices might be relatively sympathetic to established groups and liberals might be relatively sympathetic to groups in the other two categories. Adapting the Way and Burt classification, I labeled their "established" category as "mainstream" and combined the other two categories into a "non-mainstream" category.[84]

In all but one of the thirty-three non-unanimous decisions, the claimant could be assigned to one category or the other. The difference between the two sets of cases was striking. The sixteen cases involving mainstream religious groups were divided evenly between those in which the pro-claimant justices were more liberal than their colleagues and those in which they were more conservative. In contrast, in all but one of the sixteen cases involving non-mainstream groups, the pro-religion justices were more liberal than their colleagues. The mean ideological difference between the two sides was +0.15 in mainstream religion cases, compared with +2.86 in non-mainstream cases. (Positive difference scores indicate that the justices who voted for the religious freedom claim or a religious actor were more liberal than justices on the other side.) When cases that involved religious actors but not religious freedom were removed from the analysis, there was still a substantial difference between decisions involving mainstream and non-mainstream religious groups by both measures of polarity.[85]

83. Way and Burt (1983), 655.

84. However, I modified their scheme by classifying fundamentalists as mainstream. The classic example of a non-mainstream group in the Supreme Court is the Jehovah's Witnesses. In the 1937–45 Terms, the Witnesses participated in most of the religious freedom and religious-actor cases that the Court decided. But in the 1946–2012 Terms, the Witnesses were involved in only five cases that met the criteria for inclusion.

85. Analyzing conflicts between the speech rights of Christian groups in public schools and establishment clause considerations that the Court decided between 1981 and 2001, Stephen Feldman (2013, 124–30) pointed to a pattern of support for the speech rights of Christian groups on the part of the Court's conservative justices, one in which the liberal justices did not share. Feldman contrasted this pattern with the conservatives' rejection of the free speech claim by a decidedly non-mainstream religious group in *Pleasant Grove City v. Summum* (2009).

This pattern might be connected with equality as a value, in that those justices who give a high priority to equality would seek to help religious groups that they perceive as disadvantaged because those groups are outside the mainstream. But it seems more straightforward to explain the pattern in terms of group affect. In light of the widespread identification of religious freedom as a liberal value, it is noteworthy that liberal justices were no more favorable to religious freedom claims than their conservative colleagues in the cases involving mainstream groups.

Religious freedom increasingly has become a conservative cause among political elites. In the past several years this development has been most visible on two types of questions. One concerns requirements in the Obama-sponsored health care program that employers fund coverage for contraception or, for one category of employers, that they ask for an exemption from inclusion of that coverage. The first situation resulted in the Court's 5–4 decision along ideological lines in *Burwell v. Hobby Lobby Stores*.[86] The second resulted in a kind of non-decision from a Court that likely had been divided 4–4 along ideological lines in *Zubik v. Burwell*.[87] The other conflict arises from the desire of some merchants and public officials to avoid participation in same-sex weddings. If religious freedom becomes identified primarily with mainstream religious groups and with opposition to causes that liberals favor, there may be a broad ideological realignment on religious freedom issues. Alternatively, the difference in ideological polarity between cases involving mainstream and non-mainstream groups may become even wider.[88]

Establishment clause cases were separated out because it is difficult to identify the religious affiliations (or non-affiliations) of many challengers to government actions related to religion and because the actions they challenge are seldom identified with a particular religious

86. *Burwell v. Hobby Lobby Stores* (2014).
87. *Zubik v. Burwell* (2016).
88. However, that difference will narrow if conservative justices become more favorable to religious freedom claims of all types. In *Holt v. Hobbs* (2015), the Court's conservatives joined its liberals in a unanimous decision supporting a statutory religious freedom claim by a Muslim prisoner.

group. One study indicates that many of the claimants in establishment cases are religious, while many others are not.[89] Still, most establishment claims can be understood as raising questions about government policies that support mainstream religious practices.[90]

The Court decided few establishment cases prior to 1961. In the 1960–2012 Terms, it reached twenty-one non-unanimous decisions in cases in which the establishment clause played more than a peripheral role. In each case, the justices supporting the party that invoked the clause were more liberal than the justices on the other side. The ideological difference between the two sides generally was substantial. To take a small but representative example, in the long natural court of the 1994–2004 Terms, the Court decided eight establishment clause cases. There were at least two dissenting votes in all eight cases, and five were decided by 5–4 votes. Ruth Bader Ginsburg and John Paul Stevens favored all eight establishment claims; William Rehnquist, Antonin Scalia, and Clarence Thomas favored none.

The strong polarity of the establishment clause cases is interesting in light of the pattern of polarity in the other religion cases. As noted earlier, government accommodations of religion that are challenged in establishment cases ordinarily reflect the preferences of mainstream religious groups. Although other considerations contribute to the disagreements between conservative and liberal justices in establishment cases, their affect toward mainstream religious groups and the outsiders who challenge ties between government and religion undoubtedly plays a role as well.

## Economics

Takings is an economic issue, but it is unusual in the current era because it is about constitutional rights. In contrast, the great preponderance of the Supreme Court's economic agenda is statutory.

89. Sorauf (1976), 145–47.
90. However, in some establishment cases there are mainstream religious groups that oppose such policies. Morgan (1972), ch. 4.

Thus, it is useful to examine more typical economic issues that are primarily statutory.

## REGULATION OF BUSINESS

Regulation of business practices is an issue on which there are generally sharp differences between conservatives and liberals. But in the 1970s there were signs that liberals had rethought their support for some forms of regulation, based on new perceptions of how regulation affected consumers.[91] Some studies after that time found that the dimensionality of Supreme Court voting on business regulation had become more complicated.[92] That possible complication makes business regulation especially interesting to examine.

Since the New Deal Court established broad interpretations of federal power over the economy, the preponderance of cases involving regulation of business involve interpretation of federal regulatory statutes. I identified cases in the 1946–2012 Terms in which the question concerned business regulation in either of two forms: a government regulatory action was challenged, or a lawsuit between private parties was based on a regulatory statute. Altogether, there were 403 non-unanimous decisions. The justices' votes were coded as pro-regulation if they favored the government party or the private party that invoked a regulatory statute.

In the non-unanimous decisions during that period, the pro-regulation justices were more liberal than their colleagues on the other side about two-thirds of the time (68 percent). That proportion was fairly stable over time, ranging from 64 percent in the Burger Court to 76 percent in the Rehnquist Court. The absence of a stronger polarity throughout the period is noteworthy.

The stability of the Court's polarity across that period does not necessarily mean that the justices responded in the same ways to the same kinds of cases throughout that time; as some studies suggest,

91. Derthick and Quirk (1985).
92. Hagle and Spaeth (1992, 1993); see Dudley and Ducat (1986); Ducat and Dudley (1987).

the Court's dimensionality might have shifted in certain ways. But the key question is what accounted for the fairly mixed polarity of business regulation cases across the whole period. One possible explanation is the configuration of economic interests. Most of the time, a government decision that is challenged in court involves an effort to regulate a business activity or, in a field such as antitrust, to protect smaller businesses from larger competitors. Similarly, private lawsuits that invoke regulatory statutes are usually brought by individuals against businesses or, in disputes between businesses, by smaller businesses against larger businesses.

Still, there are exceptions. Sometimes governments act on behalf of economic "upperdogs," and occasionally those upperdogs bring lawsuits under regulatory statutes. Because justices might respond to cases on the basis of their sympathies toward underdogs and upperdogs, I coded cases based on the configuration of interests. About three-quarters of the time, the pro-regulatory side was also the underdog side. But in 10 percent of the cases, the pro-regulatory side represented the upperdog, and in another 15 percent of the cases, neither side was clearly the underdog.

The configuration of economic interests made an enormous difference. In cases in which regulation favored an underdog, the pro-regulation side on the Court was more liberal than the anti-regulation side 80 percent of the time. When there was no clear underdog, the proportion was 47 percent. And when regulation favored an upperdog, the proportion was 17 percent. The mean ideological differences between the two sides in the three categories of cases, in the same order, were +1.54, +0.03, and −2.30. (A positive difference score means that the pro-regulation justices were more liberal than the anti-regulation justices.) The relationship between the configuration of interests and the Court's orientation strengthened after the Vinson Court.

The impact of the configuration of interests was reflected in the voting patterns of most individual justices. Among the eighteen justices who participated in at least eight non-unanimous decisions in which regulation favored an upperdog, fifteen had a difference of more than 20 percentage points in their voting tendencies between

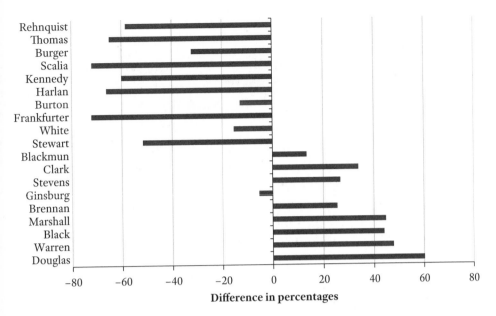

FIGURE 5.1. Difference between support for pro-underdog and pro-upperdog government regulation, non-unanimous decisions, 1946-2012 Terms, by justice.
*Notes*: The justices are listed in order of their proportions of conservative votes in orally argued cases across all issues in the 1946-2012 Terms, as coded in the Supreme Court Database. The differences shown are percentages of votes favoring pro-underdog regulation minus percentages for pro-upperdog regulation. Justices are included if they participated in at least eight non-unanimous decisions involving pro-upperdog regulation.

pro-underdog and pro-upperdog interests. Although the magnitude of these differences reflects the absence of unanimous decisions, it is still striking. Moreover, for all of those fifteen justices, the difference was in the expected direction: liberal justices were more favorable to pro-underdog regulation, and conservatives to pro-upperdog regulation.[93] That pattern is shown in figure 5.1.

More than one-third of the business regulation cases involved antitrust law, defined broadly to include antitrust-related provisions of any federal statutes. These cases evoked strong ideological divisions, with a mean difference between the two sides of

93. Tom Clark is often thought of as a conservative because of his positions in civil liberties. But he was more liberal on economic issues, and Rohde and Spaeth (1976, 143) characterized him as a "New Dealer."

+2.06.[94] Antitrust suits can be brought against governments and labor unions as well as businesses. In the 1946–2012 Terms there were eleven non-unanimous decisions in which unions were the sole parties charged with violating the antitrust laws or were jointly charged with businesses or trade associations. In all but one of those decisions, the pro-antitrust justices were more conservative than their colleagues, and the mean ideological difference between the two sides was −2.27. That difference is striking, since unions were the sole defendants in only five of the eleven cases; the Court's polarity was even stronger in those five cases.[95]

The findings for business regulation cases as a whole and for antitrust cases indicate that justices do not respond ideologically to government economic regulation in itself. Rather, they respond to the identities of the organizations that are subject to regulation. At least relative to each other, liberal justices favor underdogs and conservatives favor upperdogs. When they apply the antitrust laws, conservatives and liberals react quite differently to lawsuits against corporations and labor unions. These strong tendencies might be interpreted as reflections of broad values relating to economic equality. But more directly, justices seemed to be acting on their affect toward the subjects of regulation.

## FEDERAL TAXES

The Supreme Court hears substantial numbers of civil cases involving interpretation of the federal tax statutes, though these cases became relatively scarce (and non-unanimous decisions nearly disappeared) in the Roberts Court. Like business regulation as a whole, federal taxation is an issue on which political elites tend to divide

94. In a small number of these cases, a government regulator took a position opposed to application of the antitrust laws. For this analysis the justices' votes were recoded in terms of their position on antitrust rather than their support or opposition to regulatory action.

95. The mean differences between the two sides were −2.45 in the union-only cases and −2.11 in the other cases; the median differences were −2.92 and −1.80, respectively.

along ideological lines, with liberals more sympathetic to government's role as collector of taxes.[96] The justices might be expected to respond to federal tax cases along the same ideological lines.

A study of decisions involving interpretation of federal tax laws in the 1940–2003 terms produced noteworthy findings.[97] The study analyzed the ideological position of the Court's median justice over time rather than the votes of individual justices. It found that relatively liberal Courts and relatively conservative Courts did not differ significantly in their likelihood of ruling for individual taxpayers who contended with the federal government. However, the Court's propensity to rule for business taxpayers increased substantially with its conservatism. This finding indicates that at least some individual justices responded differentially to tax cases based on the type of claimant.

To probe the justices' responses to tax cases, I analyzed the relationship between litigants' identities and the Court's polarity in federal tax cases for the 1946–2012 terms. The overall polarity of cases was quite mixed, with the pro-government side more liberal than the pro-taxpayer side in 45 percent of all cases. Thus overall, justices did not differ substantially along ideological lines in their responses to tax disputes. Because the Court typically deals with tax questions in narrow and specific terms, it may be that tax cases are of low salience to them[98] and that the ideological divide on tax policy in the other branches of government has only limited relevance to their decisions.

As in the Court-level study described earlier, I dichotomized tax cases based on the presence of business or individual taxpayers; a small number involved other types of taxpayers and were dropped, leaving 146 non-unanimous decisions. If polarity is dichotomized, there was a moderately strong relationship between litigant type and polarity: the justices voting in favor of the government in disputes

96. In 2016, for instance, the Democratic Party platform did not mention the Internal Revenue Service (IRS), but the Republican Party platform denounced the IRS as "toxic" and recommended its eventual abolition. The platforms are archived at http://www.presidency.ucsb.edu/platforms.php.

97. Staudt, Epstein, and Wiedenbeck (2006).

98. According to Chief Justice Roberts, "you can always give all the tax opinions to a justice, if you want to punish them." Greenburg (2006).

with individuals were more liberal than justices on the other side 37.5 percent of the time, compared with 55.2 percent of the time for business cases. The mean ideological differences between business and individual taxpayer cases were −1.02 for individual cases and −0.26 for business cases. (A negative difference score means that the pro-government side was more conservative.)

Although the difference between the two types of litigants is not enormous, it is noteworthy that there is a meaningful difference at all. After all, many if not most of the individual taxpayers whose cases are heard by the Supreme Court have high incomes. To the extent that justices respond to upperdogs and underdogs differently, upperdogs are well represented among individuals as well as businesses. Still, relative to liberals, conservatives were drawn more to businesses than to individuals. In that respect, tax cases seem similar to cases involving government regulation of business.

## PERSONAL INJURIES AND MONETARY CLAIMS ON GOVERNMENT

The Supreme Court hears some cases arising from personal injuries, cases that have several different legal bases. In the 1946–2012 Terms, those cases were most common in the Vinson and Warren Courts. The largest share of these cases arises from two federal workers' compensation statutes, the Federal Employers' Liability Act (FELA) for railroad workers and the Longshore and Harbor Workers Compensation Act. I analyzed cases in which individuals who claimed compensation for injuries sued non-governmental defendants, nearly always businesses.

In the last few decades, tort law has become a strongly ideological issue in the states. Liberal supreme court justices tend to favor plaintiffs in personal injury cases, while conservatives tend to favor defendants, and interest groups spend substantial sums to elect justices on their ideological side.[99] At the federal level, Glendon Schubert noted the Court's ideological divide in FELA cases and

99. Cheek and Champagne (2005).

posited that liberal justices acted strategically to bring employees' petitions before the Court.[100]

In light of these patterns, it is not surprising that personal injury cases brought by individuals show a strong polarity. Of the eighty-two non-unanimous decisions in the 1946–2012 Terms, in seventy-six (93 percent) the pro-plaintiff justices were more liberal than the pro-defendant justices, and the mean ideological difference between the two sides across all eight-two cases was +2.32. (A positive difference score means that the justices who voted for plaintiffs were more liberal than colleagues on the other side.) Faced with conflicts between injured individuals and businesses that are asked to pay compensation, conservative and liberal justices diverged sharply when there was disagreement on the Court.[101]

Because the analysis of personal injury cases necessarily focused on individual plaintiffs, it is useful to examine as well an issue in which both individuals and businesses frequently bring claims. That is true of cases involving monetary claims against government bodies. These claims arise from a wide array of situations, ranging from an allegedly illegal search to a contract to do work for an agency. They are also brought under an array of legal provisions. Altogether, there were eighty non-unanimous decisions on this issue in the 1946–2012 Terms.

On the whole, monetary claims on government may seem unlikely to trigger ideological responses. On the other hand, it might be that conservative and liberal justices respond differently to them on the basis of attitudes toward government, the kinds of claimants who appeared in these cases, or the substantive issues raised by the claims.

As it turned out, these cases as a whole had a strong ideological polarity—though not as strong as personal injury cases. Across the full period, the justices who favored the party with a monetary claim were more liberal than their colleagues 83 percent of the time. Only

100. Schubert (1959), 210–54; Schubert (1962); but see Provine (1980), 158–70.
101. The results changed little when the two cases with individuals as defendants were set aside.

53 percent in the Vinson Court cases had that liberal orientation, but the proportion increased after that time. In the Rehnquist and Roberts Courts, all but one of the twenty-seven cases had a liberal orientation.

Strong as this polarity was, there was enough variation to merit exploration.[102] One possibility is that the identity of the parties made a difference. The great majority of claims were against the federal government, but there were eleven cases brought against state governments or their subsidiaries. Most claims were brought by individuals, but about one-third were by businesses. Cases on the two sides of each dichotomy did differ in other respects: state cases and cases brought by individuals often arose from accidents or from the criminal justice system, which seldom were involved in cases brought by businesses. Still, all these cases have in common that the financial interests of government and those of non-governmental actors are in conflict.

In bivariate analyses, both the type of claimant and the level of government made a difference. In every state case, the pro-claimant justices were more liberal than the anti-claimant justices. And even if the state cases are set aside, the pro-claimant justices were far more likely to have a liberal orientation in individuals' cases than in business cases, 89 percent to 54 percent.[103] In multivariate analyses with the Court's dichotomized orientation and the ideological distance between the two sides as dependent variables, the identity of the claimant had a strong impact but the level of the defendant government did not.

Twenty of the cases were brought under the Federal Tort Claims Act (FTCA), so those cases could be analyzed to keep the statutory basis for the suit constant. In this subset there was a substantial difference in polarity between cases brought by businesses and those

102. Because there was almost no variation in the Rehnquist and Roberts Courts, the analyses described below were replicated without cases from those Courts. The results were quite similar with that omission.

103. These figures exclude the intermediate category of individuals acting in a business capacity (as contrasted with named businesses) as well as non-business organizations.

brought by individuals. The mean ideological difference between pro-claimant and anti-claimant justices in FTCA cases was +3.17 in those brought by individuals and +0.57 in those brought by businesses; the difference between the two is about the same magnitude as for all of the claims on government. (A positive score indicates that pro-claimant justices were more liberal than justices on the other side.)

Even for a single statute, differences between cases brought by businesses and individuals differ in the subject matter of claims. However, it is still striking that the justices responded so differently to cases based on the type of plaintiff. That finding strongly suggests that liberal and conservative justices saw these cases through the filter of who the claimants were.

## Conclusions

Because this chapter covered several different issues, it is useful to summarize the findings and their implications. That summary is presented in table 5.1.

The clearest implication of these inquiries is that the shared understandings that develop about which issue positions are conservative and liberal rest only in part on logical premises. The table refers to that implication directly in racial and sex discrimination. In the two categories of discrimination, the positions of advocates in the elite world and in the Supreme Court defined the ideological polarity of questions arising from laws and practices that favored members of disadvantaged groups. The results for racial and gender discrimination differed fundamentally, and the difference stemmed primarily from the distinctive position of the ACLU's Women's Rights Project on traditional laws that favored women.

Even on those issues, it is possible to construct explanations for the Court's ideological polarity that rest on general premises relating to values or affect toward social and political groups. But without prior knowledge of what the Court's polarity ended up looking like, it might not have been easy to predict that polarity. The same is true of other findings in the chapter, such as the difference between

TABLE 5.1. Summary of inquiries in the chapter

| Issue | Key findings | Implications |
|---|---|---|
| Racial discrimination | Liberals more favorable than conservatives to discrimination claims from racial minority groups; opposite polarity for claims from whites. | Importance of advocates in defining liberal and conservative positions; influence of values related to equality, group affect, or a combination of the two as basis for issue positions. |
| Sex discrimination | Liberals more favorable to discrimination claims by women and claims by men. | |
| Religion | Liberals more favorable to claims from non-mainstream religions and to claims under establishment clause; no clear polarity in cases with claims from mainstream religions. | Likely influence of affect toward mainstream and non-mainstream groups in shaping ideological positions. |
| Regulation of business | Liberals more favorable to regulation that favors economic underdogs; opposite polarity when regulation favors upperdogs (including antitrust suits against labor unions). | Likely influence of affect toward social groups in shaping ideological positions; possible role of values related to equality. |
| Federal taxes | Relative to liberals, conservatives somewhat more favorable to businesses than to individuals. | Likely influence of affect toward the business community. |
| Personal injuries | Strong polarity, with liberals more favorable to injured parties suing businesses. | Likely influence of affect toward injured individuals and businesses, values related to equality, or both. |
| Monetary claims on government | Relative to conservatives, liberals more inclined to support claims by individuals than by businesses. | Likely influence of affect toward the business community. |

mainstream and non-mainstream religion cases and the differential treatment of individuals and businesses in taxes and monetary claims on government.

To the extent that the premises of liberalism and conservatism provide at least post hoc explanations of the patterns found in the chapter's inquiries, it can be difficult to separate values from affect toward social and political groups. In particular, the differences between liberal and conservative justices in their responses to higher-status and lower-status social groups might be interpreted as a product of the place of equality in their hierarchy of values or instead as a product of their affect toward the groups in themselves. As a broad explanation, however, group affect stands out. Across several issue areas, liberals and conservatives diverged in their responses to businesses as litigants even in contexts (such as federal taxes) in which considerations related to equality do not seem very relevant. The differential responses of justices to cases involving mainstream religious groups and non-mainstream groups are easier to understand as a result of affect toward stronger and weaker social groups than as an expression of equality as a value.

One pattern in the findings of this chapter's inquiries is the frequency with which the Court's polarity differs systematically between subsets of cases on an issue. Of course, the extent to which such differences appear depends in part on how cases are categorized into issues and on the criteria for coding of justices' votes. Even so, the variation in conservative and liberal responses to cases with different attributes under headings such as religious freedom is striking.

The inquiries in this chapter provide substantial evidence about ideological polarity in the Court. The first section of the final chapter pulls together these inquiries and the more extensive inquiries in the preceding three chapters to reach broader judgments about the mechanisms and sources of polarity.

# 6

# Implications of the Study

In this book I have analyzed one aspect of decision making in the Supreme Court, the mechanisms and sources of linkages between ideology and issues in the Court. The findings of the book's inquiries were not homogeneous, and they can be interpreted in multiple ways. For both reasons, I see this study not as definitive but as a first step in probing the phenomena it considers. Even so, I think that its theoretical perspective and its findings have significant implications for our understanding of the Court and of ideology as an element of elite politics. In this chapter I discuss those implications.

## Mechanisms and Sources of Ideological Linkages

The book's inquiries focused on the questions of how and why certain positions on issues are defined as conservative or liberal on the Court, definitions that translate justices' general ideological stances into particular issue positions. On the "how" question I argued that the linkages are best understood as products of a social process in the world of elite politics and in the Court itself, a process by which shared understandings of liberal and conservative positions on issues develop. To a degree those shared understandings rest on logical deduction from broad premises. But the translation of premises into issue positions is not always obvious and direct, and the premises that justices and others hold are more relevant to some issues than to others. Primarily for these reasons, logical deduction can explain shared understandings only in part.

I think that the evidence from the book's inquiries provides considerable support for that argument. In themselves, the changes that have occurred in the ideological polarity of some issues indicate the fluidity of the relationship between ideological stances and issue positions. Takings, for instance, had a strong ideological polarity that disappeared and then reappeared. These shifts in takings could be interpreted as a product of broad premises about government regulatory policy. But if so, the justices and other elites still had to work out the relationship between those premises and the questions that arose in takings.

The limits of general premises as a basis for issue positions are underlined by situations in which their application is uncertain. When people with low incomes and members of racial minority groups are found disproportionately among both criminal defendants and victims of crime, are those segments of society better served by pro-prosecution or pro-defendant positions in criminal justice? The answer to that question was worked out not through logical deduction but through the reactions of justices and others to what they saw in the operation of the criminal justice system.

The justices' own perceptions of which issue positions are conservative and which are liberal tend to coincide with the perceptions of other political elites. That similarity arises largely from the influence of the shared understandings that develop in the elite world as a whole. But even if justices developed their perceptions in isolation from the rest of that world, they would sort out the meaning of liberalism and conservatism partly on the basis of the same considerations as other elites. Further, justices play a role in the development of shared understandings. Under certain circumstances, that role can be substantial. For instance, this may have been true of the polarity on criminal justice that the Court began to establish in the 1940s.

What are the sources of these shared understandings? Put differently, to the extent that the shared understandings do rest on premises, what form do those premises take? Explicitly or implicitly, analyses of ideology tend to treat values as the primary basis for liberal and conservative issue positions. I agree that values play an important part in linking ideology with issues. But I also think that the justices' affect toward social groups that potentially gain or lose from particular policies and toward political groups that advocate those policies are important to this linkage. The inquiries in this book probed the relative importance of values and group affect.

These inquiries have shown that it is frequently difficult to distinguish empirically between these two potential sources of ideological polarity. To take the example that arises most frequently, certain issue positions might be understood as a product of attitudes toward equality as a value or instead as a product of attitudes toward relatively advantaged and disadvantaged groups in society. This is not simply a methodological problem. Rather, it reflects the fact that values and group affect are intertwined, shaping and reinforcing each other.

In light of this intertwining, much of the evidence in the book's inquiries is open to different interpretations. An advocate of the traditional position that values reign supreme in linking ideology to issues could read that portion of the evidence as consistent with the traditional position. But some important pieces of the evidence from these inquiries are not easily interpreted in terms of values:

- During the period from the mid-1940s to the late 1970s, pro-claimant justices in takings cases were more liberal than their anti-claimant colleagues, but not in cases brought by companies. Across the 1946–2012 Terms, the appearance of a business as a litigant also modified the Court's polarity in cases involving monetary claims on government and, to a lesser extent, tax cases.
- In the transitional period of the 1937–45 Terms, the justices who voted in favor of criminal defendants were usually more liberal than their colleagues, but that tendency disappeared and was mildly reversed when defendants had acted on behalf of a business. In the 1946–2012 Terms, the Court's strong

ideological polarity weakened when a white-collar crime was involved, and that effect was especially strong in the second half of that period.

- In the 1946–2012 Terms, government policies on regulation of business received highly disproportionate support from liberal justices when those policies favored economic "underdogs," but that pattern was reversed when they favored "upperdogs."
- In religious freedom cases during that period, pro-claimant justices were considerably more liberal than other justices when the claimant was from a non-mainstream religion, but that tendency disappeared for mainstream claimants.
- In free expression cases during the same period, the strong tendency for claimants to receive disproportionate support from more liberal justices was weakened considerably— and, from the mid-1990s on, actually reversed—when those claimants came from the mainstream political right or from the business community.

These pieces of evidence relate to differences in polarity between subsets of cases on the same issue during the same time period. While it is possible to construct value-based explanations of such differences, it is more straightforward and more reasonable to explain them on the basis of justices' affect toward the groups with which they associated litigants and toward the broader interests they represented.

All these examples involve social groups that are potential beneficiaries of decisions. In that respect they tie in with the conception of Court clienteles that Martin Shapiro articulated.[104] For most liberal justices in and after the New Deal period, the labor movement[105] and racial minority groups seemed to function as something like clientele groups. That function seems clear in freedom of expression and, for racial minority groups, in criminal justice. Especially noteworthy was the effort of the Court collectively, and especially

---

104. M. Shapiro (1978), 188–94.
105. Kersch (2006).

its liberal members, to protect the civil rights movement from attack by Southern legislatures and law enforcement officials.[106] Perhaps most striking was the Court's decision in *New York Times v. Sullivan,* which revolutionized the constitutional law of libel—apparently as a means to protect the news media and civil rights advocates from punitive libel suits in the South.[107] As two scholars pointed out, *Sullivan* "at heart was a civil rights case."[108]

Some commentators depict the business community as a clientele of the conservative majority in the Roberts Court.[109] More broadly, it appears that business has long served as a reference group for justices, distinctly more positive for conservatives than for liberals. Across several issues, the impact of litigants from the business world on the Court's ideological polarity during certain periods is striking.

Some advocates in the Court are associated with groups that are objects of the justices' affect, and advocates also provide clues to justices about the ideological polarity of issues and of specific questions that arise in cases. Both roles are reflected in the impact of conservative advocates for broad interpretations of the takings clause in the current era. A more specific manifestation of these roles concerns the function of civil rights advocates in defining which positions were in the interests of their groups when laws and private practices were challenged as discriminatory because they favored disadvantaged groups. This was especially true of Ruth Bader Ginsburg's opposition to traditional laws favoring women when she represented the Women's Rights Project of the ACLU.

If affect toward social and political groups plays a major role in shaping the ideological polarity of the Supreme Court, that reality has implications for the ways we think about the Court. To return to the point that I made in chapter 1, affect toward social and political groups as an element in the justices' responses to cases is not limited to occasional "low politics" decisions such as *Bush v. Gore.*

---

106. See Kalven (1966).
107. *New York Times Co. v. Sullivan* (1964).
108. K. Hall and Urofsky (2011), 117.
109. Liptak (2013).

Rather, this affect is an important element in Supreme Court decision making as a whole.

This does not mean that all manifestations of group affect are the same. Legal scholar Lawrence Solum responded to the distinction between high and low politics by making finer distinctions on a continuum from "high high high" to "low low low," putting *Bush v. Gore* in the latter category.[110] Although Solum was not talking about group affect as such, his multiple categories are a reminder that there is a difference between decision making based on partisan loyalties and other manifestations of affect toward groups. Developing issue positions partly on the basis of affect toward groups that are associated with an issue is "higher" than purely partisan responses to cases.

When the ideological lineup of justices on an issue varies with the social groups to which litigants belong, that pattern of behavior can be regarded as an intermediate case—"higher" than purely partisan responses to cases, but without the element of broad principle that exists when justices respond ideologically to an issue in a more consistent way. The most prominent illustration is freedom of expression, in which the relative willingness of liberal and conservative justices to support free expression claims depends to a considerable degree on the kinds of people and institutions that make those claims.

When the justices differentiate among individual cases on an issue in this way, they are relatively free from the definitions of conservative and liberal issue positions that develop in the larger elite world. In the period when the Court's polarity in takings cases was based in part on who was making a takings claim, there was no shared understanding in the elite world that liberal and conservative positions on takings should differ by the type of claimant.

This point relates to the question of *whose* affect shapes the Court's ideological polarity. At the level of issues, as I have emphasized, the definitions of conservative and liberal positions that shape decision making in the Court are developed primarily in the larger political world. As a result, justices who were absolutely neutral toward political and social groups except for their self-identifications

110. Solum (2003).

as conservative or liberal would be influenced by the group affect of other elites. In reality, justices' own affect tends to reinforce that of other elites and sometimes exerts an independent force in shaping issue positions. At the level of the questions in individual cases, when the Court's polarity varies with the attributes of litigants and advocates, the affect of the justices themselves appears to play an even more powerful part in shaping that polarity.

Ideological polarity is only one aspect of decision making in the Supreme Court, so the role of affect toward social and political groups in shaping that polarity is not necessarily the same as its role in decision making as a whole. But group affect undoubtedly plays into patterns of decisional behavior by justices that cannot be characterized in ideological terms—more idiosyncratic choices by individual justices that are based in part on their likes and dislikes for particular groups. For that reason the potential impact of justices' attitudes toward groups goes well beyond the ideological structure of decision making, and this impact and the processes that bring it about merit further inquiries by students of the Supreme Court.

This is one of the contexts in which it is useful to keep in mind that the justices are human beings. In a world in which other people have positive and negative feelings about social and political groups, it is inevitable that Supreme Court justices also have those feelings. And since they do, it is inevitable that these feelings shape their responses to the issues and questions that they address as decision makers. In this respect, as in others, taking into account justices' emotions and cognitions alongside their conscious goals provides us with a richer understanding of why they do what they do.

## Ideology in the Study of the Supreme Court

The concept of ideology is central to scholarship on the Supreme Court. That concept is used in a variety of ways. It is sometimes treated as an attribute of the justices' attitudes, sometimes as an attribute of their votes and opinions. It is employed as a description, an independent variable, and a dependent variable.

In this study I have focused on one pair of questions about ideology in the Supreme Court: how and why certain policy positions are identified as conservative or liberal and are held primarily by conservatives or liberals. These are important questions that have received relatively little attention, and I hope that in addressing them I have contributed to the understanding of ideology as an element in decision making by the justices. Beyond what the study's findings show in themselves, they have some implications for the ways that ideology is used in research on the Court.

The implications arise in part from the role of affect toward groups in ideological decision making, but even more from three other findings. First, the definitions of certain positions on issues as liberal or conservative are not simply a matter of logical deduction from general premises; rather, they arise from shared understandings in which that logic is only one element. Second, the ideological polarity of issues in the Court is subject to change, sometimes quite substantial change. Finally, the ideological polarity of an issue at a particular time is not necessarily homogeneous; differences in the attributes of cases on an issue are sometimes associated with quite different lineups of liberal and conservative justices.

One possible reaction to these findings is that we should avoid treating ideology as an attribute of either the justices or their decision making. If the content of liberal and conservative positions on issues is both changeable and sometimes arbitrary, does ideology actually matter much? My own reaction is different: I think that the findings do not detract from the importance of ideology but rather underline its complexity. For one thing, ideology is not just a product of justices' values; it reflects their affect toward social and political groups as well. And ideology is also a part of their social identities, drawing them toward positions that they perceive as appropriate for conservatives or liberals to take. When scholars think about the justices' behavior in ideological terms, they should keep the complex meaning of ideology in mind.

The value of doing so is especially relevant when ideology is treated as an explanatory variable. If the justices' ideological positions correlate with their votes in some set of cases, that relationship could derive from any of the elements of ideology or from some combination of those elements. This complexity should be taken into account in interpreting these statistical relationships. Measures of the justices' ideological positions are often used primarily as control variables, to serve as a kind of baseline from which to gauge the statistical impact of other determinants of choice. That practice seems quite justifiable, but in this context as well it is good to keep in mind the multiple elements of ideology when interpreting what the baseline means.[111]

If the justices' ideological positions are to be analyzed for any purposes, how should they be measured? One fundamental choice is between coding justices' positions in cases according to specified rules or using the structure of the justices' votes (or, as it becomes possible, the structure of the opinions they write and join) to identify ideological positions.[112] At least on its face, the Supreme Court Database is the dominant version of the first approach in research by political scientists; the Martin-Quinn scores are the dominant version of the second.[113]

The Martin-Quinn approach is almost entirely inductive: votes are analyzed without regard to their content, and patterns of agreement among the justices are used to array them along a scale. Defining one end of the scale as liberal and the other as conservative is based on common knowledge, which can hardly be contested. This inductive approach made the Martin-Quinn scores attractive for this study, for which the ideological polarity of the justices across all cases had to be free from any assumptions about which positions on an issue or in a specific case are liberal and conservative.

The corresponding limitation of the scores is their lack of direct substantive meaning. In freedom of expression, to take one example, cases in which four liberals vote for a claimant and five conservatives vote against the claimant contribute to the Court's ideological dimension in the same way as cases in which the conservatives vote for a claimant and the liberals against. Thus use of this measure

111. The Court's collective ideological position is sometimes used as an independent variable or as a baseline. The appropriateness of that usage depends heavily on the comparability of measures of that position over time. Ho and Quinn (2010), 844–46; Bailey (2013), 822.

112. See C. Shapiro (2010), 87–88.

113. Martin and Quinn (2002).

incorporates the conception that a conservative vote in a case is a vote that conservatives were more likely than liberals to cast. But this limitation is not necessarily problematical. So long as that conception and other attributes of the Martin-Quinn scores are consistent with the goals of a study, then these scores are a valuable resource.[114]

The use of coding rules for liberal and conservative votes and decisions in the Supreme Court Database makes any resulting scores for justices appear to be fundamentally different from the Martin-Quinn scores.[115] In reality, there is a substantial inductive element to the Database coding. The designation of particular positions on an issue as conservative or liberal is largely a product of patterns of voting by the justices that were identified in the research on which the Database was built. Similarly, the assignment of cases to particular issues and issue areas is partly a product of voting patterns. Still, the existence of the coding rules makes the designation of ideological direction less than fully inductive.

This hybrid quality of the Database coding procedures makes it especially important for some purposes to check and modify the codings of issues and of the direction of votes and decisions. The analyses in this book required that cases be assigned to issues on the basis of their content without regard to voting patterns and that votes on an issue be coded in terms of the outcome for the two sides (such as criminal defendants and the prosecution) rather than any characterization of which sides were conservative and liberal that had a different basis. For those reasons, as described in the appendix, the codings of issues and votes in the Database could only be a starting point.

All this leads to a more specific and a more general point. The specific point is that there is not necessarily a best ideological coding of the two sides in a case. The appropriate coding of the two sides depends on the underlying purposes of a study.

---

114. Ho and Quinn (2010, 846–47) argue that, for at least most purposes, the scores should be converted into rank orders. My reasons for using the original interval-level scores are discussed in the appendix.

115. The rules are listed at http://scdb.wustl.edu/documentation.php?var=decision Direction.

The general point is that we should avoid reifying ideology as it applies to decisions and to the justices' positions in decisions. As I have emphasized, the meaning of ideology is both fluid and complicated. When scholars describe individual or collective behavior in ideological terms or treat ideological positions as a determinant of that behavior, most of the time they implicitly treat ideology as fixed and simple. Doing so can be justifiable and useful, but the distance between that practice and the reality of ideology should be kept in mind in interpreting the findings of inquiries into ideology in decision making.

Beyond the concerns that arise from the findings of this study, scholars have noted other reasons to be careful when analyzing the Supreme Court in ideological terms. Strong as the forces that create ideological divisions may be, many of the Court's decisions are unanimous and some others feature divisions that diverge from ideological lines.[116] To the extent that patterns of votes are multidimensional, focusing on a single ideological dimension may oversimplify the pattern of response to cases.[117] Further, the process of case selection may distort the picture of ideological thinking that emerges from the Court's decisions on the merits.[118]

To reiterate what I said earlier, none of this means that we should abandon analysis of the Court in ideological terms. But to reiterate another theme, there is considerable reason to be self-conscious and explicit about the meaning of ideology when we employ it to help understand judicial decision making.

## The Court in Its Political Environment

Students of the Supreme Court have given considerable attention to the influence of the larger political world on the Court. A substantial body of scholarship probes the impact of the legislative and executive branches and the general public on justices' choices as

---

116. Edelman, Klein, and Lindquist (2008, 2012).
117. Lauderdale and Clark (2012, 2014).
118. Kastellec and Lax (2008); McGuire et al. (2009); Yates, Cann, and Boyea (2013).

decision makers.[119] While adherents to attitudinal perspectives on the Court perceive the impact of the Court's political environment as quite limited, many other scholars see that impact as substantial and even pervasive.

The influence of the political environment is usually portrayed as a force that is distinct from the justices' own preferences. The question for most scholars is how much, and in what ways, the environment moves justices to take positions that depart from their own conceptions of good law and good policy. But the Court's environment may have a more integral impact by shaping the justices' preferences themselves rather than moving the justices away from their preferred positions, and that impact is one theme of some scholarship that takes a historical institutionalist perspective on the Court.[120]

The findings of this study point to one of the most powerful ways that the larger world shapes the justices' preferences: shaping ideologically oriented behavior by the justices. The linkages between ideology and issue positions in the Court are generally similar to the linkages that exist among other political elites. That similarity is typically taken for granted, as it should be if both Supreme Court justices and other political elites develop issue positions through logical deduction from the premises of conservatism and liberalism. As I have argued, however, the linkages between issues and ideology develop through a social process among political elites, one that is driven by logic only in part.

Inevitably, the shared understandings that develop from this social process structure the justices' thinking. This does not mean that justices always conceive of liberal and conservative positions in the same way as do most people outside the Court. Nor does it mean that they are simply passive recipients of the understandings of other elites. Indeed, the Court helps to create and reinforce shared understandings about the ideological meaning of issues. But justices do take in the ways that issues are defined ideologically among political

119. Examples of recent work that addresses this impact are B. Friedman (2009), Bailey and Maltzman (2011), Clark (2011), Harvey (2013), and Black et al. (2016).

120. E.g., Rabban (1997); Kersch (2004).

elites as a whole, and those definitions shape justices' own perceptions of liberal and conservative positions.

Of course, this is hardly the only way that the elite world affects the justices' policy preferences. As attitudes toward problems connected with illegal drugs or toward the roles of women change in that world, the justices' attitudes are likely to change with them. But the impact of shared understandings about the ideological meaning of issues is especially significant, because it can structure justices' approaches to whole fields of legal policy.

The high level of polarization in elite politics in the current era may also have an impact on the justices' perspectives. This polarization does not necessarily mean that affect toward political groups is stronger among justices today than it was in earlier eras. But just as partisan and ideological lines have come to be quite similar in bodies such as Congress, those lines have coincided in the Court since the appointment of Elena Kagan in 2010. The mutual reinforcement of party and ideology may have created favorable conditions for the justices' affect toward political groups to shape decisions in which both ideological and partisan considerations come into play.[121]

## Ideology in the World of Elite Politics

Throughout the book I have emphasized the connections between the Supreme Court and the larger world elite of which it is part, but I have focused on the workings of ideology in the Court. It is worthwhile to consider more directly some implications of the book's inquiry for other policy-making bodies.

Lower federal courts are a good place to start. Almost surely, ideology plays a more limited role in decision making in the courts of appeals and district courts than in the Supreme Court. This is

---

121. That is one possible interpretation of the justices' votes in cases about the health care program sponsored by President Obama: *National Federation of Independent Business v. Sebelius* (2012); *Burwell v. Hobby Lobby Stores, Inc.* (2014); and *King v. Burwell* (2015). But it should be kept in mind that only in *Hobby Lobby* and on the commerce clause question in *Sebelius* did the justices divide perfectly along partisan and ideological lines.

primarily because lower courts hear relatively high proportions of cases in which the law and facts leave relatively little room for the judges' ideological stances to influence their choices.

To the extent that lower-court judges do act on an ideological basis, the mechanisms and sources of the linkages between their ideological stances and their issue positions should be similar to those that operate in the Supreme Court in most respects. One possible difference stems from the fact that judges in the district courts and courts of appeals have the Supreme Court as an additional source of information about the polarity of issues. Because the Court addresses issues in the form of disputes over federal law, as other federal courts do, the ways that liberal and conservative justices line up on those issues are especially relevant to lower-court judges. This possible influence might be probed by analyzing how lower courts respond to changes in the polarity of issues in the Supreme Court, taking into account other developments in the world of political elites.

Different as federal courts are from the other branches of government, I have emphasized similarity across branches in the identification of certain issue positions as liberal and others as conservative.[122] This similarity arises both from similarities in reasoning and from the development of shared understandings of the ideological meaning of issues. As suggested in chapter 1, however, there is one major difference between the Supreme Court (and other federal courts) and segments of the political elites for which electoral considerations are more directly relevant. That difference is the role of what I called politics: the adoption of issue positions with the goal of maximizing political support. Politics and group affect can have similar effects, but they arise from different motivations. For a member of Congress, adopting positions that favor a particular group in order to maximize

---

122. The body of scholarship that treats the ideological dimensions in the Court and the other branches as comparable incorporates the assumption that justices and other policy makers define ideological positions in the same ways. That assumption is especially clear in studies that use the polarity of positions in the other branches to define the polarity of positions in the Supreme Court. Bailey (2013), 827; Harvey (2013), 144–47. Specifics of measurement strategies aside, the findings of this study support that assumption.

the chances of reelection is different from adopting such positions because of an affinity for that group or identification with it.

Politics as I have defined it is not entirely absent from the Supreme Court, in that justices may act to promote the policies they favor and to enhance support for the Court in the political world and the country as a whole. Still, the justices' relatively high level of independence from external constraints limits the impact of political considerations on the justices. And those considerations are unlikely to have a direct effect on the ideological polarity of issues in the Court.[123] On the whole, the same is true of lower federal courts.[124]

Of course, officeholders in the other branches have a direct interest in their personal electoral success, the success of the political party with which they are affiliated, or both. Thus it is reasonable to posit that members of Congress act primarily on their interest in retaining their offices.[125] But it is not just officeholders who have a stake in partisan outcomes. Prospective officeholders, party officials, and commentators who hope to influence a presidential administration, among others, also have considerable stake in those outcomes.

One consequence is that American politics scholars have given considerably more attention to the development of political parties' issue positions and change in those positions than they have to the linkages between ideology and issue positions.[126] The central

123. However, as discussed earlier, they may have an indirect effect by shaping shared understandings from which the justices draw in defining issues ideologically.

124. Judges who face elections might differ in this respect. That is especially true of state supreme courts, because the ideological structure of decisions is visible in the same way that it is in the US Supreme Court and because justices have more reason to worry about retaining their positions than do judges on lower state courts. In states such as Wisconsin, electoral rivalries seem to have reinforced ideological divisions on the supreme court. See Kritzer (2015), 8–21. More fundamentally, justices' interest in retaining support from their core constituencies, including campaign contributors, may reinforce the identification of certain positions on issues such as tort law as conservative or liberal. But it appears that the basic polarity of those issues in state supreme courts results primarily from shared understandings that are based in part on values and group affect.

125. Mayhew (1974).

126. But see Noel (2013).

theme of this scholarship is unsurprising: although parties adopt and modify positions on issues for a variety of reasons, electoral incentives are the most important source of those choices.[127] An implicit corollary is that incentives to maintain and expand electoral coalitions make party positions on issues less stable than the positions of ideological camps.

Because electoral incentives are so strong, they might crowd out group affect as a source of ideological polarity in sectors of the elite that are involved in electoral politics, including policy-making bodies such as Congress. I think, however, that there is room for affect toward social and political groups to have substantial effects on the positions of conservatives and liberals in those sectors.

To begin with, people who are active in electoral politics do hold strong positive or negative affect toward social groups, affect that is structured largely along ideological lines.[128] This affect can be expected to influence their views on issues even in the presence of strong electoral incentives. In chapter 1, I quoted David Karol's judgment that "it seems more apt to say politicians are consistent in their views of 'who' is good and deserving of help than 'what' is good in terms of policy and principles of governmental action."[129] Although politicians' ideas about who is good and deserving stem in part from the composition of their electoral coalitions, they are also shaped by more fundamental attitudes toward segments of society. Indeed, those attitudes likely have considerable impact on politicians' own ideological identifications. And active participants in the contentious world of politics have especially strong positive and negative feelings toward political groups, based on which side they are on. Those feelings sometimes outweigh political considerations in determining what positions they take on issues.

Although polarization among political elites in the current era surely affects the functioning of ideology in the courts, it is even more relevant to the other branches. Affective polarization, a growth

127. E.g., Carmines and Stimson (1989); Wolbrecht (2000); Karol (2009).
128. Zinni, Mattei, and Rhodebeck (1997); Devine (2011), 99–164.
129. Karol (2009), 47.

in hostility between partisan and ideological rivals,[130] undoubtedly has increased the impact of attitudes toward political groups on the issue positions connected with liberalism and conservatism. The effect of partisan sorting is less certain. On the one hand, the merging of ideological and partisan camps might give political considerations a more pervasive impact in the development of shared understandings of conservative and liberal positions. On the other hand, these strengthened ties may bind the parties more closely to the ideological positions that develop outside the arena of electoral politics— positions that are based in considerable part on affect toward social groups.

Regardless of the effects of polarization, I think that the role of group affect in shaping the ideological polarity of issues in the executive and legislative branches merits more consideration than it has received. This role is not as obvious as the ways that political considerations shape the adoption of issue positions by individual politicians or their political parties. But the deep-seated affect of political elites toward social and political groups may have a fundamental impact on the positions adopted by people in the conservative and liberal segments of those elites.

Still, the relatively limited impact of political considerations in the Supreme Court means that there is even more room for group affect to function in the Court than in most other segments of the political elite. In the Court as well, affect toward social and political groups has had a more powerful impact than observers of the Court recognize. By giving more attention to group affect as a source of polarity, scholars can gain a richer sense of ideology as an element in decision making in the Supreme Court.

130. Iyengar, Sood, and Lelkes (2012).

# APPENDIX: METHODOLOGY FOR ANALYSIS OF CASES AND DECISIONS

The analyses presented in chapters 2–4 are of the cases that the Supreme Court heard on each issue and the votes and decisions in those cases. This appendix discusses several aspects of the methods used to gather, code, and analyze data related to cases and decisions. I also discuss the shorter case studies in chapter 5 more briefly.

In this appendix I refer to the researcher as "I," both for simplicity and to make it clear where the responsibility for methodological choices lies. However, that is a serious oversimplification. Most of the identification and coding of cases was done in collaboration with the student assistants whom I thank in the acknowledgments. Those students played integral parts in the research process, both in the development of general rules and in the application of those rules to individual cases.

## Identification of Cases for the Datasets

On each of the three issues analyzed in chapters 2–4, relevant cases from the Supreme Court's 1910–2012 Terms were identified. For the 1946–2012 Terms, all cases whose subject matter met the criteria for inclusion (described below) became part of the dataset to be analyzed. For freedom of expression, the same rule was used for the 1910–45 Terms. For criminal justice, only non-unanimous decisions were included for the 1910–45 Terms; for takings, only non-unanimous decisions were included for the 1910–36 Terms. The limitation for criminal cases was adopted because of the very large number of decisions in criminal cases, especially for the era prior to the Court's receipt of broad discretionary jurisdiction in 1925. The limitation for takings was adopted because of the great difficulty of identifying takings cases before the mid-1930s, a product of the Court's frequent failure to specify the constitutional provision on which its decision was based. By focusing on non-unanimous decisions, I could give closer attention to the question of whether individual decisions (and the votes of individual justices) were based on the takings clause. The limitation to non-unanimous decisions in those early periods for two issues did not affect the central concern of the analyses, the polarity of the Court in decisions that divided the justices.

Issue domains can be defined in multiple ways. I developed detailed rules to determine whether cases involved each issue analyzed in the study. The original or "Modern" Supreme Court Database includes cases from the 1946 Term on. For the criminal and free expression issues, that Database was the starting point for identification of cases to include for the 1946–2012 Terms, but additional steps were undertaken to select cases for those two datasets on the basis of my coding rules. Other information in the Database, other sources, and direct examination of individual cases were used to create datasets of criminal and free expression cases. The Database was less useful in identifying relevant takings cases because of the frequent presence of other issues, often more prominent, in cases involving the takings clause. For that reason, I relied primarily on other sources to compile the set of takings cases.

An early version of the "Legacy" Supreme Court Database that covers the Court's full history was issued after the analyses of the 1910–45 Terms had been carried out. On each of the three issues I used the Legacy Database to identify cases that were potential additions to the datasets on the three issues. A few cases were added to the datasets as a result. The sources that I initially used to identify relevant cases from the 1910–45 Terms are discussed below under the headings for each issue.

One key question is the criteria for classifying an action by the Court as a decision. My main criterion was similar to the standard one: decisions are included only if they are on the merits. Thus, denials of certiorari, summary affirmances and dismissals of appeals, and dismissals because certiorari was improvidently granted (DIGs) were not included. Some other actions by the Court were announced in very brief opinions, so that they did not seem to be "real" decisions. With a few exceptions, cases were excluded if the opinions were only one paragraph in length.

### FREEDOM OF EXPRESSION

The subject-matter criterion for inclusion of cases in this issue is that they involve the rights protected by the non-religion clauses of the First Amendment: speech, press, petition, and peaceable assembly. It would be reasonable to include cases only if they were decided on the basis of the First Amendment. But that rule seems unduly restrictive, because the Court often decides cases involving free expression on other bases, such as interpretation of statutes or procedural rights, even though First Amendment considerations seem to motivate the justices. I included these cases in the dataset and in the primary analyses of free expression with a variable that distinguished them from cases decided on the basis of the First Amendment. That variable was used to conduct supplementary analyses from which they were excluded. The findings of those analyses were similar to those of the analyses that included these cases.

The Supreme Court Database was the starting point for identification of cases in the 1946–2012 Terms. I began with all cases in the First Amendment issue area except for those with issues based on the religion clauses, and I examined each case to determine whether it met the criterion for inclusion. The great majority met the criterion.

Some cases involving First Amendment rights are placed in other issue areas in the Database. One example is cases involving protests at abortion clinics, which are classified as involving abortion rather than freedom of expression. I identified issues in the Database to examine (in the Database, issues are subsets of issue areas) from lists of free expression decisions in two sources, the section on freedom of expression in the Congressional Research Service publication, *The Constitution of the United States of America: Analysis and Interpretation*[131] and the discussion of freedom of expression in *Corwin and Peltason's Understanding the Constitution.*[132] When one or more cases in those sources fell under a non-free expression issue, I read cases classified under that issue in the Database to see which should be included. That procedure led to the inclusion of a substantial number of additional cases.

For the 1910–45 Terms, potential cases were identified primarily from Lexis searches, and these cases were then read. This step was supplemented with examination of First Amendment cases that were cited in standard sources. These techniques likely identified nearly all eligible cases.

### CRIMINAL JUSTICE

Identification of criminal cases might seem straightforward, but in fact it is a complicated process. For one thing, in many criminal prosecutions the issue is really about something else. For instance, a good many free expression cases in areas such as obscenity take the form of criminal prosecutions. Another complication is that some cases that are not criminal prosecutions involve criminal procedure issues. For instance, questions concerning the legality of searches may arise in civil cases.

The rule that I adopted was that cases would be included if they arose from criminal prosecutions and if they were decided on the basis of issues in criminal law or criminal procedure. These criteria are easily applied to the great majority of cases, but there are some borderline cases, and more specific rules were adopted to address those borderline cases.

For the 1946–2012 Terms, the starting point for identification of cases was the criminal procedure issue area in the Supreme Court Database. With a few exceptions, the Database included cases in this issue area only if the decision rested on criminal law or criminal procedure issues, but there were some exceptions. Appropriately for

131. Congressional Research Service (2013).
132. Peltason (1997).

the purposes of the Database, a number of cases that did not involve criminal prosecutions were included in this issue area. Each case in this issue area was examined to determine if it was criminal, and a substantial number of cases were excluded.

The Database puts a great many criminal prosecutions into issue areas other than criminal procedure. These cases can be identified from the variables for the identities of the petitioner and respondent. Many of these cases clearly should be excluded because they are decided on the basis of non-criminal issues, but others clearly meet my criteria for inclusion, and some additional cases are on the margins. I examined each case in which the petitioner or respondent was a criminal defendant or a similar party, as identified in the Database, and applied the inclusion rules to it. A substantial number of these cases were added to the dataset.

The cases that had elements of non-criminal issues were the most difficult to classify. As noted earlier, my criterion was the basis for decision. Thus, to take one example, obscenity cases were included if they were decided on the basis of interpretation of a statute or a procedural issue, but they were excluded if they were decided on the basis of the First Amendment.

For the 1910–45 Terms, potential cases were identified from reading of the United States Reports and through searches of the Lexis database with various search terms, some of which were based on a reading of cases. These cases were then read to determine whether they met the criteria for classification as criminal decisions and whether they were non-unanimous. For a supplementary analysis of the Court's agenda in that period, all criminal cases—whether unanimous or non-unanimous—at five-year intervals from 1910 to 1940 (as well as the 1942 Term) were analyzed.

## TAKINGS

Identification of takings cases is challenging because cases with takings questions quite often have other questions as well. Further, in the early twentieth century, the Court's opinions in state-level cases were often quite unclear about whether they were deciding an issue under the takings clause as incorporated in the Fourteenth Amendment or on another basis, typically substantive due process independent of the takings clause.

Because of the frequent conjunction of takings and other issues, the Supreme Court Database was not used as a starting point for the identification of cases in the 1946–2012 Terms: appropriately, the Database classified some cases with takings claims as involving other issues instead. Multiple sources were employed to find decisions. A list of certain types of takings cases in one source[133] and citations in the section on takings in the Congressional Research Service volume on constitutional law[134] provided a substantial start in locating decisions. A Lexis word search of decisions was undertaken to locate additional decisions, based on a reading of opinions that indicated the most useful terms to search. The cases obtained from these sources were read to identify those in which the opinion for the Court (or, for decisions without a majority opinion, any opinion on the majority side) actually decided a question under the takings clause or a question with clear implications for that clause.[135]

For the period in which the Court has been explicit about its use of the takings clause, beginning around the 1930s, it is likely that all relevant cases were identified. For the period prior to that time, the Court's frequent ambiguity about what it was deciding makes it difficult to determine the effectiveness of the search techniques. However, when the Legacy Database became available, only one additional case that met the criteria for inclusion was identified from that source. Because of the Court's ambiguity, decisions whether or not to include some cases from this early period were difficult, and in those cases a different judgment certainly could be justified. But the Court's polarity in takings in the 1910–36 Terms was so strong, including the cases that came close to inclusion in the

---

133. Meltz (2005).

134. Congressional Research Service (2013).

135. Thus, cases were included if a statute was interpreted in a particular way in order to avoid a possible violation of the takings clause, if a litigant made a takings claim and the Court ruled that the takings question was not yet ripe, or if the Court ruled on whether a litigant had the right to make a takings claim in court.

dataset, that decisions about inclusion and exclusion did not affect the dominant pattern.

Cases in which takings was one of multiple issues were included if (a) the majority opinion decided a takings question and (b) any other opinion took the opposing position on that takings question. Even in those cases, the takings question was often subordinate to questions involving other issues. As with freedom of expression, the primary analyses were conducted on all cases, but supplementary analyses were limited to those cases in which the takings question was coded as central to the decision. On this issue too, the supplementary analyses produced similar results.

## Votes

The justices' votes in cases were coded dichotomously in terms of their positions on the issue under analysis: for or against free expression claimants, criminal defendants, or takings claimants. Following the practice in the Supreme Court Database, if the justices divided differently on different questions in the case, each set of votes was treated as a separate case. However, there were few such cases.

In criminal and free expression cases, I followed the standard procedure of coding votes on the basis of which side they predominantly favored in the outcome of the case. I began with the coding of votes in the Supreme Court Database as liberal or conservative. But because that ideological coding scheme does not always coincide with voting for or against criminal defendants or free expression claimants, the coding of each case had to be checked. On each issue, more often freedom of expression, I changed the coding of some votes where the Database's ideological coding produced a different result from party-based coding. Thus, the final coding of votes was based on whether a justice voted in favor of criminal defendants or free expression claimants rather than whether the vote would generally be regarded as liberal or conservative.

The frequent existence of other issues in takings cases made it less than ideal to code votes on the basis of the outcome of the case for the party with a takings claim. It was common for only a subset of justices to address the takings question in a case, and justices' positions on the takings question often went in the opposite direction from their positions on the outcome of the case. For these reasons, I coded votes according to a justice's position on the takings question or questions in the case. One result was that the votes of one or more justices who participated in a decision frequently were not coded, because those justices did not address a takings question.

## Ideological Polarity

For purposes of this study, the ideological polarity of the justices' positions in each non-unanimous decision is defined as the relationship between the justices' liberalism and conservatism across decisions on all issues (or, as I will discuss, nearly all decisions) and the divisions between justices on the two sides in the specific decision. A statistical measure of polarity can be calculated for each case. That measure can be used, or it can be broken down into dichotomous or finer categories. The mean polarity of the justices across all cases on an issue for a particular time period can be calculated from the measures of polarity for each case.

This approach raises three questions that overlap in some respects. The first is whether it is appropriate to use decisional behavior to measure justices' overall ideological positions. This has been one key issue in the debate among students of judicial behavior over measures of ideological positions.[136]

The answer depends largely on the purpose for which a measure is used. For causal analyses that are aimed at determining the impact of justices' policy preferences on their choices as decision makers, a measure of ideological positions independent of decisional behavior is generally preferable even if it is imperfect. For that reason the Segal-Cover measure based on newspaper editorials at the time of a justice's nomination appropriately has received wide use in causal analyses.[137] For analyses that are concerned with the dimensionality

136. Fischman and Law (2009).
137. Segal and Cover (1989).

of justices' positions in cases relative to each other, however, a measure of ideological position that is based on those positions is preferable. Thus I wanted to use a measure based on decisional behavior.

Another aspect of this question arises from the existence of change in the ideological polarity of issues. If that polarity can change, then justices' positions on an ideological scale based on the full set of their votes might itself be an unstable benchmark. But even if there were a great deal of instability, considerably more than actually exists, the overall polarity of the justices across issues at any given time would be an appropriate benchmark.

In her analysis of congressional voting, Frances Lee raises a related concern.[138] Many of the votes that divide Republicans from Democrats in Congress do not involve issues that have much (or any) ideological meaning as we understand conservatism and liberalism. Thus, to interpret those votes in ideological terms simply because they correlate with votes that do have ideological meaning might be problematic. As Lee shows, however, those votes stem from partisan interests—interests that are not irrelevant to the Court but that affect only a small proportion of cases directly.

The second question is whether changes in ideological polarity can be identified meaningfully from the Court's decisions when the set of cases that the Court decides on an issue changes in content over time. Supreme Court scholars have pointed to the distorting effects of analyzing the justices' behavior on the basis of the set of cases that the Court decides on the merits.[139] The cases that the Court decides are unrepresentative of all cases brought to the Court, let alone all the cases that might be brought to the Court. The subset of cases in which the justices disagree on the outcome is even less representative.

Even in a study that is concerned with polarity only at a specific time, the Court's agenda-setting might have a distorting effect. Depending on the Court's choices of cases on an issue, the consistency

---

138. Lee (2009), 47–56.

139. Kastellec and Lax (2008); McGuire et al. (2009); Yates, Cann, and Boyea (2013). Other scholars have pointed to similar distorting effects in Congress. Vandoren (1990); Crespin, Rohde, and Vander Wielen (2011); Harbridge (2015).

of the ways that the justices divide and the extent to which polarity on that issue reflects the Court's overall ideological polarity might be enhanced or weakened. To the extent that these distortions are fairly constant over time, as they probably are for the most part, their effects are reduced in a study that is focused on change over time. But when the Court's agenda on an issue evolves over time, as it frequently does,[140] agenda change could create a false impression of change in the Court's polarity.

The effects of change in the Court's agenda are best addressed in a study of this type by taking those effects into account directly. When the Court's ideological polarity on an issue changes, agenda change can and should be treated as one possible source of change in polarity. That is the approach I take in this study. Of course, agenda change does not occur in isolation. It reflects changes in the world outside the Court, especially as those changes are reflected in the set of cases brought to the Court, along with changes in the justices' own thinking. But that complication, inherent to any study of changes in institutional behavior, can also be taken into account.

The third question is whether justices' overall positions and their positions in individual cases are reasonable to measure in terms of votes on case outcomes rather than the legal doctrines they support.[141] Votes provide only a partial picture of justices' positions, and the doctrines that justices support ultimately are more consequential. Scholars' reliance on votes rather than doctrine has rested primarily on the difficulty of measuring doctrinal positions systematically. But if the use of votes is largely a matter of necessity, it can also be defended on two grounds. First, the justices' votes are a good gauge of their positions on an issue relative to each other: concurring opinions notwithstanding, almost surely the justices' votes on an issue correlate highly with their doctrinal positions. Second, outcomes are important in themselves. Justices do care about outcomes, and their votes on outcomes may illuminate their affect

---

140. Pacelle (1991, 1995).

141. As noted earlier, in takings it is votes on the takings claim that are measured rather than votes on the case outcome, though the two usually coincide.

toward groups associated with litigants more clearly than do their doctrinal positions in cases.

Thus, I sought a vote-based measure of the justices' overall ideological positions. The most prominent measure of this type is the ideological scores developed by Andrew Martin and Kevin Quinn, which are available for the 1937–2012 Terms.[142] The Martin-Quinn scores place each justice in each Court term on an ideological scale. Because they are based on the structure of votes rather than a coding of votes as liberal or conservative, the Martin-Quinn scores do not rest on assumptions about the ideological direction of votes. That quality is important to the purposes of this study. In comparison with simple percentages of liberal and conservative votes, the Martin-Quinn scores have two other advantages: they are designed to reduce the impact of idiosyncratic variation from term to term that results from changes in the Court's agenda, and they avoid the distortions that result when justices who participated in different subsets of decisions are compared. For those reasons, I use those scores to identify the overall ideological structure of the justices' positions in each term.

That choice requires justification in light of the limitations of the Martin-Quinn scores discussed by Ho and Quinn[143] and Bailey.[144] Perhaps the most important limitation, emphasized by Bailey, is that the scores are not well suited to the comparison of justices' positions over time. Because I focus on the justices' positions relative to each other at the same time, that limitation is not relevant to this study. Bailey points to the element of circularity in defining ideological positions on the basis of the justices' voting patterns.[145] But that approach is appropriate to this study, in which the task is not to analyze the relationship between ideology and the justices' votes but rather to ascertain how voting on a particular issue relates to the overall ideological pattern of voting in the Court. In other words, use of the Martin-Quinn scores allows comparison of votes for one side or the

142. Martin and Quinn (2002).
143. Ho and Quinn (2010).
144. Bailey (2013).
145. Bailey, 825.

other on a particular issue (such as free expression claimants and those who oppose the claim) with the overall ideological structure of voting in the Court.

Because the standard Martin-Quinn scores are based on all the Court's decisions, they are affected by votes on the issues that are analyzed. That effect potentially biases the relationship between the justices' overall positions and their positions on the issue in question in a positive direction. Analyses by Martin and Quinn suggest that any such bias is quite small.[146] Even so, it seemed preferable to use modified Martin-Quinn scores that were based on an estimation procedure from which cases on the issue in question were omitted, and I did so for freedom of expression and criminal justice.[147] Because takings cases constitute a very small portion of the Court's agenda, I used the original Martin-Quinn scores for that issue.

The one limitation of the Martin-Quinn scores that is potentially problematic for the analyses in the book is that their placement of justices on an interval scale is inexact. The most visible aspect of this quality is a pattern in which the distances between justices who stand at the far end of the ideological spectrum and their colleagues on the same side of that spectrum are often exaggerated considerably. This quality of the scores led Ho and Quinn to conclude that the scores should be treated only as ordinal.[148] But treating the scores as standing on an ordinal scale loses information about relative distances between justices that the scores capture with some accuracy despite the distortions. Further, when justices are close to each other ideologically, their rank orders sometimes jump around from term to term in a way that creates distortions of its own.

For this reason I treated the scores as interval-level, though with a step (discussed below) to reduce the effect of exaggerated extreme scores. But I was interested in the effect of that choice. For freedom

146. Martin and Quinn (2005), 3.

147. These modified scores were calculated by Alicia Uribe, working with Andrew Martin; I appreciate their assistance. The cases omitted from calculation of the scores are not defined in exactly the same way as the cases that I analyzed in the two fields, but they are close enough to make the omissions appropriate and useful.

148. Ho and Quinn (2010), 846–47.

of expression cases in the 1946–2012 Terms, I compared the relationship between the justices' votes in individual cases and their overall ideological stances based on the interval-level Martin-Quinn scores with the same relationship based on ranked version of the scores. Among the 397 non-unanimous decisions, there were ten in which justices on the two sides were ideologically identical based on the ranked version of the scores. Leaving those cases aside, there were only three cases (0.8%) in which the Court's dichotomized ideological orientation (that is, whether the pro-expression justices were more liberal or more conservative than their colleagues on the other side) differed between the two versions. For each version of the scores, I calculated the magnitude of the ideological differences between the two sides in a decision—ranging from very positive (pro-expression justices much more liberal than their colleagues) to very negative. The correlation between these magnitudes for the two versions was +.891. Thus, the choice between those versions did not make a great deal of difference. To the extent that they differ, however, I think that the original interval-level scores are at least marginally preferable.

Bailey developed a measure of the justices' ideological positions on the basis of "bridge observations" that connect cases to each other and to positions taken by policy makers in the other branches of government.[149] His method, which produces ideal point estimates for each justice in each term during the 1950–2011 period, is intended to overcome some limitations of the Martin-Quinn scores. The Bailey measure is quite appealing, but it is not fully suitable for purposes of this study. It covers a somewhat shorter period than the Martin-Quinn scores, and it has not been applied to economic issues.[150]

For those reasons, the Martin-Quinn scores were preferable. But that leaves the same question that I raised for the ranked Martin-Quinn scores: how much difference does it make to use the original

149. Bailey (2013); see Bailey (2007); Bailey and Maltzman (2011).
150. There are also two minor disadvantages to the Bailey measure for purposes of the study: scores are calculated for calendar years rather than Court terms, and scores for justices based on sets of cases that exclude freedom of expression or criminal justice are not available.

Martin-Quinn scores rather than the Bailey measure? I was uncertain what to expect. On the one hand, the ideological polarity of many decisions is so strong that the choice of measures seems unlikely to affect the direction of that polarity. On the other hand, the sharp differences between the methods on which the two sets of scores are based could easily produce differences between the two measures in decisions in which the two sides are not so polarized.

The results were striking. Among the 382 free expression cases for which the Bailey measure was available, there was one tie score with that measure for the dichotomized ideological orientation, and only six cases (1.6%) had different dichotomized orientations with the Bailey and Martin-Quinn measures. The correlation between the magnitude of ideological differences between the two sides in cases with the two measures was +.914. The degree of similarity between the two measures in this respect was surprising, given the very different ways that they were created.

In utilizing the Martin-Quinn scores, I began with the mean estimate of the score for each justice in each term, the score that Martin and Quinn recommend using. In each non-unanimous decision, I then compared the median of the mean estimates for the justices on each side—in free expression, for instance, the side that favored the party with a free expression claim or the side that opposed the claimant. I chose the median rather than the mean in order to reduce the impact of the exaggerated scores for extreme justices. As noted earlier, in takings I used the justices' votes on the takings claim rather than their votes on the outcome of the case for the parties.

Thus, for each case there was a score for the ideological difference between the justices on each side. A positive difference indicated that the justices who supported someone who made a takings claim, a criminal defendant, or a free expression claimant were more liberal than the justices on the other side.

For any set of cases that I analyzed, I summarized the difference scores from individual cases in multiple ways. The first was the mean of the difference scores across those cases. The others involved categorization of scores. Most often, I created a simple dichotomy. How frequently were the justices supporting the rights claimant more liberal than the justices opposing the claimant, and how often were they more conservative? I made considerable use of this measure to show the overall pattern of polarity over time. Occasionally I put scores into more than two categories in order to show patterns of polarity in greater detail. Undoubtedly, the imperfect linearity of the Martin-Quinn scores affects these finer distinctions more than the simple dichotomy. But the distribution of decisions across the categories still provides useful information about the ideological polarity of those decisions.

For the 1910–36 Terms of the Court, for which Martin-Quinn scores were not yet available when I completed the book, I used two other measures of the justices' ideological positions. Donald Leavitt developed measures for the 1910–20 Terms on the basis of dimensional analysis of the justices' votes—one measure for the 1910–15 Terms, the other for the 1916–20 Terms.[151] For the 1921–36 Terms, I used Eloise Snyder's division of the justices into three ideological "cliques" for each natural court on the basis of her own dimensional analysis of their votes in cases interpreting constitutional amendments.[152] These measures can be used to gain a picture of the polarity of the justices' votes on an issue in the period for which Martin-Quinn scores are not available.

Because these scores are not on the same scales as the Martin-Quinn scores (or as each other), I did not try to compare the magnitudes of the differences between justices on the two sides between periods in which different measures were used. But I did track the dichotomous orientation of the Court's decisions on an issue over periods that used the three different measures, and these comparisons

151. Leavitt (1970), 146, 186. Leavitt developed several measures. The one that I used is the first principal axis loadings from Q-analysis, which seems to capture the overall pattern of ideological voting best.

152. Snyder (1958), 235. I gave numerical scores to each clique. I treated the intervals between liberal and moderate cliques and between moderate and conservative cliques as equal. Because there were only three possible scores for any period, in a few cases the medians for the justices on the two sides were the same. I broke that tie with the mean. The one case in which the means for the two sides were also the same was not used in the analysis of polarity.

were important to the analyses of criminal justice and takings. Thus, the comparability of the measures is a potential concern.

The Leavitt measure consists of interval-level scores based on dimensional analyses of all votes, so these scores seem broadly comparable—though certainly not identical—with the Martin-Quinn scores. The Snyder measure differs from both the other measures in that it was based on a subset of decisions and differences among justices were simplified by placing justices in three ordinal categories (occasionally in two). Thus, the comparability question is more serious for the Snyder measure.

It was possible to compare the results based on Snyder scores and the Martin-Quinn scores directly, because the Snyder scores extend beyond the 1936 Term. For free expression cases in the 1937–45 Terms, I computed the difference in the mean Snyder scores between the two sides, using the mean rather than the median because Snyder's grouping of justices into categories produced some ties between the two sides when the median was used. The correlation between the Martin-Quinn difference in median and the Snyder difference in mean was .750. Of the twenty-seven non-unanimous decisions in that period, all but one had the same dichotomous ideological polarity with the two measures. This result indicates a high level of comparability in the patterns that the two measures identify, though it does not eliminate the need for caution in comparing time periods in which different measures were employed.

## Amicus Curiae Participation

Amicus curiae briefs in the Supreme Court can be a significant source of information for the justices. Aside from providing arguments about the merits of cases in terms of law and policy, they inform the justices about how political and social groups perceive their stakes in a case. As a result, amicus briefs facilitate responses to cases on the basis of justices' affect toward those groups. In turn, the lineup of amicus briefs in a case serves as a useful indicator of the justices' perceptions of the stakes in that case for social and political groups. Thus, interest group participation in amicus briefs is a valuable resource for the research in this book, one that I used in the analysis of each issue.

I sought to identify amicus briefs filed at the merits stage of decision in all takings and free expression cases. Although I gathered information on amicus briefs in free expression and takings prior to the 1946 Term, analysis was limited to the 1946–2012 Terms because of the paucity of amicus briefs prior to that time. In criminal justice, because of the large number of cases and the small numbers of amicus briefs for most of the study period, I gathered amicus information for only a sample of the cases decided in the 1946–2012 Terms. That sample included all cases involving white-collar crimes or defendants acting on behalf of businesses and an equal number of other cases, matched with the white-collar and business cases by time of decision. This sampling scheme was used because of the importance of white-collar and business cases for understanding of the Court's polarity in criminal justice.

Identification of the groups that submit amicus briefs is a more complicated task than it initially appears to be. In its bound volumes, the U.S. Reports lists amicus briefs, but it usually provides the name of only the first signer of a brief, it does not always indicate which side a brief takes even when a brief is clearly on one side, and it simply omits some briefs. To gain fuller information on amicus briefs, I supplemented the U.S. Reports with other sources: the collections of briefs in Lexis-Nexis in the period for which they are available, the Court's docket sheets in the period for which they are available, and the microfiche *United States Supreme Court Records and Briefs* throughout the study period. For decisions too recent to be in the bound volumes of the U.S. Reports, with their lists of amicus briefs, I relied on these other sources.

Briefs were coded for the side they took. Briefs in which the U.S. Reports did not indicate a side, or that were not in the Reports, were read to determine which side they took. Many briefs indicate on the cover which side they are taking. Other briefs were read to determine whether the body of the brief was explicit as to which side it supported. Briefs that did not indicate which side they took were coded as "neither." This information was compiled to provide the total numbers of briefs and the numbers on each side and to characterize the positions of specific groups and types of groups in individual cases and across cases.

Even with the use of multiple sources, full information about some briefs was unavailable. For that reason, and because of ambiguities in some of the information used, there undoubtedly are errors in the data on amicus briefs. But those errors are infrequent, so they should not affect any broad patterns in the data.

## Certiorari Petitions and Appeals

Because the mix of cases that the Supreme Court decides on an issue can affect the ideological polarity of that issue, it is worthwhile to examine the cases in which certiorari petitions and appeals are brought to the Court. Doing so allows consideration of the relationship between the potential agenda created by litigants and the actual agenda.

Paid petitions for certiorari and appeals have been catalogued in the print version of *United States Law Week* for several decades and in an online version of *Law Week* since the 1996 Term. Because the preponderance of petitions in criminal cases comes from indigent defendants in the current era, *Law Week* is not a good source of information on the composition of petitions on that issue. In any event, because defendants who were sentenced to substantial prison terms have strong incentives to bring petitions, large and heterogeneous sets of criminal cases come to the Court each term. As a result, there is no need to verify the Court's capacity to determine the composition of its agenda in this field.

In takings and freedom of expression, the keyword search function in the online version of *Law Week* makes it possible to identify takings cases and cases involving freedom of speech or freedom of the press. On those two issues I analyzed petitions submitted in the first six months of the 1996, 2001, 2006, and 2011 Terms, and I coded variables related to the type of case and litigant that were also coded for cases decided on the merits. Where the case summaries in *Law Week* provided insufficient information for coding, I used lower-court opinions and the briefs that were available in the micro-fiche *United States Supreme Court Records and Briefs* cases and in Lexis. (Briefs were unavailable in either source for some 2011 Term cases, so some data were missing.)

For terms prior to 1996, the print version of *Law Week* is not very useful for identifying takings cases, which are submerged within several categories of cases. Thus, this period could not be analyzed. Freedom of expression cases are also divided among several categories in the print version, but cross-references make it possible to identify what appear to be the great majority of cases. Thus, I analyzed free expression petitions in the first six months of the 1966, 1976, and 1986 Terms. However, the possibility that the identified cases were not fully representative of all petitions in freedom of expression required some caution in interpreting patterns in the subject matter of these petitions. More broadly, analysis of certiorari petitions for only a limited portion of the study period allows only a partial picture of the impact of case selection by the Court.

## Other Case Attributes

On each issue, I coded attributes of cases that were potentially relevant to explaining the Court's ideological polarity and changes in that polarity. Supreme Court opinions in cases were the basic source of information for this coding, though other sources (most often lower-court opinions) were occasionally used to fill in gaps.

Each attribute presented its own coding challenges. There were two general challenges. One is that there were some instances in which information was too limited to make a confident judgment about an attribute in a specific case. The other and more important is that some cases did not fit comfortably within a single coding category. This situation sometimes arose because of inevitable ambiguities in the definitions of categories. In other instances, a case was mixed. For instance, for attributes of litigants, multiple parties on one side of a case might fit into different categories. In all these instances, my rule was to put a case in the category that best characterized the case as a whole. To state the obvious, there is considerable room to disagree with my judgments about some attributes for some cases.

### FREEDOM OF EXPRESSION

The most basic attribute was the *type of question* that the Court addressed. Cases were divided into ten broad categories, most of which had subsets, and a miscellaneous category. Some of the categories were familiar ones, such as national security, libel, and obscenity. Others were less familiar, such as government funding/employment and mainstream politics.

Free expression *claimants* were put into eleven categories on the basis of the roles that were related to their speech activities. Individuals were placed in six categories, such as government employees, consumers, and participants in politics; organizations and people associated with them were placed in five categories, such as news media, other businesses, and political organizations. There were "other" categories for individuals and for organizations.

The *countervailing value* in a case was the justification for limiting expression. There were fifteen categories for countervailing values, such as avoiding offensiveness, protecting reputations, and serving the interests of government as an employer. The countervailing value is not always explicit in the justices' opinions, but most of the time it was clear. The justification did not necessarily coincide with what appeared to be the actual motives of those who sought to limit expression in the circumstances of a case. A miscellaneous category included a few cases in which no legitimate countervailing value could be identified.

The *ideological coloration* of the expression involved in a case related to the speaker who was making a free expression claim or, where there was no actual speaker involved in a case, the kinds of speakers at whom a challenged policy was aimed. Ideological coloration was defined in two ways, designated as broad and narrow. For both variables, there were three categories: left, right, and neither.

For the narrow variable, expression was put into the left or right categories only when the speech was directly political and when the speaker or speakers in a case clearly fit on one side of the ideological spectrum. Based on this rule, a high proportion of cases did not fit into the left and right categories. When there was an actual speaker in a case, as there was the great majority of the time, the coding was based on that speaker rather than on the potential long-term beneficiary of a pro-expression decision. One subcategory on the left, the Communist Party and associated groups, required special handling because many people who challenged policies aimed at those groups were not actual members of, or even sympathetic with, those groups. But because of the aims behind these policies, such claimants were put in this category. Extreme right groups were not put in the right category because of traditional liberal support for their free expression rights; there were few cases involving the extreme right.

For the broad variable, all left and right cases by the narrow definition remained in those categories. In addition, all cases in which free expression claims were made by labor unions, leaders, or members were put in the left category, and all claims by businesses or businesspeople other than the news media were put in the right category. Cases in which labor or business acted in a political role were already classified as left or right for the narrow variable, so the broad variable differs by including labor and business when they engaged in non-political speech.

### CRIMINAL JUSTICE

The *type of question* that the Court addressed in a case was dichotomized as substantive or procedural. For the most part, this dichotomy is easy to apply. Cases in categories that involve definitions of criminal offenses and sentencing standards under federal law clearly are substantive. Similarly, cases in categories involving criminal procedure under the Constitution, federal statutes, or federal rules clearly are procedural. But more ambiguous are cases involving the constitutional rights of defendants that have strong substantive elements, primarily those arising under the Eighth Amendment.

Following convention, I treated all cases involving constitutional rights as procedural.[153]

The *level of prosecution* was dichotomized as federal or state. Prosecutions in the District of Columbia and the territories were treated as federal. There were a few cases involving extradition to other nations; these were counted as neither state nor federal.

A third dichotomy was between *white-collar crimes* and other offenses. As noted in chapter 3, there is an array of definitions of white-collar crime; I adopted the definition that white-collar crime involves an effort to obtain financial gain without physical force or the threat of force. That definition is reflected in the list of white-collar offenses compiled by the Legal Information Institute at Cornell University,[154] a list used in another study of the Supreme Court.[155] With a few additions of offenses similar to those on the list, I adopted the Institute's definition. One ambiguous category of cases arises from charges under federal tax laws that are aimed at illegal activity of other types—typically liquor, drug, or gambling offenses. Although tax offenses ordinarily are white-collar, I did not treat cases in this category as white-collar. When there were multiple charges against a defendant, a case was counted as white-collar if any of the offenses were white-collar.

The final dichotomy was between *business crimes* and other crimes. An offense was treated as a business crime if any defendant was a named business, a business proprietor acting in a business capacity, or another individual acting on behalf of a business. Businesses were defined broadly to include any economic enterprise, such as farms. But an entity was not treated as a business if it was illegal by definition, such as an organization created to trade in illegal drugs.

153. For the 1946–2012 Terms, cases were coded as substantive or procedural on the basis of the issue coding in the Supreme Court Database. In the criminal procedure issue area, from which the preponderance of cases come, issues 10010-10370 and 10580-10600 were coded as procedural; 10380-10570 were coded as substantive. For cases in other issue areas in the Database, the content of cases was examined to determine whether a particular category was predominantly substantive or procedural. Similar criteria were applied to cases in the 1910–45 Terms.

154. The list is at http://www.law.cornell.edu/wex/white-collar_crime.

155. L. Epstein, Landes, and Posner (2013a), 360.

I created three other variables relating to white-collar and business status. One was whether there was a white-collar defendant who held a high position in a business. The other two were combinations of the white-collar and business categories: whether the defendant was either business or white-collar and whether the defendant fell in both categories. These variables were used in some analyses. Those analyses are not presented in the text because their results did not add substantial information beyond what the analyses with white-collar and business variables provided.

### TAKINGS

*Claimants* in takings cases were put into six categories. "Business" and "company" are distinguished from each other by whether the claimant involved in business activity was a named company or an individual. "Individual or business" is an individual for whom there was insufficient information to determine whether the individual was engaged in a business activity. When there were multiple claimants that fell into different categories, company took precedence over business and organizations took precedence over individuals. "Indian tribe or Native American" includes all Native Americans whose property rights are related to tribal lands. "Individual" is a residual category for individuals who do not fit into other categories. "Other" includes governments, private organizations other than companies, and plots of land.

In coding of *legal question*, I started with the standard categories described in the text: whether there was a taking, whether the taking was for a public use, and whether adequate compensation was provided. The first category was divided in two between regulatory takings and other takings. In regulatory takings, property remains in an owner's hand but the government issued rules for how that property could be used and the question is whether a taking occurred.

For the *political issue* category, environmental policy includes cases in which the claimant challenged a policy aimed at protecting the environment. Environmental protection was defined in terms of the goals of legislation that was enacted beginning in the 1970s.

Land-use regulations that might have an indirect impact on environmental goals were not put in this category. It would have been possible for pre-1970s cases to be defined as environmental, working backwards from the goals of later environmental laws, but in practice no cases prior to the late 1970s fit into this category. "Other liberal policy" includes challenges to regulations that were designed to advance non-environmental policies generally defined as liberal. Examples include racial equality, freedom of expression, rent control, and legal assistance to low-income individuals.

## Analyses in Chapter 5

The analyses that were used in the discussions of several issues in chapter 5 were more limited than those in chapters 2–4. Those analyses generally focused on the overall polarity of an issue during the period that was examined and comparisons of the polarity of subsets of cases.

Like the analyses presented more extensively in the earlier chapters, each of the analyses in chapter 5 had its own attributes. Those issue-specific attributes are described in the discussions of each issue. However, the methodology for identification of the ideological polarity of issues and of subsets of cases within issues was the same as that used in earlier chapters. Thus the direction and strength of that polarity can be compared across all the issues analyzed in the book.

As in the analyses of freedom of expression and criminal justice, the identification of relevant cases and the coding of justices' votes were based in part on the Supreme Court Database. On the whole, I relied more on the Database for the analyses in chapter 5 than in those earlier analyses. (The analysis of takings was not based on the Database at all.) As a result, those analyses reflect the coding choices that were made in building the Database more than do the analyses in chapters 2 and 3. However, in addition to coding new variables to capture relevant case attributes, I usually created my own sets of cases by reading the cases that were coded under one or more categories of the "issue" variable in the Database and

deleting those cases that did not match my own definition of the
issue to be analyzed.

## A Note on Significance Tests

The book's analyses of the sources and mechanisms of ideological
polarity include many bivariate analyses of questions such as how the
polarity of an issue has changed over time, how attributes of cases
on an issue have changed, and how case attributes relate to polarity.
There are also some multivariate analyses of potential determinants
of polarity.

The usual practice would be to report tests of the statistical
significance of relationships in these analyses. That practice has
received considerable criticism, with many statistical methodolo-
gists arguing that significance tests and standard criteria for identification of significant relationships are inappropriate under most
conditions.[156] The rationales for those criticisms are especially per-
suasive as they apply to the set of analyses that is presented in this
book. These analyses are used to explore possible relationships
between variables, and I give the most attention to analyses whose
results help in understanding the bases for ideological polarity and
for changes in that polarity. That approach creates the kinds of
biases that critics of significance tests have identified and warned
against, so presentation of significance levels would be misleading.
Instead, I focus on the strength of relationships, keeping in mind
the numbers of cases that are the subject of an analysis and noting where small numbers of cases require caution in interpreting
a relationship.

The inquiries in chapters 2–4 each involve examination of an
array of quantitative and qualitative data as a means to probe the
book's concerns. It is the aggregate of those analyses that provides
a picture of how and why that polarity changed and, more broadly,
what sources and mechanisms are responsible for the polarity of
an issue at any given time. With or without significance tests for

---

156. Greenland et al. (2016); Wasserstein and Lazar (2016).

particular quantitative analyses, drawing inferences from the analyses necessarily involves judgment. In this and other respects, my goal was to provide readers with sufficient information to reach their own judgments about the conclusions that can be drawn from the evidence that I present.

# REFERENCES

Abrams, Floyd. 2013. *Friend of the Court: On the Front Lines with the First Amendment.* New Haven, CT: Yale University Press.

Adams, Greg D. 1997. "Abortion: Evidence of an Issue Evolution." *American Journal of Political Science* 41: 718–37.

Anderson, Martin. 1964. *The Federal Bulldozer: A Critical Analysis of Urban Renewal, 1949–1962.* Cambridge, MA: M.I.T. Press.

Anderson, Michelle J. 2002. "From Chastity Requirement to Sexuality License: Sexual Consent and a New Rape Shield Law." *George Washington Law Review* 70: 51–162.

Asher, Herbert B., and Herbert F. Weisberg. 1978. "Voting Change in Congress: Some Dynamic Perspectives on an Evolutionary Process." *Midwest Journal of Political Science* 22: 391–425.

Associated Press. 2016a. Associated Press/NORC Poll, January 2016, produced by National Opinion Research Center.

Associated Press. 2016b. Associated Press/NORC Poll, February 2016, produced by National Opinion Research Center.

Auerbach, Jerold S. 1966. *Labor and Liberty: The La Follette Committee and the New Deal.* Indianapolis: Bobbs Merrill.

Avery, Michael, and Danielle McLaughlin. 2013. *The Federalist Society: How Conservatives Took the Law Back from Liberals.* Nashville: Vanderbilt University Press.

Baer, Judith A. 1978. *The Chains of Protection: The Judicial Response to Women's Labor Legislation.* Westport, CT: Greenwood Press.

Bailey, Michael A. 2007. "Comparable Preference Estimates across Time and Institutions for the Congress and Presidency." *American Journal of Political Science* 351: 433–48.

Bailey, Michael A. 2013. "Is Today's Court the Most Conservative in Sixty Years? Challenges and Opportunities in Measuring Judicial Preferences." *Journal of Politics* 75: 821–34.

Bailey, Michael A., Brian Kamoie, and Forrest Maltzman. 2005. "Signals from the Tenth Justice: The Political Role of the Solicitor General in Supreme Court Decision Making." *American Journal of Political Science* 49: 72–85.

Bailey, Michael A., and Forrest Maltzman. 2011. *The Constrained Court: Law, Politics, and the Decisions Justices Make.* Princeton, NJ: Princeton University Press.

Balkin, Jack M. 1990. "Some Realism about Pluralism: Legal Realist Approaches to the First Amendment." *Duke Law Journal* 1990: 375–430.

Balkin, Jack M. 1993. "Ideological Drift and the Struggle over Meaning." *Connecticut Law Review* 25: 869–91.

Balkin, Jack M. 2001. "*Bush v. Gore* and the Boundary between Law and Politics." *Yale Law Journal* 110: 1407–58.

Balkin, Jack M., and Sanford Levinson. 2001. "Understanding the Constitutional Revolution." *Virginia Law Review* 87: 1045–104.

Barkow, Rachel E. 2006. "Originalists, Politics, and Criminal Law on the Rehnquist Court." *George Washington Law Review* 74: 1043–77.

Bartels, Brandon L. 2009. "The Constraining Capacity of Legal Doctrine on the U.S. Supreme Court." *American Political Science Review* 103: 474–95.

Baum, Lawrence. 2006. *Judges and Their Audiences: A Perspective on Judicial Behavior.* Princeton, NJ: Princeton University Press.

Baum, Lawrence. 2011. *Specializing the Courts.* Chicago: University of Chicago Press.

Baum, Lawrence. 2016. *The Supreme Court,* 12th ed. Washington, DC: CQ Press.

Baybeck, Brady, and William Lowry. 2000. "Federalism Outcomes and Ideological Preferences: The U.S. Supreme Court and Preemption Cases." *Publius* 30(3): 73–97.

Benedict, Jeff. 2009. *Little Pink House: A True Story of Defiance and Courage.* New York: Grand Central Publishing.

Berger, Lawrence. 1995. "Public Use, Substantive Due Process and Takings—An Integration." *Nebraska Law Review* 74: 843–85.

Berkman, Michael B. 1993. *The State Roots of National Politics: Congress and the Tax Agenda, 1978–1986.* Pittsburgh: University of Pittsburgh Press.

Bernstein, David E. 2003. *You Can't Say That!: The Growing Threat to Civil Liberties from Antidiscrimination Laws.* Washington, DC: Cato Institute.

Black, Ryan C., and Ryan J. Owens. 2012. *The Solicitor General and the United States Supreme Court: Executive Branch Influence and Judicial Decisions.* New York: Cambridge University Press.

Black, Ryan C., Ryan J. Owens, Justin Wedeking, and Patrick C. Wohlfarth. 2016. *U.S. Supreme Court Opinions and Their Audiences.* New York: Cambridge University Press.

Bollinger, Lee C., and Geoffrey R. Stone. 2002. "Dialogue." In *Eternally Vigilant: Free Speech in the Modern Era,* ed. Lee C. Bollinger and Geoffrey R. Stone, 1–31. Chicago: University of Chicago Press.

Boyd, Christina L., Lee Epstein, and Andrew D. Martin. 2010. "Untangling the Causal Effects of Sex on Judging." *American Journal of Political Science* 54: 389–411.

Braeman, John. 1988. *Before the Civil Rights Revolution: The Old Court and Individual Rights.* New York: Greenwood Press.

Braithwaite, John. 1993. "Review Essay: Crime and the Average American." *Law and Society Review* 27: 215–31.

Buckley, William F., Jr., ed. 1962. *The Committee and Its Critics: A Calm Review of the House Committee on Un-American Activities.* Chicago: Henry Regnery.

Burns, John W. 1997. "Party Policy Change: The Case of the Democrats and Taxes, 1956–68." *Party Politics* 3: 513–32.

Campbell, Amy Leigh. 2002. "Raising the Bar: Ruth Bader Ginsburg and the ACLU Women's Rights Project." *Texas Journal of Women and the Law* 11: 157–243.

Campbell, Angus, Philip E. Converse, Warren E. Miller, and Donald E. Stokes. 1960. *The American Voter.* New York: John Wiley and Sons.

Carmines, Edward G., and James A. Stimson. 1989. *Issue Evolution: Race and the Transformation of American Politics.* Princeton, NJ: Princeton University Press.

Carp, Robert A., Kenneth L. Manning, and Ronald Stidham. 2009. "The Decision-Making Behavior of George W. Bush's Judicial Appointees." *Judicature* 92: 312–19.

Casillas, Christopher J., Peter K. Enns, and Patrick C. Wohlfarth. 2011. "How Public Opinion Constrains the U.S. Supreme Court." *American Journal of Political Science* 55: 74–88.

Castleton, Tom. 1992. "Claims Court Crusader: Chief Judge Smith Puts Property Rights Up Front." *Legal Times*, August 17, 1, 16–17.

Cawley, R. McGreggor. 1993. *Federal Land, Western Anger: The Sagebrush Rebellion and Environmental Politics.* Lawrence: University Press of Kansas.

Cheek, Kyle, and Anthony Champagne. 2005. *Judicial Politics in Texas: Partisanship, Money, and Politics in State Courts.* New York: Peter Lang.

Clark, Tom S. 2011. *The Limits of Judicial Independence.* New York: Cambridge University Press.

Clark, Tom S., and Benjamin Lauderdale. 2010. "Locating Supreme Court Opinions in Doctrine Space." *American Journal of Political Science* 54: 871–90.

Clarke, Stevens H., and Gary G. Koch. 1976. "The Influence of Income and Other Factors on Whether Criminal Defendants Go to Prison." *Law and Society Review* 11: 57–92.

Cloud, Morgan. 1996. "The Fourth Amendment during the *Lochner* Era: Privacy, Property, and Liberty in Constitutional Theory." *Stanford Law Review* 48: 555–631.

Cohen, Geoffrey L. 2003. "Party over Policy: The Dominating Impact of Group Influence on Political Beliefs." *Journal of Personality and Social Psychology* 85: 808–22.

Cole, David. 1999. *No Equal Justice: Race and Class in the American Criminal Justice System.* New York: New Press.

Collins, Ronald K. L. 2012. "Exceptional Freedom—The Roberts Court, the First Amendment, and the New Absolutism." *Albany Law Review* 76: 409–66.

Congressional Research Service. 2013. *The Constitution of the United States of America: Analysis and Interpretation, Centennial Edition, Interim Edition.* Washington, DC: Government Printing Office.

Congressional Research Service. 2016. *The Constitution of the United States of America: Analysis and Interpretation, Centennial Edition, Interim Edition.* Washington, DC: Government Printing Office.

Conover, Pamela Johnston. 1984. "The Influence of Group Identifications on Political Perception and Evaluation." *Journal of Politics* 46: 760–85.

Conover, Pamela Johnston. 1988. "The Role of Social Groups in Political Thinking." *British Journal of Political Science* 19 (January): 51–76.

Conover, Pamela Johnston, and Stanley Feldman. 1984. "Group Identification, Values, and the Nature of Political Beliefs." *American Politics Research* 12: 151–75.

Converse, Philip E. 1964. "The Nature of Belief Systems in Mass Publics." In David E. Apter, ed., *Ideology and Discontent*, 206–61. New York: Free Press.

Coombs, Clyde H. 1964. *A Theory of Data.* New York: John Wiley and Sons.

Corwin, Edward S. 1909. "The Supreme Court and the Fourteenth Amendment." *Michigan Law Review* 7: 643–72.

Coyle, Marcia. 1997. "Fight over Plan to Widen Claims Court Jurisdiction." *National Law Journal*, September 29, A10.

Crespin, Michael H., David W. Rohde, and Ryan J. Vander Wielen. 2011. "Measuring Variations in Party Unity Voting: An Assessment of Agenda Effects." *Party Politics* 19: 432–57.

Crespo, Andrew Manuel. 2016. "Regaining Perspective: Constitutional Criminal Adjudication in the U.S. Supreme Court." *Minnesota Law Review* 100: 1985–2042.

Davis, Michael J., and Robert L. Glicksman. 1989. "To the Promised Land: A Century of Wandering and a Final Homeland for the Due Process and Taking Clauses." *Oregon Law Review* 68: 393–458.

Dawley, Alan. 2003. *Changing the World: American Progressives in War and Revolution.* Princeton, NJ: Princeton University Press.

Delgado, Richard. 1982. "Words That Wound: A Tort Action for Racial Insults, Epithets, and Name-Calling." *Harvard Civil Rights-Civil Liberties Law Review* 17: 133–81.

Derthick, Martha, and Paul J. Quirk. 1985. *The Politics of Deregulation.* Washington, DC: Brookings Institution.

Devine, Christopher John. 2011. "Ideological Social Identity: How Psychological Attachment to Ideological Groups Shapes Political Attitudes and Behaviors." PhD dissertation, Ohio State University.

Devine, Christopher J. 2015. "Ideological Social Identity: Psychological Attachment to Ideological In-Groups as a Political Phenomenon and a Behavioral Influence." *Political Behavior* 37: 509–35.

Dickinson, W. B., Jr. 1963. "Urban Renewal under Fire." *Editorial Research Reports 1963*, vol. 2. Washington, DC: CQ Press.

Dinnerstein, Leonard. 1968. *The Leo Frank Case.* New York: Columbia University Press.

Dorsen, Norman, and Joel Gora. 1982. "Free Speech, Property, and the Burger Court: Old Values, New Balances." *Supreme Court Review* 1982: 195–241.

Dowd, Maureen. 1988. "Bush Portrays His Opponent as Sympathetic to Criminals." *New York Times,* October 8, 35.

Downs, Donald Alexander. 1985. *Nazis in Skokie: Freedom, Community, and the First Amendment.* Notre Dame, IN: University of Notre Dame Press.

Druckman, James N., Erik Peterson, and Rune Slothuus. 2013. "How Elite Partisan Polarization Affects Public Opinion Formation." *American Political Science Review* 107: 57–79.

Ducat, Craig R., and Robert L. Dudley. 1987. "Dimensions Underlying Economic Policymaking in the Early and Later Burger Courts." *Journal of Politics* 49 (May): 521–39.

Dudley, Robert L., and Craig R. Ducat. 1986. "The Supreme Court and Economic Liberalism." *Western Political Quarterly* 39: 236–49.

Echeverria, John D. 1997. "The Politics of Property Rights." *Oklahoma Law Review* 50: 351–75.

Edelhertz, Herbert. 1970. *The Nature, Impact and Prosecution of White Collar Crime.* Washington, DC: U.S. Department of Justice.

Edelman, Paul H., David E. Klein, and Stefanie A. Lindquist. 2008. "Measuring Deviations from Expected Voting Patterns on Collegial Votes." *Journal of Empirical Legal Studies* 5: 819–52.

Edelman, Paul H., David E. Klein, and Stefanie A. Lindquist. 2012. "Consensus, Disorder, and Ideology on the Supreme Court." *Journal of Empirical Legal Studies* 9: 129–48.

Ely, James W., Jr. 1996. "The Fuller Court and Takings Jurisprudence." *Journal of Supreme Court History* 2: 120–35.

Ely, James W., Jr. 2001. *Railroads and American Law.* Lawrence: University Press of Kansas.

Ely, James W., Jr. 2008. *The Guardian of Every Other Right: A Constitutional History of Property Rights.* New York: Oxford University Press.

Emerson, Thomas I. 1970. *The System of Freedom of Expression.* New York: Random House.

Enns, Peter K., and Patrick C. Wohlfarth. 2013. "The Swing Justice." *Journal of Politics* 75: 1089–107.

Epstein, Lee, and Jack Knight. 1998. *The Choices Justices Make.* Washington, DC: CQ Press.

Epstein, Lee, William M. Landes, and Richard A. Posner. 2013a. *The Behavior of Federal Judges: A Theoretical and Empirical Study of Rational Choice.* Cambridge, MA: Harvard University Press.

Epstein, Lee, William M. Landes, and Richard A. Posner. 2013b. "How Business Fares in the Supreme Court." *Minnesota Law Review* 97: 1431–72.

Epstein, Lee, Christopher M. Parker, and Jeffrey A. Segal. 2013. "Do Justices Defend the Speech They Hate?: In-Group Bias, Opportunism, and the First Amendment." Paper presented at the annual meeting of the American Political Science Association, Chicago.

Epstein, Lee, and Jeffrey A. Segal. 2000. "Measuring Issue Salience." *American Journal of Political Science* 44: 66–83.

Epstein, Lee, and Jeffrey A. Segal. 2006. "Trumping the First Amendment." *Washington University Journal of Law and Policy* 21: 81–121.

Epstein, Lee, Jeffrey A. Segal, Harold J. Spaeth, and Thomas G. Walker. 2015. *The Supreme Court Compendium,* 6th ed. Los Angeles: CQ Press.

Epstein, Richard A. 1985. *Takings: Private Property and the Power of Eminent Domain.* Cambridge, MA: Harvard University Press.

Erikson, Robert S., Norman R. Luttbeg, and Kent L. Tedin. 1980 *American Public Opinion: Its Origins, Content, and Impact,* 2d ed. New York: John Wiley and Sons.

Estlund, Cynthia L. 1997. "Freedom of Expression in the Workplace and the Problem of Discriminatory Harassment." *Texas Law Review* 75: 687–741.

Farnsworth, Ward. 2005. "Signatures of Ideology: The Case of the Supreme Court's Criminal Docket." *Michigan Law Review* 104: 67–100.

Farnsworth, Ward. 2009. "Dissents against Type." *Minnesota Law Review* 93: 1535–59.

Federico, Christopher M. 2004. "When Do Welfare Attitudes Become Racialized? The Paradoxical Effects of Education." *American Journal of Political Science* 48: 374–91.

Feldman, Stanley. 2013. "Political Ideology." In *Oxford Handbook of Political Psychology*, 2d ed., ed. Leonie Huddy, David O. Sears, and Jack S. Levy, 591–626. New York: Oxford University Press.

Feldman, Stanley, and Christopher Johnston. 2014. "Understanding the Determinants of Political Ideology: Implications of Structural Complexity." *Political Psychology* 35: 337–58.

Feldman, Stephen M. 2013. *Neoconservative Politics and the Supreme Court*. New York: New York University Press.

Feygina, Irina, and Tom R. Tyler. 2009. "Procedural Justice and System-Justifying Motivations." In *Social and Psychological Bases of Ideology and System Justification*, ed. John T. Jost, Aaron C. Kay, and Hulda Thorisdottir, 351–70. New York: Oxford University Press.

Fischel, William A. 1995. *Regulatory Takings: Law, Economics, and Politics*. Cambridge, MA: Harvard University Press.

Fischman, Joshua B. 2015. "Do the Justices Vote Like Policy Makers? Evidence from Scaling the Supreme Court with Interest Groups." *Journal of Legal Studies* 44: S269–93.

Fischman, Joshua B., and Tonja Jacobi. 2016. "The Second Dimension of the Supreme Court." *William and Mary Law Review* 57: 1671–715.

Fischman, Joshua B., and David S. Law. 2009. "What Is Judicial Ideology, and How Should We Measure It?" *Washington University Journal of Law and Policy* 29: 133–214.

Fiss, Owen M. 1986. "Free Speech and Social Structure." *Iowa Law Review* 71: 1405–25.

Flamm, Michael W. 2005. *Law and Order: Street Crime, Civil Unrest, and the Crisis of Liberalism in the 1960s*. New York: Columbia University Press.

Fordham, Benjamin O. 2007. "The Evolution of Republican and Democratic Positions on Cold War Military Spending: A Historical Puzzle." *Social Science History* 31: 603–36.

Fortner, Michael Javen. 2015. *Black Silent Majority: The Rockefeller Drug Laws and the Politics of Punishment*. Cambridge, MA: Harvard University Press.

Fried, Charles. 1991. *Order and Law: Arguing the Reagan Revolution—A Firsthand Account*. New York: Simon and Schuster.

Friedman, Barry. 2009. *The Will of the People: How Public Opinion Has Influenced the Supreme Court and Shaped the Meaning of the Constitution*. New York: Farrar, Strauss and Giroux.

Friedman, Lawrence M. 1986. "A Search for Seizure: *Pennsylvania Coal Co. v. Mahon* in Context," *Law and History Review* 4: 1–22.

Friedman, Lawrence M. 1993. *Crime and Punishment in American History*. New York: Basic Books.

Friedman, Lawrence M., and Robert V. Percival. 1981. *The Roots of Justice: Crime and Punishment in Alameda County, California 1870–1910*. Chapel Hill: University of North Carolina Press.

Funk, Carolyn L., Kevin B. Smith, John R. Alford, Matthew V. Hibbing, Nicholas R. Eaton, Robert E. Krueger, Lindon J. Eaves, and John R. Hibbing. 2013. "Genetic and Environmental Transmission of Political Orientations." *Political Psychology* 34: 805–19.

Gaba, Jeffrey M. 2007. "Taking 'Justice and Fairness' Seriously: Distributive Justice and the Takings Clause." *Creighton Law Review* 40(3): 569–94.

Galanter, Marc. 1974. "Why the 'Haves' Come Out Ahead: Speculations on the Limits of Social Change." *Law and Society Review* 9: 95–160.

Garrett, Brandon L. 2011. *Convicting the Innocent: Where Criminal Prosecutions Go Wrong*. Cambridge, MA: Harvard University Press.

Garrett, Brandon L. 2014. *Too Big to Jail: How Prosecutors Compromise with Corporations*. Cambridge, MA: Harvard University Press.

Gelfand, Mark I. 1975. *A Nation of Cities: The Federal Government and Urban America, 1933–1965*. New York: Oxford University Press.

Gerber, Scott Douglas. 1999. *First Principles: The Jurisprudence of Clarence Thomas*. New York: New York University Press.

Gerring, John. 1997. "Ideology: A Definitional Analysis." *Political Research Quarterly* 50: 957–94.

Gerring, John. 1998. *Party Ideologies in America, 1828–1996*. New York: Cambridge University Press.

Gibson, James L. 2012. *Electing Judges: The Surprising Effects of Campaigning on Judicial Legitimacy*. Chicago: University of Chicago Press.

Giles, Micheal W., Bethany Blackstone, and Richard L. Vining. 2008. "The Supreme Court in American Democracy: Unraveling the Linkages between Public Opinion and Judicial Decision Making." *Journal of Politics* 70: 293–306.

Gillman, Howard. 2001. *The Votes That Counted: How the Court Decided the 2000 Presidential Election*. Chicago: University of Chicago Press.

Goldberger, David. 1978. "Skokie: The First Amendment under Attack by Its Friends." *Mercer Law Review* 29: 761–72.

Goldman, Sheldon. 1975. "Voting Behavior on the United States Courts of Appeals Revisited." *American Political Science Review* 69: 491–506.

Gould, Jon B. 2005. *Speak No Evil: The Triumph of Hate Speech Regulation*. Chicago: University of Chicago Press.

Graber, Mark A. 1991. *Transforming Free Speech: The Ambiguous Legacy of Civil Libertarianism*. Berkeley: University of California Press.

Graetz, Michael J., and Linda Greenhouse. 2016. *The Burger Court and the Rise of the Judicial Right*. New York: Simon and Schuster.

Grant, J. Tobin, and Thomas J. Rudolph. 2003. "Value Conflict, Group Affect, and the Issue of Campaign Finance." *American Journal of Political Science* 47: 453–69.

Green, Donald, Bradley Palmquist, and Eric Schickler. 2002. *Partisan Hearts and Minds: Political Parties and the Social Identities of Voters*. New Haven, CT: Yale University Press.

Greenberg, Jack. 1994. *Crusaders in the Courts: How a Dedicated Band of Lawyers Fought for the Civil Rights Revolution*. New York: Basic Books.

Greenburg, Jan Crawford. 2006. "Interview with Chief Justice Roberts." ABC News, November 28, http://abcnews.go.com/Nightline/story?id=2661589&page=6.

Greenhouse, Linda. 2005. *Becoming Justice Blackmun: Harry Blackmun's Supreme Court Journey*. New York: Times Books.

Greenland, Sander, Stephen J. Senn, Kenneth J. Rothman, John B. Carlin, Charles Poole, Steven N. Goodman, and Douglas G. Altman. 2016. "Statistical Tests, $P$-values, Confidence Intervals, and Power: A Guide to Misinterpretations." *American Statistician* 70(2): 1–12. Online Supplement.

Greve, Michael S., and Jonathan Klick. 2006. "Preemption in the Rehnquist Court: A Preliminary Empirical Assessment." *Supreme Court Economic Review* 14: 43–94.

Gries, Peter Hays. 2014. *The Politics of American Foreign Policy: How Ideology Divides Liberals and Conservatives over Foreign Affairs*. Stanford: Stanford University Press.

Grofman, Bernard, and Timothy J. Brazill. 2002. "Identifying the Median Justice on the Supreme Court through Multidimensional Scaling: Analysis of 'Natural Courts' 1953–1991." *Public Choice* 112: 55–79.

Grossman, Joel B. 1969. "A Model for Judicial Policy Analysis: The Supreme Court and the Sit-In Cases." In *Frontiers of Judicial Research*, ed. Joel B. Grossman and Joseph Tanenhaus, 405–60. New York: John Wiley and Sons.

Hagan, John. 2010. *Who Are the Criminals? The Politics of Crime Policy from the Age of Roosevelt to the Age of Reagan*. Princeton, NJ: Princeton University Press.

Hagle, Timothy M., and Harold J. Spaeth. 1992. "The Emergence of a New Ideology: The Business Decisions of the Burger Court." *Journal of Politics* 54: 120–34.

Hagle, Timothy M., and Harold J. Spaeth. 1993. "Ideological Patterns in the Justices' Voting in the Burger Court's Business Cases." *Journal of Politics* 55 (May): 492–505.

Hagner, Paul R., and John C. Pierce. 1982. "Correlative Characteristics of Levels of Conceptualization in the American Public 1956–1976." *Journal of Politics* 44: 779–807.

Hall, Kermit L., and Melvin I. Urofsky. 2011. New York Times v. Sullivan: *Civil Rights, Libel Law, and the Free Press*. Lawrence: University Press of Kansas.

Hall, Livingston. 1937. "The Substantive Law of Crimes—1887–1936." *Harvard Law Review* 50: 616–53.

Ham, Mary Katherine, and Guy Benson. 2015. *End of Discussion: How the Left's Outrage Industry Shuts Down Debate, Manipulates Voters, and Makes America Less Free*. New York: Crown Forum.

Hamilton, Walton. 1957. *The Politics of Industry*. New York: Alfred A. Knopf.

Harbaugh, William H. 1973. *Lawyer's Lawyer: The Life of John W. Davis*. New York: Oxford University Press.

Harbridge, Laurel. 2015. *Is Bipartisanship Dead? Policy Agreement and Agenda-Setting in the House of Representatives*. New York: Cambridge University Press.

Harcourt, Bernard E. 1995. "Imagery and Adjudication in the Criminal Law; The Relationship between Images of Criminal Defendants and Ideologies of Criminal Law in Southern Antebellum and Modern Appellate Decisions," *Brooklyn Law Review* 61: 1165–246.

Harlow, Caroline Wolf. 2000. *Defense Counsel in Criminal Cases*. Washington, DC: Bureau of Justice Statistics, U.S. Department of Justice.

Harrell, Erika, Lynn Langton, Marcus Berzofsky, Lance Couzens, and Hope Smiley-McDonald. 2014. *Household Poverty and Nonfatal Violent Victimization, 2008–2012*. Washington, DC: Bureau of Justice Statistics, U.S. Department of Justice.

Harvey, Anna L. 2013. *A Mere Machine: The Supreme Court, Congress, and American Democracy.*

Harvey, Anna, and Michael J. Woodruff. 2013. "Confirmation Bias in the United States Supreme Court Database." *Journal of Law, Economics, and Organization* 29: 414–59.

Hentoff, Nat. 1992. *Free Speech for Me—but Not for Thee: How the Left and Right Relentlessly Censor Each Other*. New York: HarperCollins.

Hillman, Arye L. 2010. "Expressive Behavior in Economics and Politics." *European Journal of Political Economy* 26: 403–18.

Ho, Daniel E., and Kevin M. Quinn. 2010. "How Not to Lie with Judicial Votes: Misconceptions, Measurement, and Models." *California Law Review* 98: 813–76.

Hogg, Michael A., and Joanne R. Smith. 2007. "Attitudes in Social Context: A Social Identity Perspective." *European Review of Social Psychology* 18: 89–131.

Hollis-Brusky, Amanda. 2015. *Ideas with Consequences: The Federalist Society and the Conservative Counterrevolution*. New York: Oxford University Press.

"House Votes." 1997. In *CQ Almanac 1996*, 52nd ed., edited by Jan Austin, H1-H148. Washington, DC: Congressional Quarterly.

Horwitz, Morton J. 1993. "The Constitution of Change: Legal Fundamentality without Fundamentalism." *Harvard Law Review* 107: 30–117.

Huffman, James L. 1995. "Judge Plager's 'Sea Change' in Regulatory Takings Law." *Fordham Environmental Law Journal* 6: 597–617.

Hutchinson, Dennis J. 1998. *The Man Who Once Was Whizzer White: A Portrait of Justice Byron R. White*. New York: Free Press.

Iyengar, Shanto, Gaurav Sood, and Yphtach Lelkes. 2012. "Affect, Not Ideology: A Social Identity Perspective on Polarization." *Public Opinion Quarterly* 76: 405–31.

Iyengar, Shanto, and Sean Westwood. 2015. "Fear and Loathing across Party Lines: New Evidence on Group Polarization." *American Journal of Political Science* 59: 690–707.

Jackson, Thomas H., and John Calvin Jeffries, Jr. 1979. "Commercial Speech: Economic Due Process and the First Amendment." *Virginia Law Review* 65: 1–41.

Jackson, Robert A., and Thomas M. Carsey. 2002. "Group Effects on Party Identification and Party Coalitions across the United States." *American Politics Research* 30: 66–92.

Jacobs, James B., and Kimberly Potter. 1998. *Hate Crimes: Criminal Law and Identity Politics*. New York: Oxford University Press.

Jacoby, William G. 2014. "Is There a Culture War? Conflicting Value Structures in American Public Opinion." *American Political Science Review* 108: 754–71.

Jennings, M. Kent. 1992. "Ideological Thinking among Mass Publics and Political Elites." *Public Opinion Quarterly* 56: 419–41.

Jewitt, Caitlin E., and Paul Goren. 2016. "Ideological Structure and Consistency in the Age of Polarization." *American Politics Research* 44: 81–105.

Johnson, Donald. 1963. *The Challenge to American Freedoms: World War I and the Rise of the American Civil Liberties Union*. Lexington: University of Kentucky Press.

Jost, John T., Christopher M. Federico, and Jaime L. Napier. 2009. "Political Ideology: Its Structure, Functions, and Elective Affinities." *Annual Review of Psychology* 60: 307–37.

Judd, Dennis R., and Todd Swanstrom. 1998. *City Politics: Private Power and Public Policy*, 2nd ed. New York: Longman.

Kalven, Harry. 1966. *The Negro and the First Amendment*. Chicago: University of Chicago Press.

Kang, Michael S., and Joanna M. Shepherd. 2016. "The Long Shadow of *Bush v. Gore*: Judicial Partisanship in Election Cases." *Stanford Law Review* 68: 1411-52.

Kansal, Tusha. 2005. *Racial Disparity in Sentencing: A Review of the Literature*. Washington, DC: The Sentencing Project.

Karol, David. 2009. *Party Position Change in American Politics: Coalition Management*. New York: Cambridge University Press.

Kastellec, Jonathan P. 2013. "Racial Diversity and Judicial Influence on Appellate Courts." *American Journal of Political Science* 57: 167–83.

Kastellec, Jonathan P., and Jeffrey R. Lax. 2008. "Case Selection and the Study of Judicial Politics." *Journal of Empirical Legal Studies* 5: 407–46.

Katz, Jack. 1979. "Legality and Equality: Plea Bargaining in the Prosecution of White-Collar and Common Crimes." *Law and Society Review* 13: 431–59.

Kearney, Joseph D., and Thomas W. Merrill. 2000. "The Influence of Amicus Curiae Briefs on the Supreme Court." *University of Pennsylvania Law Review* 148: 743–855.

Kendall, Douglas T., and Charles P. Lord. 1998. "The Takings Project: A Critical Analysis and Assessment of the Progress So Far." *Boston College Environmental Affairs Law Review* 25(3): 509–88.

Kennedy, Randall. 1994. "The State, Criminal Law, and Racial Discrimination: A Comment." *Harvard Law Review* 107: 1255–78.

Kerlinger, Fred N. 1984. *Liberalism and Conservatism: The Nature and Structure of Social Attitudes*. Hillsdale, NJ: Lawrence Erlbaum Associates.

Kersch, Ken I. 2004. *Constructing Civil Liberties: Discontinuities in the Development of American Constitutional Law*. New York: Cambridge University Press.

Kersch, Ken I. 2006. "The New Deal Triumph as the End of History? The Judicial Negotiation of Labor Rights and Civil Rights." In *The Supreme Court and American Political Development*, ed. Ronald Kahn and Ken I. Kersch, 169–226. Lawrence: University Press of Kansas.

King, Gary, Michael Tomz, and Jason Wittenberg. 2000. "Making the Most of Statistical Analyses: Improving Interpretation and Presentation." *American Journal of Political Science* 44: 341–55.

King, Gilbert. 2011. "The Man Who Busted the 'Banksters.'" Smithsonian.com, Nov. 11, http://www.smithsonianmag.com/ist/?next=/history/the-man-who-busted-the-banksters-932416/.

King, Gilbert. 2012. *Devil in the Grove: Thurgood Marshall, the Groveland Boys, and the Dawn of a New America.* New York: Harper Collins.

Klarman, Michael J. 2000. "The Racial Origins of Modern Criminal Procedure." *Michigan Law Review* 99: 48–97.

Klein, Ezra. 2012. "Unpopular Mandate." *New Yorker,* June 25, 30–33.

Kmiec, Douglas W. 1992. *The Attorney General's Lawyer: Inside the Meese Justice Department.* New York: Praeger.

Kopko, Kyle C. 2008. "Partisanship Suppressed: Judicial Decision-Making in Ralph Nader's 2004 Ballot Access Litigation." *Election Law Journal* 7: 301–24.

Kopko, Kyle C. 2015. "Litigant Partisan Identity and Challenges to Campaign Finance Policies: An Examination of U.S. District Court Decisions, 1971–2007." *Justice System Journal* 36: 212–32.

Kraft, Michael E., and Norman J. Vig. 2000. "Environmental Policy from the 1970s to 2000: An Overview." In *Environmental Policy: New Directions for the Twenty-First Century,* 4th ed., ed. Norman J. Vig and Michael E. Kraft, 1–31. Washington, DC: CQ Press.

Kritzer, Herbert M. 1978. "Ideology and American Political Elites." *Public Opinion Quarterly* 42: 484–502.

Kritzer, Herbert. 2003. "The Government Gorilla: Why Does Government Come Out Ahead in Appellate Courts?" In *In Litigation: Do the "Haves" Still Come Out Ahead?,* ed. Herbert M. Kritzer and Susan Silbey, 342–70. Stanford: Stanford University Press.

Kritzer, Herbert M. 2015. *Justices on the Ballot: Continuity and Change in State Supreme Court Elections.* New York: Cambridge University Press.

Kuklinski, James H., Daniel S. Metlay, and W. D. Kay. 1982. "Citizen Knowledge and Choices on the Complex Issue of Nuclear Energy." *American Journal of Political Science* 26: 615–42.

Landes, William M., and Richard A. Posner. 2009. "Rational Judicial Behavior: A Statistical Study." *Journal of Legal Analysis* 1: 775–831.

Lane, Robert E. 1973. "Patterns of Political Belief." In *Handbook of Political Psychology,* ed. Jeanne N. Knutson, 83–116. San Francisco: Jossey-Bass.

Lauderdale, Benjamin E., and Tom S. Clark. 2012. "The Supreme Court's Many Median Justices." *American Political Science Review* 106: 847–66.

Lauderdale, Benjamin E., and Tom S. Clark. 2014. "Scaling Politically Meaningful Dimensions Using Texts and Votes." *American Journal of Political Science* 58: 754–71.

Lavine, Amy. 2010. "Urban Renewal and the Story of *Berman v. Parker.*" *Urban Lawyer* 42(2): 423–75.

Lazarus, Richard J. 1997. "Counting Votes and Discounting Holdings in the Supreme Court's Takings Cases." *William and Mary Law Review* 38(3): 1099–141.

Leavitt, Donald Carl. 1970. "Attitudes and Ideology on the White Supreme Court 1910–1920." PhD dissertation, Michigan State University.

Lee, Frances E. 2009. *Beyond Ideology: Politics, Principles, and Partisanship in the U.S. Senate.* Chicago: University of Chicago Press.

Levinson, Sanford. 2001. "Return of Legal Realism." *Nation,* January 8–15, 8.

Levinson, Sanford. 2013. "Same-Sex Marriage Cases," March 28. Posting to Law and Courts Discussion List.

Levitin, Teresa E., and Warren E. Miller. 1979. "Ideological Interpretations of Presidential Elections." *American Political Science Review* 73: 751–71.

Lewis, Neal A. 1993. "2 Years after His Bruising Hearing, Justice Thomas Still Shows the Hurt." *New York Times*, November 27, 6.

Lewis-Beck, Michael S., William G. Jacoby, Helmut Norpoth, and Herbert F. Weisberg. 2008. *The American Voter Revisited*. Ann Arbor: University of Michigan Press.

Light, Michael T. 2014. "The New Face of Legal Inequality: Noncitizens and the Long-Term Trends in Sentencing Disparities across U.S. District Courts, 1992–2009." *Law and Society Review* 48: 447–78.

Lillquist, R. Erik. 1995. "Constitutional Rights at the Junction: The Emergence of the Privilege against Self-Incrimination and the Interstate Commerce Act." *Virginia Law Review* 81: 1989–2042.

Liptak, Adam. 2013. "Friend of the Corporation." *New York Times*, May 5, BU1.

Lloyd, Randall D. 1995. "Separating Partisanship from Party in Judicial Research: Reapportionment in the U.S. District Courts." *American Political Science Review* 89: 413–20.

Long, Carolyn N. 2006. Mapp v. Ohio: *Guarding against Unreasonable Searches and Seizures*. Lawrence: University Press of Kansas.

Lupton, Robert N., William M. Myers, and Judd R. Thornton. 2015. "Political Sophistication and the Dimensionality of Elite and Mass Attitudes, 1980–2004." *Journal of Politics* 77: 368–80.

MacKinnon, Catharine A. 1986. "Pornography as Sex Discrimination." *Law and Inequality* 4: 38–49.

MacKinnon, Catharine A., and Reva B. Siegel, eds. 2004. *Directions in Sexual Harassment Law*. New Haven, CT: Yale University Press.

Malka, Ariel, and Yphtach Lelkes. 2010. "More than Ideology: Conservative-Liberal Identity and Receptivity to Political Cues." *Social Justice Research* 23: 156–88.

Marcuse, Herbert. 1965. "Repressive Tolerance," in Robert Paul Wolff, Barrington Moore, Jr., and Herbert Marcuse, *A Critique of Pure Tolerance*, 81–117. Boston: Beacon Press.

Martin, Andrew D., and Kevin M. Quinn. 2002. "Dynamic Ideal Point Estimation via Markov Chain Monte Carlo for the U.S. Supreme Court, 1953–1999." *Political Analysis* 10: 134–53.

Martin, Andrew D., and Kevin M. Quinn. 2005. "Can Ideal Point Estimates Be Used as Explanatory Variables?", mqscores.berkeley.edu/media/resnote.pdf.

Martin, Jonathan. 2014. "As G.O.P. Wedge, the Common Core Cuts Both Ways." *New York Times*, April 20, A1.

Marzulla, Nancie G. 1995. "The Property Rights Movement: How It Began and Where It Is Headed." In *Land Rights: The 1990s' Property Rights Rebellion*, ed. Bruce Yandle, 1–30. Lanham, MD: Rowman and Littlefield.

Matsuda, Mari J., Charles R. Lawrence III, Richard Delgado, and Kimberlè Williams Crenshaw. 1993. *Words That Wound: Critical Race Theory, Assaultive Speech, and the First Amendment*. Boulder, CO: Westview Press.

Mauro, Tony. 1998. "A Journalist's Perspective," in *The Burger Court: Counter-Revolution or Confirmation?*, ed. Bernard Schwartz, 216–21. New York: Oxford University Press.

Mayhew, David R. 1974. *Congress: The Electoral Connection*. New Haven, CT: Yale University Press.

McClosky, Herbert. 1964. "Consensus and Ideology in American Politics." *American Political Science Review* 58: 361–82.

McClosky, Herbert, Paul J. Hoffmann, and Rosemary O'Hara. 1960. "Conflict and Consensus among Party Leaders and Followers." *American Political Science Review* 54: 406–27.

McClosky, Herbert, and John Zaller. 1984. *The American Ethos: Public Attitudes toward Capitalism and Democracy*. Cambridge, MA: Harvard University Press.

McGuire, Kevin T. 1998. "Explaining Executive Success in the U.S. Supreme Court." *Political Research Quarterly* 51: 505–26.

McGuire, Kevin T., and James A. Stimson. 2004. "The Least Dangerous Branch Revisited: New Evidence on Supreme Court Responsiveness to Public Preferences." *Journal of Politics* 66: 1018–35.

McGuire, Kevin T., George Vanberg, Charles E. Smith, Jr., and Gregory A. Caldeira. 2009. "Measuring Policy Content on the U.S. Supreme Court." *Journal of Politics* 71: 1305–20.

McKenzie, Mark Jonathan. 2012. "The Influence of Partisanship, Ideology, and the Law on Redistricting Decisions in the Federal Courts." *Political Research Quarterly* 65: 799–813.

Meltsner, Michael. 1973. *Cruel and Unusual: The Supreme Court and Capital Punishment*. New York: Random House.

Meltz, Robert. 1991. *When the United States Takes Property: Legal Principles,* rev. ed., Congressional Research Service, Library of Congress, Report 91-339A.

Meltz, Robert. 1995. *The Property Rights Issue*. Congressional Research Service, Library of Congress, Report 95-200A.

Meltz, Robert. 2007. "Takings Law Today: A Primer for the Perplexed." *Ecology Law Quarterly* 34: 307–80.

Meltz, Robert. 2015. *Takings Decisions of the U.S. Supreme Court: A Chronology*. Washington, DC: Congressional Research Service.

Meltz, Robert, Dwight H. Merriam, and Richard M. Frank. 1999. *The Takings Issue: Constitutional Limits on Land Use Control and Environmental Regulation*. Washington, DC: Island Press.

Milkis, Sidney M. 1999. "Introduction." In *Progressivism and the New Democracy*, ed. Sidney M. Milkis and Jerome M. Mileur, 1–39. Amherst: University of Massachusetts Press.

Miller, Banks. 2010. "Describing the State Solicitors General." *Judicature* 93: 238–46.

Miller, Lisa L. 2010. "The Invisible Black Victim: How American Federalism Perpetuates Racial Inequality in Criminal Justice." *Law and Society Review* 44: 805–42.

Moore, W. John. 1992. "'Just Compensation.'" *National Journal*, June 13, 1404–7.

Morgan, Richard E. 1972. *The Supreme Court and Religion*. New York: Free Press.

Morin, Jason L. 2014. "The Voting Behavior of Minority Judges in the U.S. Courts of Appeals: Does the Race of the Claimant Matter?" *American Politics Research* 42: 34–64.

Murakawa, Naomi. 2014. *The First Civil Right: How Liberals Built Prison America*. New York: Oxford University Press.

Murchison, Kenneth M. 1994. *Federal Criminal Law Doctrines: The Forgotten Influence of National Prohibition*. Durham, NC: Duke University Press.

Murphy, Paul L. 1972. *The Meaning of Freedom of Speech: First Amendment Freedoms from Wilson to FDR*. Westport, CT: Greenwood Press.

Murphy, Paul L. 1979. *World War I and the Origin of Civil Liberties in the United States*. New York: W. W. Norton.

Nadler, Janice, and Shari Seidman Diamond. 2008. "Eminent Domain and the Psychology of Property Rights: Proposed Use, Subjective Attachment, and Taker Identity." *Journal of Empirical Legal Studies* 5(4): 713–49.

Nagel, Stuart S. 1961. "Political Party Affiliation and Judges' Affiliations." *American Political Science Review* 55: 843–50.

Nelson, Thomas E., and Donald R. Kinder. 1996. "Issue Frames and Group-Centrism in American Public Opinion." *Journal of Politics* 58: 1055–78.

Noel, Hans. 2013. *Political Ideologies and Political Parties in America*. New York: Cambridge University Press.

Norton, Gale A. 1990. "Takings Analysis of Regulations." *Harvard Journal of Law and Public Policy* 13: 84–90.

Nosek, Brian A., Mahzarin R. Banaji, and John T. Jost. 2009. "The Politics of Intergroup Attitudes." In *Social and Psychological Bases of Ideology and System Justification*, ed. John T. Jost, Aaron C. Kay, and Hulda Thorisdottir, 480–506. New York: Oxford University Press.

Novkov, Julie. 2001. *Constituting Workers, Protecting Women: Gender, Law, and Labor in the Progressive Era and New Deal Years*. Ann Arbor: University of Michigan Press.

Okrent, Daniel. 2010. *Last Call: The Rise and Fall of Prohibition*. New York: Scribner.

Olivetti, Alfred M., Jr., and Jeff Worsham. 2003. *This Land Is Your Land, This Land Is My Land: The Property Rights Movement and Regulatory Takings*. New York: LFB Scholarly Publishing.

*The Onion Book of Known Knowledge*. 2012. New York: Little, Brown.

Pacelle, Richard L., Jr. 1991. *The Transformation of the Supreme Court's Agenda from the New Deal to the Reagan Administration*. Boulder, CO: Westview Press.

Pacelle, Richard L., Jr. 1995. "The Dynamics and Determinants of Agenda Change in the Rehnquist Court." In *Contemplating Courts*, ed. Lee Epstein, 251–74. Washington, DC: CQ Press.

Pacelle, Richard L., Jr. 2003. *Between Law and Politics: The Solicitor General and the Structuring of Race, Gender, and Reproductive Rights Litigation*. College Station: Texas A & M University Press.

Packer, Herbert L. 1968. *The Limits of the Criminal Sanction*. Stanford, CA: Stanford University Press.

Parker, Christopher M. 2011. "Ideological Voting in Supreme Court Federalism Cases, 1953–2007." *Justice System Journal* 32: 206–34.

Peffley, Mark A., and Jon Hurwitz. 1985. "A Hierarchical Model of Attitude Constraint." *American Journal of Political Science* 29: 871–90.

Peltason, J. W. 1997. *Corwin and Peltason's Understanding the Constitution*, 14th ed. Fort Worth: Harcourt Brace.

Peresie, Jennifer L. 2005. "Female Judges Matter: Gender and Collegial Decisionmaking in the Federal Appellate Courts." *Yale Law Journal* 114: 1759–90.

Piety, Tamara R. 2012. *Brandishing the First Amendment: Commercial Expression in America*. Ann Arbor: University of Michigan Press.

Piper, J. Richard. 1997. *Ideologies and Institutions: American Conservative and Liberal Governance Prescriptions since 1933*. Lanham, MD: Rowman and Littlefield.

Poole, Keith T., and Howard Rosenthal. 1997. *Congress: A Political-Economic History of Roll-Call Voting*. New York: Oxford University Press.

Polsky, Andrew J. 1989. "The Odyssey of the Juvenile Court: Policy Failure and Institutional Persistence in the Therapeutic State." *Studies in American Political Development* 3: 157–98.

Pound, Roscoe. 1930. *Criminal Justice in America*. New York: Henry Holt.

Powe, Lucas A., Jr. 2000. *The Warren Court and American Politics*. Cambridge, MA: Harvard University Press.

Powers, Kirsten. 2015. *The Silencing: How the Left Is Killing Free Speech*. Washington, DC: Regnery.

Pralle, Sarah, and Michael W. McCann. 2000. "New Property Rights Debates: The Dialectics of Naming, Blaming, and Claiming." In *Land in the American West: Private Claims and the Common Good*, ed. William G. Robbins and James C. Foster, 53–74. Seattle: University of Washington Press.

Prislin, Radmila, and Wendy Wood. 2005. "Social Influence in Attitudes and Attitude Change." In *The Handbook of Attitudes*, ed. Dolores Albarracin, Blair T. Johnson, and Mark P. Zanna, 671–706. Mahwah, NJ: Lawrence Erlbaum Associates.

Pritchett, C. Herman. 1948. *The Roosevelt Court: A Study in Judicial Politics and Values 1937–1947*. New York: Macmillan.

Provine, Doris Marie. 1980. *Case Selection in the United States Supreme Court*. Chicago: University of Chicago Press.

Rabban, David M. 1997. *Free Speech in Its Forgotten Years*. New York: Cambridge University Press.

Reaves, Brian A. 2013. *Felony Defendants in Large Urban Counties, 2009—Statistical Tables*. Washington, DC: Bureau of Justice Statistics, U.S. Department of Justice.

Reinert, Alexander A. 2010. "Measuring the Success of Bivens Litigation and Its Consequences for the Individual Liability Model." *Stanford Law Review* 62: 809–62.

Richards, Mark J. 2013. *The Politics of Freedom of Expression: The Decisions of the Supreme Court of the United States*. New York: Palgrave Macmillan.

Robinson, Rob, and Brendon Swedlow. 2015. "Toward a Cultural Theory of Judicial Behavior: Identifying and Overcoming Limitations in the Attitudinal Model." Paper presented at the annual meeting of the American Political Science Association, San Francisco.

Rohde, David W., and Harold J. Spaeth. 1976. *Supreme Court Decision Making*. San Francisco: W. H. Freeman.

Rokeach, Milton. 1968. *Beliefs, Attitudes, and Values: A Theory of Organization and Change*. San Francisco: Jossey-Bass.

Rokeach, Milton. 1973. *The Nature of Human Values*. New York: Free Press.

Rose, Carol M. 1984. "*Mahon* Reconstructed: Why the Takings Issue Is Still a Muddle." *Southern California Law Review* 57(4): 561–99.

Ross, Edward Alsworth. 1907. *Sin and Society: An Analysis of Latter-Day Iniquity*. Boston: Houghton Mifflin.

Rossum, Ralph A. 2014. *Understanding Clarence Thomas: The Jurisprudence of Constitutional Restoration*. Lawrence: University Press of Kansas.

Rothman, David J. 1978. "The State as Parent: Social Policy in the Progressive Era." In *Doing Good: The Limits of Benevolence*, by Willard Gaylin, Ira Glasser, Steven Marcus, and David J. Rothman, 67–96. New York: Pantheon.

Sanbonmatsu, Kira. 2002. *Democrats, Republicans, and the Politics of Women's Place*. Ann Arbor: University of Michigan Press.

Sanneh, Kelefa. 2015. "The Hell You Say." *New Yorker*, August 10–17, 30–34.

Schauer, Frederick. 2002. "First Amendment Opportunism." In *Eternally Vigilant: Free Speech in the Modern Era*, ed. Lee C. Bollinger and Geoffrey R. Stone, 175–97. Chicago: University of Chicago Press.

Scheiber, Harry N. 1989. "The Jurisprudence—and Mythology—of Eminent Domain in American Legal History." In *Liberty, Property, and Government: Constitutional Interpretation before the New Deal*, ed. Ellen Frankel Paul and Howard Dickman, 217–38. Albany: State University of New York Press.

Scheurer, Katherine Felix. 2012. "Gender and the U.S. Supreme Court: An Analysis of Voting Behavior in Gender-Based Claims and Civil-Rights and Economic-Activity Cases." *Justice System Journal* 33: 294–317.

Schmidt, Christopher W. 2016. "The Civil Rights-Civil Liberties Divide." *Stanford Journal of Civil Rights and Civil Liberties* 12: 1–41.

Schroeder, Jeanne L. 1996. "Never Jam To-Day: On the Impossibility of Takings Jurisprudence." *Georgetown Law Journal* 84(5): 1531–69.

Schubert, Glendon A. 1959. *Quantitative Analysis of Judicial Behavior*. Glencoe, IL: Free Press.

Schubert, Glendon A. 1962. "Policy without Law: An Extension of the Certiorari Game." *Stanford Law Review* 14: 284–327.

Schubert, Glendon. 1965. *The Judicial Mind: Attitudes and Ideologies of Supreme Court Justices 1946–1963*. Evanston, IL: Northwestern University Press.

Schultz, David. 2010. *Evicted! Property Rights and Eminent Domain in America*. Santa Barbara, CA: Praeger.

Segal, Jeffrey A., and Albert Cover. 1989. "Ideological Values and the Votes of Supreme Court Justices." *American Political Science Review* 83: 557–65.

Segal, Jeffrey A., and Harold J. Spaeth. 2002. *The Supreme Court and the Attitudinal Model Revisited*. New York: Cambridge University Press.

Seidman, Louis Michael. 1995. "The Problems with Privacy's Problems." *Michigan Law Review* 93: 1079–101.

Seidman, Louis Michael. 2004. "Left Out." *Law and Contemporary Problems* 67 (Summer): 23–32.

Shapiro, Carolyn. 2009. "Coding Complexity: Bringing Law to the Empirical Analysis of the Supreme Court." *Hastings Law Journal* 60: 477–539.

Shapiro, Carolyn. 2010. "The Context of Ideology: Law, Politics, and Empirical Legal Scholarship." *Missouri Law Review* 75: 79–142.

Shapiro, Martin. 1978. "The Supreme Court: From Warren to Burger." In *The New American Political System*, ed. Anthony King, 179–211. Washington, DC: American Enterprise Institute.

Shapiro, Martin. 1979. "Judicial Activism." In *The Third Century: America as a Post-Industrial Society*, ed. Seymour Martin Lipset, 109–31. Stanford: Hoover Institution Press.

Sheehan, Reginald S., William Mishler, and Donald R. Songer. 1992. "Ideology, Status, and the Differential Success of Direct Parties before the Supreme Court." *American Political Science Review* 86: 464–71.

Shoch, James. 2001. *Trading Blows: Party Competition and U.S. Trade Policy in a Globalizing Era*. Chapel Hill: University of North Carolina Press.

Slothuus, Rune, and Claes H. de Vreese. 2010. "Political Parties, Motivated Reasoning, and Issue Framing Effects." *Journal of Politics* 72: 630–45.

Smith, Kevin B., Douglas R. Oxley, Matthew V. Hibbing, John R. Alford, and John R. Hibbing. 2011. "Linking Genetics and Political Attitudes: Reconceptualizing Political Ideology." *Political Psychology* 32: 369–97.

Sniderman, Paul M., Richard A. Brody, and Philip E. Tetlock. 1991. *Reasoning and Choice: Explorations in Political Psychology*. New York: Cambridge University Press.

Sniderman, Paul M., and Philip E. Tetlock. 1986. "Interrelationship of Political Ideology and Public Opinion." In *Political Psychology*, ed. Margaret G. Hermann, 62–96. San Francisco: Jossey-Bass.

Snyder, Eloise C. 1958. "The Supreme Court as a Small Group." *Social Forces* 36: 232–38.

Solum, Lawrence. 2003. "I'm Gonna Get High, High, High, or Deconstructing the Up-Down Distinction Revisited." *Legal Theory Blog*, May 4. http://lsolum.typepad.com/legaltheory/2003/05/im_gonna_get_hi.html.

Somin, Ilya. 2012. "Ezra Klein on 'Motivated Reasoning' and the Struggle over the Individual Mandate." *The Volokh Conspiracy*, June 21. http://www.volokh.com/2012/06/21/ezra-klein-on-motivated-reasoning-and-the-struggle-over-the-individual-mandate/.

Somin, Ilya, 2015. *The Grasping Hand:* Kelo v. City of New London *and the Limits of Eminent Domain*. Chicago: University of Chicago Press.

Songer, Donald, Reginald S. Sheehan, and Susan Brodie Haire. 2003. "Do the 'Haves' Come Out Ahead over Time? Applying Galanter's Framework to Decisions of the U.S. Court of Appeals, 1925–1988." In *In Litigation: Do the "Haves" Still Come Out Ahead?*, ed. Herbert M. Kritzer and Susan Silbey, 85–107. Stanford: Stanford University Press.

Sorauf, Frank J. 1976. *The Wall of Separation: The Constitutional Politics of Church and State*. Princeton, NJ: Princeton University Press.

Sotomayor, Sonia. 2013. *My Beloved World*. New York: Alfred A. Knopf.

Southworth, Ann. 2008. *Lawyers of the Right: Professionalizing the Conservative Coalition.* Chicago: University of Chicago Press.

Spaeth, Harold J., David B. Meltz, Gregory J. Rathjen, and Michael V. Haselswerdt. 1972. "Is Justice Blind: An Empirical Investigation of a Normative Ideal." *Law and Society Review* 7: 119–37.

Spaeth, Harold J., and Douglas R. Parker. 1969. "Effects of Attitude toward Situation upon Attitude toward Object." *Journal of Psychology* 73 (November): 173–82.

Spohn, Cassia, and David Holleran. 2000. "The Imprisonment Penalty Paid by Young, Unemployed Black and Hispanic Male Offenders." *Criminology* 38: 281–306.

Staudt, Nancy, Lee Epstein, and Peter Wiedenbeck. 2006. "The Ideological Component of Judging in the Taxation Context." *Washington University Law Review* 84: 1797–821.

Steffensmeier, Darrell, and Chester L. Britt. 2001. "Judges' Race and Judicial Decision Making: Do Black Judges Sentence Differently?" *Social Science Quarterly* 82: 749–64.

Steffensmeier, Darrell, and Stephen Demuth. 2006. "Does Gender Modify the Effects of Race-Ethnicity on Criminal Sentencing? Sentences for Male and Female White, Black, and Hispanic Defendants." *Journal of Quantitative Criminology* 22: 241–61.

Stephenson, Donald Grier, Jr. 1999. *Campaigns and the Court: The U.S. Supreme Court in Presidential Elections.* New York: Columbia University Press.

Stern, Mark Joseph. 2015. "Does the First Amendment Protect Professionals?" *Slate,* November 23, http://www.slate.com/articles/news_and_politics/jurisprudence /2015/11/does_the_first_amendment_protect_medical_professionals.html.

Stevens, John Paul. 2012. "Kelo, Popularity, and Substantive Due Process." *Alabama Law Review* 63: 941–54.

Stewart, Potter. 1983. "The Road to *Mapp v. Ohio* and Beyond: The Origins, Development and Future of the Exclusionary Rule in Search-and-Seizure Cases." *Columbia Law Review* 83: 1365–404.

Strader, J. Kelly. 1999. "The Judicial Politics of White Collar Crime." *Hastings Law Journal* 50: 1199–273.

Strebeigh, Fred. 2009. *Equal: Women Reshape American Law.* New York: W. W. Norton.

Strum, Philippa. 1999. *When the Nazis Came to Skokie: Freedom for Speech We Hate.* Lawrence: University Press of Kansas.

Stuntz, William J. 1995a. "Privacy's Problem and the Law of Criminal Procedure." *Michigan Law Review* 93: 1016–78.

Stuntz, William J. 1995b. "The Substantive Origins of Criminal Procedure." *Yale Law Journal* 105: 393–447.

Stuntz, William J. 2011. *The Collapse of American Criminal Justice.* Cambridge, MA: Harvard University Press.

Sullivan, John L., James Piereson, and George E. Marcus. 1982. *Political Tolerance and American Democracy.* Chicago: University of Chicago Press.

Sunstein, Cass R. 1993. *Democracy and the Problem of Free Speech.* New York: Free Press.

Sunstein, Cass R., David Schkade, Lisa M. Ellman, and Andres Sawicki. 2006. *Are Judges Political? An Empirical Analysis of the Federal Judiciary.* Washington, DC: Brookings Institution Press.

Sutherland, Edwin H. 1949. *White Collar Crime*. New York: Dryden Press.

Sutherland, Edwin H. 1983. *White Collar Crime: The Uncut Version*. New Haven, CT: Yale University Press.

Swedlow, Brendon, and Mikel L. Wyckoff. 2009. "Value Preferences and Ideological Structuring of Attitudes in American Public Opinion." *American Politics Research* 37: 1048–87.

Szmer, John, Donald R. Songer, and Jennifer Bowie. 2016. "Party Capability and the US Courts of Appeals." *Journal of Law and Courts* 4: 65–102.

Tajfel, Henri. 1978. "Social Categorization, Social Identity and Social Comparison." In *Differentiation between Social Groups: Studies in the Social Psychology of Intergroup Relations*, ed. Henri Tajfel, 61–76. London: Academic Press.

Tanenhaus, David S. 2004. *Juvenile Justice in the Making*. New York: Oxford University Press.

Taylor, Stuart, Jr. 1985. "Sentences Getting Stiffer," *New York Times*, May 9, D4.

Teaford, Jon C. 2000. "Urban Renewal and Its Aftermath." *Housing Policy Debate* 11: 443–65.

Tedin, Kent. 1987. "Political Ideology and the Vote." *Research in Micropolitics* 2: 63–94.

Teles, Steven M. 2008. *The Rise of the Conservative Legal Movement*. Princeton, NJ: Princeton University Press.

Thomas, Clarence. 2007. *My Grandfather's Son: A Memoir*. New York: HarperCollins.

Thorpe, Rebecca U., Michael C. Evans, Stephen A. Simon, and Wayne V. McIntosh. 2010. "Legal Mobilization and US Supreme Court Decision Making in Property and Civil Rights Cases, 1978–2003." In *Property Rights and Neoliberalism: Cultural Demands and Legal Actions*, ed. Wayne V. McIntosh and Laura J. Hatcher, 29–58. Burlington, VT: Ashgate.

Tillman, Robert, and Henry N. Pontell. 1992. "Is Justice 'Collar-Blind'?: Punishing Medicaid Provider Fraud." *Criminology* 30: 547–73.

Treanor, William Michael. 1985. "The Origins and Original Significance of the Just Compensation Clause of the Fifth Amendment." *Yale Law Journal* 94: 694–716.

Tribe, Laurence, and Joshua Matz. 2014. *Uncertain Justice: The Roberts Court and the Constitution*. New York: Henry Holt.

Truman, Jennifer L., and Lynn Langton. 2014. *Criminal Victimization, 2013*. Washington, DC: Bureau of Justice Statistics, U.S. Department of Justice.

Tushnet, Mark. 1984. "An Essay on Rights." *Texas Law Review* 62: 1363–1403.

Tushnet, Mark V. 1994. *Making Civil Rights Law: Thurgood Marshall and the Supreme Court, 1936–1961*. New York: Oxford University Press.

Tushnet, Mark. 2006. "The Supreme Court and the National Political Order: Collaboration and Confrontation." In *The Supreme Court and American Political Development*, ed. Ronald Kahn and Ken I. Kersch, 117–37. Lawrence: University Press of Kansas.

Twiss, Benjamin. 1942. *Lawyers and the Constitution: How Laissez Faire Came to the Supreme Court*. Princeton, NJ: Princeton University Press.

U.S. House of Representatives. 1997. *Tucker Act Shuffle Relief Act of 1997*. House Report 105–424, Judiciary Committee.

Vandoren, Peter M. 1990. "Can We Learn the Causes of Congressional Decisions from Roll-Call Data?" *Legislative Studies Quarterly* 15: 311–40.

Volokh, Eugene. 1992. "Freedom of Speech and Workplace Harassment." *UCLA Law Review* 6: 1791–872.

Volokh, Eugene. 2001. "How the Justices Voted in Free Speech Cases, 1994–2000." *UCLA Law Review* 48: 1191–202.

Walker, Samuel. 1994. *Hate Speech: The History of an American Controversy.* Lincoln: University of Nebraska Press.

Walker, Samuel. 1999. *In Defense of American Liberties: A History of the ACLU,* 2d ed. Carbondale: Southern Illinois University Press.

Wanner, Craig. 1975. "The Public Ordering of Private Relations, Part Two: Winning Civil Cases." *Law and Society Review* 9: 293–306.

Wasserstein, Ronald L., and Nicole A. Lazar. 2016. "The ASA's Statement on *p*-Values: Context, Process, and Purpose." *American Statistician* 70: 129–33.

Way, Frank, and Barbara J. Burt. 1983. "Religious Marginality and the Free Exercise Clause." *American Political Science Review* 77: 652–65.

Weissman, Robert. 2011. "Let the People Speak: The Case for a Constitutional Amendment to Remove Corporate Speech from the Ambit of the First Amendment." *Temple Law Review* 83: 979–1005.

Welch, Susan, Michael Combs, and John Gruhl. 1988. "Do Black Judges Make a Difference?" *American Journal of Political Science* 32: 126–36.

Wheeler, Stanton, Bliss Cartwright, Robert Kagan, and Lawrence Friedman. 1987. "Do the 'Haves' Come Out Ahead? Winning and Losing in State Supreme Courts, 1870–1970." *Law and Society Review* 8: 421–40.

Wheeler, Stanton, Kenneth Mann, and Austin Sarat. 1988. *Sitting in Judgment: The Sentencing of White-Collar Criminals.* New Haven, CT: Yale University Press.

White, G. Edward. 1996. "The First Amendment Comes of Age: The Emergence of Free Speech in Twentieth-Century America." *Michigan Law Review* 95: 299–392.

Wilkerson, William R. 2010. "*Kelo v. New London,* the Institute for Justice, and the Idea of Economic Development Takings." In *Property Rights and Neoliberalism: Cultural Demands and Legal Actions,* ed. Wayne V. McIntosh and Laura J. Hatcher, 59–74. Burlington, VT: Ashgate.

Willrich, Michael. 2003. *City of Courts: Socializing Justice in Progressive Era Chicago.* New York: Cambridge University Press.

Winkler, Adam. 2011. *Gunfight: The Battle over the Right to Bear Arms in America.* New York: W. W. Norton.

Wlezien, Christopher, and Arthur H. Miller. 1997. "Social Groups and Political Judgments." *Social Science Quarterly* 78: 625–40.

Wolbrecht, Christina. 2000. *The Politics of Women's Rights: Parties, Positions, and Change.* Princeton, NJ: Princeton University Press.

Wolf, Michael Allan. 2008. "Hysteria versus History: Public Use in the Public Eye." In *Private Property, Community Development, and Eminent Domain,* ed. Robin Paul Malloy, 15–33. Burlington, VT: Ashgate.

Wolfskill, George. 1962. *The Revolt of the Conservatives: A History of the American Liberty League 1934–1940.* Boston: Houghton Mifflin.

Wright, J. Skelly. 1982. "Money and the Pollution of Politics: Is the First Amendment an Obstacle to Political Equality?" *Columbia Law Review* 82: 609–45.

Wu, Tim. 2013. "The Right to Evade Regulation: How Corporations Hijacked the First Amendment." *New Republic*, web edition, June 3.

Yates, Jeff, Damon M. Cann, and Brent D. Boyea. 2013. "Judicial Ideology and the Selection of Disputes for U.S. Supreme Court Adjudication." *Journal of Empirical Legal Studies* 10: 847–65.

Zinni, Frank P., Jr., Franco Mattei, and Laurie A. Rhodebeck. 1997. "The Structure of Attitudes toward Groups: A Comparison of Experts and Novices." *Political Research Quarterly* 50: 597–626.

Zinni, Frank P., Jr., Laurie A. Rhodebeck, and Franco Mattei. 1997. "The Structure and Dynamics of Group Politics: 1946–1992." *Political Behavior* 19: 247–82.

Zschirnt, Simon. 2011. "The Origins and Meaning of Liberal/Conservative Self-Identifications Revisited." *Political Behavior* 33: 685–701.

## Court Decisions and Other Legal Materials

Abramski v. United States. 2014. 189 L. Ed. 2d 262.

Adkins v. Children's Hospital. 1923. 261 U.S. 525.

Altadis U.S.A. v. Reilly. 2001. 533 U.S. 525.

Arizona Free Enterprise Club's Freedom Club PAC v. Bennett. 2011. 180 L. Ed. 2d 664.

Arnett v. Kennedy. 1974. 416 U.S. 134.

Ashcroft v. American Civil Liberties Union. 2002. 535 U.S. 564.

AT&T Mobility LLC v. Concepcion. 2011. 179 L. Ed. 742.

Ballard v. United States. 1946. 329 U.S. 187.

Bates v. State Bar of Arizona. 1977. 433 U.S. 350.

Berman v. Parker. 1954. 348 U.S. 26.

Bigelow v. Virginia. 1975. 421 U.S. 809.

Bivens v. Six Unknown Federal Narcotics Agents. 1971. 403 U.S. 388.

Blakely v. Washington. 2004. 542 U.S. 296.

Boyd v. United States. 1886. 116 U.S. 616.

Bray v. Alexandria Women's Health Clinic. 1993. 506 U.S. 263.

Brown v. Board of Education. 1954. 347 U.S. 483.

Brown v. Board of Education. 1955. 349 U.S. 294.

Brown v. Legal Foundation of Washington. 2003. 538 U.S. 216.

Brown v. Mississippi. 1936. 297 U.S. 278.

Brumfield v. Cain. 2015. 192 L. Ed. 2d 356.

Buckley v. Valeo. 1976. 424 U.S. 1.

Burdeau v. McDowell. 1921. 256 U.S. 465.

Burwell v. Hobby Lobby Stores. 2014. 189 L. Ed. 2d 675.

Bush v. Gore. 2000. 531 U.S. 98.

Carey v. Population Services International. 1977. 431 U.S. 678.

Caron v. United States. 1998. 524 U.S. 308.

Carroll v. United States. 1925. 267 U.S. 132.

Chambers v. Florida. 1940. 309 U.S. 227.

Cheek v. United States. 1991. 498 U.S. 192.

Chicago, Burlington and Quincy Railroad Co. v. Chicago. 1897. 166 U.S. 226.

Citizen Publishing Co. v. United States. 1969. 394 U.S. 131.

Citizens United v. Federal Election Commission. 2010. 558 U.S. 310.

Coker v. Georgia. 1977. 433 U.S. 584.

Counselman v. Hitchcock. 1892. 142 U.S. 547.

Cuomo v. The Clearing House Association. 2009. 557 U.S. 519.

Dames & Moore v. Regan. 1981. 453 U.S. 654.

David's Railroad Supply v. Attorney General, 807 F.3d 1235 (11th Cir. 2015).

Davis v. Federal Election Commission. 2008. 554 U.S. 724.

Davis v. Massachusetts. 1897. 167 U.S. 43.

Day v. McDonough. 2006. 547 U.S. 198.

Department of Commerce v. U.S. House of Representatives. 1999. 525 U.S. 316.

District of Columbia v. Heller. 2008. 554 U.S. 570.

Dolan v. City of Tigard. 1994. 512 U.S. 374.

Duncan v. Louisiana. 1968. 391 U.S. 145.

Eastern Enterprises v. Appel. 1998. 524 U.S. 498.

Eldred v. Ashcroft. 2003. 537 U.S. 186.

Equal Employment Opportunity Commission v. Associated Dry Goods Corp. 1981. 449 U.S. 590.

Escobedo v. Illinois. 1964. 378 U.S. 478.

Ex parte Curtis. 1882. 106 U.S. 371.

Ex parte Jackson. 1878. 96 U.S. 727.

Florida Bar v. Went for It, Inc. 1995. 515 U.S. 618.

Frank v. Mangum. 1915. 237 U.S. 309.

Friedrichs v. California Teachers Association. 2016. 194 L. Ed. 2d 255.

Furman v. Georgia. 1972. 408 U.S. 238.

Garcetti v. Ceballos. 2006. 547 U.S. 410.

Glickman v. Wileman Brothers. 1997. 521 U.S. 457.

Goesaert v. Cleary. 1948. 335 U.S. 464.

Gonzales v. United States. 2008. 553 U.S. 242.

Gouled v. United States. 1921. 255 U.S. 298.

Gratz v. Bollinger. 2003. 539 U.S. 244.

Gregg v. Georgia. 1976. 428 U.S. 153.

Grove City College v Bell. 1984. 465 U.S. 555.

Grutter v. Bollinger. 2003. 539 U.S. 306.

Hale v. Henkel. 1906. 201 U.S. 43.

Harris v. Quinn. 2014. 189 L. Ed. 2d 620.

Hawaii Housing Authority v. Midkiff. 1984. 467 U.S. 229.

Helvering v. Davis. 1937. 310 U.S. 619.

Herring v. United States. 2009. 555 U.S. 135.

Hishon v. King & Spalding. 1984. 467 U.S. 69.

Holloway v. United States. 1999. 526 U.S. 1.

Holt v. Hobbs. 2015. 190 L. Ed. 2d 747.

Horne v. Department of Agriculture. 2015. 192 L. Ed. 2d 388.

Horner v. United States. 1892. 143 U.S. 570.

In re Rapier. 1892. 143 U.S. 110.

International Franchise Association, Inc. v. City of Seattle. 2015. 97 F. Supp. 3d 1256 (W.D. Wash.).

Interstate Commerce Commission v. Oregon-Washington Railroad & Navigation Co. 1933. 288 U.S. 14.

Johanns v. Livestock Marketing Association. 2005. 544 U.S. 550.

Johnson v. Transportation Agency. 1987. 480 U.S. 616.

Kelo v. City of New London. 2005. 545 U.S. 469.

Kepner v. United States. 1904. 195 U.S. 100.

King v. Burwell. 2015. 192 L. Ed. 2d 483.

Klopfer v. North Carolina. 1967. 386 U.S. 213.

Knox v. Service Employees International Union. 2012. 183 L. Ed. 2d 281.

Koon v. United States. 1996. 518 U.S. 81.

Koontz v. St. Johns River Water Management District. 2013. 186 L. Ed. 2d 697.

Korematsu v. United States. 1944. 323 U.S. 214.

Lawrence v. Texas. 2003. 539 U.S. 558.

Leach v. Carlile. 1922. 258 U.S. 138.

Lehnert v. Ferris Faculty Association. 1991. 500 U.S. 507.

Lockhart v. United States. 2016. 194 L. Ed. 2d 48.

Louisiana ex rel. Francis v. Resweber. 1947. 329 U.S. 459.

Louisville Joint Stock Land Bank v. Radford. 1935. 295 U.S. 555.

Lucas v. South Carolina Coastal Council. 1992. 505 U.S. 1003.

Lyons v. Oklahoma. 1944. 322 U.S. 596.

Mapp v. Ohio. 1961. 367 U.S. 643.

McCleskey v. Kemp. 1987. 481 U.S. 279.

McDonald v. City of Chicago. 2010. 561 U.S. 742.

Minersville School District v. Gobitis. 1940. 310 U.S. 586.

Miranda v. Arizona. 1966. 384 U.S. 436.

Moore v. Dempsey. 1923. 261 U.S. 86.

Morehead v. New York ex rel. Tipaldo. 1936. 298 U.S. 587.

Moskal v. United States. 1990. 498 U.S. 103.

Mugler v. Kansas. 1887. 123 U.S. 623.

National Federation of Independent Business v. Sebelius. 2012. 183 L. Ed. 2d 450.

National Labor Relations Board v. Jones & Laughlin Steel Corp. 1937. 301 U.S. 1.

New York Times Co. v. Sullivan. 1964. 376 U.S. 254.

Nollan v. California Coastal Commission. 1987. 483 U.S. 825.

Norman v. B & O Railroad Co. 1935. 294 U.S. 240.

Obergefell v. Hodges. 2015. 192 L. Ed. 2d 609.

Olmstead v. United States. 1928. 277 U.S. 438.

Oregon v. Ice. 2009. 555 U.S. 160.

Parents Involved in Community Schools v. Seattle School District No. 1. 2007. 551 U.S. 701.

Patterson v. Colorado. 1907. 205 U.S. 454.

Penn Central Transportation Company v. New York City. 1978. 438 U.S. 104.

Pennell v. City of San Jose. 1988. 485 U.S. 1.

Pennsylvania Coal Co. v. Mahon. 1922. 260 U.S. 393.

Perkins v. Matthews. 1971. 400 U.S. 379.

Phillips v. Washington Legal Foundation. 1998. 524 U.S. 156.

Pittsburgh Press Co. v. Pittsburgh Commission on Human Relations. 1973. 413 U.S. 376.

Pleasant Grove City v. Summum. 2009. 555 U.S. 460.

Pliva v. Mensing. 2011. 180 L. Ed. 2d 580.

Powell v. Alabama. 1932. 287 U.S. 45.

Pumpelly v. Green Bay Company. 1872. 80 U.S. 166.

Quong Wing v. Kirkendall. 1912. 223 U.S. 59.

Railroad Retirement Board v. Alton Railroad Co. 1935. 295 U.S. 330.

Republican Party v. White. 2002. 536 U.S. 765.

Roberts v. United States Jaycees. 1984. 468 U.S. 609.

Robinson v. California. 1962. 370 U.S. 660.

Romer v. Evans. 1996. 517 U.S. 620.

Runyon v. McCrary. 1976. 427 U.S. 160.

Russello v. United States. 1983. 464 U.S. 16.

Schenck v. Pro-Choice Network. 1997. 519 U.S. 357.

Shelley v. Kraemer. 1948. 334 U.S. 1.

Silverthorne Lumber Co. v. United States. 1920. 251 U.S. 385.

Snyder v. Phelps. 2011. 179 L. Ed. 2d 172.

Sorrell v. IMS Health Inc. 2011. 180 L. Ed. 2d 544.

South Carolina v. Katzenbach. 1966. 383 U.S. 301.

Spirit Airlines, Inc. v. U.S. Department of Transportation. 2012. 486 F.3d 403 (D.C. Cir.).

Staples v. United States. 1994. 511 U.S. 600.

Thomas v. Collins. 1945. 323 U.S. 516.

Thompson v. Thompson. 1910. 218 U.S. 611.

Thompson v. Western States Medical Center. 2002. 535 U.S. 357.

Turner Broadcasting System v. Federal Communications Commission. 1997. 520 U.S. 180.

United Jewish Organizations v. Carey. 1977. 430 U.S. 144.

United States v. Booker. 2005. 543 U.S. 220.

United States v. Butler. 1937. 297 U.S. 1.

United States v. Carolene Products Co. 1938. 304 U.S. 144.

United States v. Congress of Industrial Organizations. 1948. 335 U.S. 106.

United States v. Hayes. 2009. 555 U.S. 415.

United States v. Leon. 1984. 468 U.S. 897.

United States v. Locke. 1985. 471 U.S. 84.

United States v. Resendiz-Ponce. 2007. 549 U.S. 102.

United States v. Robinson. 1988. 485 U.S. 25.

United States v. United Auto Workers. 1957. 352 U.S. 567.

United States v. United Foods. 2001. 533 U.S. 405.

United States ex rel. Turner v. Williams. 1904. 194 U.S. 279.

Virginia State Board of Pharmacy v. Virginia Citizens Consumer Council. 1976. 425
    U.S. 748.
Voisine v. United States. 2016. 195 L. Ed. 2d 736.
Weeks v. United States. 1914. 232 U.S. 383.
Weems v. United States. 1910. 217 U.S. 349.
West v. Chesapeake & Potomac Telephone Co. 1935. 295 U.S. 662.
West Coast Hotel Co. v. Parrish. 1937. 300 U.S. 379.
Wilkie v. Robbins. 2007. 551 U.S. 537.
Wisconsin v. Mitchell. 1993. 508 U.S. 476.
Wisconsin v. Yoder. 1972. 406 U.S. 205.
Wolf v. Colorado. 1949. 338 U.S. 25.
Wyeth v. Levine. 2009. 555 U.S. 555.
Zubik v. Burwell. 2016. 194 L. Ed. 2d 696.

# NAME INDEX

# SUBJECT AND CASE INDEX

## A NOTE ON THE TYPE

This book has been composed in Adobe Text and Gotham. Adobe Text, designed by Robert Slimbach for Adobe, bridges the gap between fifteenth- and sixteenth-century calligraphic and eighteenth-century Modern styles. Gotham, inspired by New York street signs, was designed by Tobias Frere-Jones for Hoefler & Co.